Shirley Bridgeforth

VIRGINIA'S
CIVIL WAR

VIRGINIA'S CIVIL WAR

EDITED BY

Peter Wallenstein and Bertram Wyatt-Brown

UNIVERSITY OF VIRGINIA PRESS
CHARLOTTESVILLE AND LONDON

University of Virginia Press
© 2005 by the Rector and Visitors of the University of Virginia
All rights reserved
Printed in the United States of America on acid-free paper

First published 2005

1 3 5 7 9 8 6 4 2

LIBRARY OF CONGRESS CATALOGING-IN-PUBLICATION DATA

Virginia's Civil War / edited by Peter Wallenstein and Bertram
Wyatt-Brown.
    p.   cm.
Derived from a select group of papers delivered at the Virginia Civil War
conference at the University of Richmond in February 2002.
Includes bibliographical references and index.
ISBN 0-8139-2315-8 (cloth : alk. paper)
    1. Virginia—History—Civil War, 1861-1865—Congresses. 2. United
States—History—Civil War, 1861-1865—Congresses. I. Wallenstein,
Peter. II. Wyatt-Brown, Bertram, 1932-
    E534.V46 2004
    973.7'09755—dc22

                                                    2004011410

For

our students, our friends in the Southern Historical Association,
and all participants in the Douglas Southall Freeman Conference,
University of Richmond, 2002

Contents

PART THREE: AFTER THE WAR

APPENDIX: Documents from Virginia's Civil War

Preface

During the spring semester of 2002, the University of Richmond generously sponsored an impressive assemblage on the topic, "Virginia's Civil War and Aftermath." The program involved jointly the Douglas Southall Freeman conference and the Southern Intellectual History symposium. As the Freeman Professor that term, Bertram Wyatt-Brown had the choice of presenting a lecture series or directing a gathering of scholars in a public forum. He chose the latter task. A call for papers aroused many more proposals—and much more general interest—than either he or Hugh West, chairman of the Department of History at the University of Richmond, had anticipated. During the conference, he invited Peter Wallenstein to join him in editing a collection of the papers for book publication.

Despite the logistical complications in handling so large an assembly, with a limited but highly efficient staff, the double conferences, held between February 21 and 24, 2002, proved most successful. With 126 participants, 29 panels, and 3 plenary sessions, the public was treated to a variety of informative and able presentations. Sessions covered the late prewar period, the war years, and the time after the war. Chairing the sessions, presenting the papers, and commenting on them were dozens of the leading scholars in American nineteenth-century history and culture. Members of the audience as well as the presenters at each session lent considerable expertise to the weekend's intellectual liveliness.

Most of the meetings took place on the campus of the University of Richmond. One plenary session, heavily attended, was held at the Virginia Historical Society, thanks to VHS director Charles Bryant, proficient sponsor of the event. A similar assembly, held at the Trede-gar Iron Works, addressed the significance of Robert E. Lee. Several of these papers appear at the beginning of this book. The topic and the exemplary publicity work of Alex Wise, director of the Tredegar Mu-seum, drew a crowd that filled the spacious foundry floor, once the chief armaments facility of the Confederacy.

We have a number of additional people to acknowledge. Four graduate students at the University of Florida contributed efficiently to the success of the enterprise. Randall Stephens and Carey Shellman helped in managing the conference itself. Jay Langdale and Margaret Macdonald were both skillfully involved in the editorial process. Con-versations with Joseph Pierro, a Virginia Tech graduate student, shaped the appendix of documents. Erin Mooney, an undergraduate at Virginia Tech, assisted with the index. As for the anonymous outside readers, their reports to the press were models of the genre, support-ive and appreciative of the project while offering any number of help-ful suggestions for improvements. Richard Holway, the history editor at the University of Virginia Press, was present at the conference and nurtured this book from its inception.

In neither the history books nor the public imagination has Vir-ginia's social or cultural experience of the Civil War era attracted as much attention as have the battle sites and the generals who won or lost those bloody engagements. The conference and the essays grow-ing from it have demonstrated that there is much of value to be learned about other matters than military, and in fact more as well to be learned about the conduct and consequences of the military dimen-sion of the war. The essays to follow explore some areas seldom treated, and they provide new insights into old questions.

Editorial Note

The editors have standardized the rendition of the term "Southern-ers," presenting it throughout the book that way, capitalized, rather than as "southerners." No such standardization applies to what writers mean by the term, a meaning that can, depending on writer and con-text, refer to the fifteen slaveholding states of 1860 or, more restric-tively, just the eleven states of the Confederacy and, similarly, can refer to all residents, all white residents, or only Confederate whites.

Abbreviations in Notes

CWM   Swem Library, The College of William and Mary
CWH   *Civil War History*
DU   Special Collections, Perkins Library, Duke University
JSH   *Journal of Southern History*
LC   Library of Congress, Washington, D.C.
NA   National Archives, Washington, D.C.
OR   U.S. War Department, *The War of the Rebellion: The Official Records of the Union and Confederate Armies*, 128 volumes (Washington, D.C., 1890–1901)
SHC   Southern Historical Collection, Wilson Library, University of North Carolina, Chapel Hill
UVA   Albert and Shirley Small Special Collections Library, University of Virginia
USC   South Caroliniana Library, University of South Carolina
VBHS   Virginia Baptist Historical Society, Richmond
VHS   Virginia Historical Society, Richmond
VMHB   *Virginia Magazine of History and Biography*
Weevils *Weevils in the Wheat: Interviews with Virginia Ex-Slaves*, eds. Charles L. Perdue Jr., Thomas E. Barden, and Robert K. Phillips (Charlottesville, Va., 1976)

VIRGINIA'S
CIVIL WAR

Introduction

PETER WALLENSTEIN AND
BERTRAM WYATT-BROWN

On April 5, 2003, several hundred celebrants watched as a bronze sculpture honoring Abraham Lincoln's brief visit to Richmond in 1865 was unveiled at the Civil War Visitor Center, adjacent to the Tredegar Iron Works in Virginia's capital city, once the capital of the Confederacy. The sculpture shows the president seated on a bench with his arm around his twelve-year-old son, Tad, who had accompanied him. The boy is looking up earnestly at his father, while Lincoln gazes down in solemn contemplation.

In keeping with Lincoln's own sense of melancholy, the statue's demeanor does not reflect the glory of a victory almost fully completed: General Lee's Army of Northern Virginia would surrender to Gen. U. S. Grant on April 10, 1865, five days after Lincoln's visit. Rather, David Frech, the sculptor, offers a tender rendition of a father and son, behind whose facsimiles on a granite wall are written: "To Bind Up the Nation's Wounds." Some 148 years before the unveiling—the same day and month as the Tredegar dedication—the Union's commander in chief had left the federal military headquarters in Virginia and toured the conquered, ruined capital of the Confederacy. Ten days later, John Wilkes Booth killed him at Ford's Theater and thereby made a martyr of the wartime president, one of the very last people to sacrifice his life in the line of wartime duty.

The Frech representation of Lincoln contrasts with the statues along Richmond's famous Monument Avenue—Robert E. Lee, Stonewall Jackson, and J. E. B. Stuart. Mounted on military steeds, the generals, with expressions brave and determined, appear ready to do battle with the hated foe. At the Richmond ceremony in 2003, moreover, a small group attended not to commemorate but to deride the sense of a reunited country that Lincoln had sought to personify by his presence. With some dressed in period costume, the naysayers flourished Confederate banners, sported derogatory signs, and shouted epithets, accusing Lincoln of being a war criminal, an American Hitler.

Ron Wilson, the national commander of the Sons of Confederate Veterans, vowed that day: "We are going to fight these people everywhere they raise their head." He and his colleagues are convinced that the bronze sculpture insults all Southern whites and the grand cause for which their forebears fought. The memorial was "a gratuitous measure of disrespect to people of Southern heritage," as a reporter summarized the sentiments. In this view, the Confederacy that the Union president had helped overcome was a government far superior to Lincoln's republic—representing not enslavement and white hegemony but the world's last best hope for freedom and justice.[1]

The 2003 incident reflects the continued struggle despite the distance separating that era of national tragedy and our own time. For that reason *Virginia's Civil War* assumes particular interest, because so much of the war was fought on the blood-drenched soil around the Richmond that Lincoln visited. Indeed, given the centrality of Virginia's part in the great struggle, the theme itself has been less thoroughly studied than one might have expected.[2] This volume will help to rectify that deficiency by probing social and cultural dimensions of Virginia's Civil War experience. It is striking that two of the dominant themes among these essays are religion and gender, rather than the military and political affairs that have been far more thoroughly aired.

Big public events—and the Civil War was surely a big public event—intersect with private lives in innumerable ways. Even a single brief encounter—as on a battlefield, or when the battlefield comes crashing into the home front—can have very different meanings for the individuals involved. In that sense of multiple experiences, there was no one Civil War in Virginia. Rather, there were many civil wars—at the time and also, later, in the ways people recalled the events and continued to be shaped by them. The essays in this book seek to recapture some of those smaller wars that made up, or stemmed from, the larger one.

Moreover, if the results of the war grew out of battlefield developments, and the battlefield itself reflected the nature of the home front, then knowing more about the home front can be expected to foster new insights as to what happened on the battlefield. In a longer view, similarly, in the reciprocal interplay between home front and battlefront, Virginians long found their lives shaped in profound ways by what had happened during four years of war.

The opening section centers on the Southern hero and mythical icon, Robert E. Lee. Given his preeminence, particularly in Richmond, the city he so long had defended, how could it be otherwise? Emory Thomas, author of *Robert E. Lee: A Biography* (1995) and many other Civil War works, leads off with an appraisal of Lee's motivations and a survey of the range of ways in which Lee has been portrayed. In Thomas's view, the financial trouble suffered by the general's father, Henry Lee, shadowed the family's honor and explains his son's determination to restore it. The son's irreproachable comportment and a genius in warfare would outshine the Revolutionary fame of "Light-Horse Harry."

Other essayists take differing approaches. Dwelling on a darker side, Michael Fellman argues that Lee, embarking surreptitiously into the politics of white restoration during Reconstruction, marred the splendor of his wartime career. Bertram Wyatt-Brown contends that uppermost in Lee's mind was a devotion to the ethic of honor as exemplified in the Stoic tradition of Marcus Aurelius and other ancient Roman and Greek classical thinkers. Far from suffering from the shame of a financially unstable father, Lee held steadfastly to his ethical principles, even though, like other white Virginians of his generation, he entertained deep racial antipathies. Charles Joyner concludes the opening section with his inimitable interpretation of Lee as "a man of constant sorrow," who was mournfully aware, from first to last, that his decision to lead the Confederate military cause by no means assured victory at the end.

Established scholars authored the essays on Robert E. Lee; the essays on other topics are, by and large, by newcomers, and all bring fresh research and offer new interpretations of Virginia in the Civil War era. Three essays concern the cultural and religious factors that kept Virginians from emulating South Carolinians in leaping at secession and, if necessary, war after Abraham Lincoln's election to the presidency. Daniel Kilbride asks why, when traveling abroad, the Virginia gentility seemed so unreflective about their peculiar racial situation. Instead, they compared themselves—favorably, of course—to the snobbish, aristocratic elements with whom they mingled. In their minds, they were Americans, not a breed apart. Perhaps, Kilbride speculates, scholars overplay proslaveryism, a point that the next contributor, Charles F. Irons, affirms in another context. Irons explores why Virginia's Protestant clergy and laity displayed so little zeal for disunion. In his view, they distinguished between a devotion to slaveholding, which they maintained, and a craving for Southern independence, which at first they resisted. Wayne Wei-siang Hsieh finds similar sentiments within the Baptist churches of Virginia, at least in the early stages of the war. Baptists displayed reluctance to enter the struggle, followed by a commitment to balance their Christian principles of love and peace with a faith in Confederate nationalism.

Hsieh's essay leads to several that concern issues of morale at home and in the Virginian ranks. One reason for an enduring Confederate sense of military and national purpose, according to Jason Phillips, was the role that religious faith played in the ranks. To be sure, not all soldiers were God-fearing churchgoers, but, with revivals extensive among soldiers from Virginia to Texas, the numbers of professing Christians grew throughout the war. Continuing the theme of popular morale, Ian Binnington examines the *Southern Illustrated News* and assesses its role in promoting Confederate nation. Success at war was essential to the Confederate experiment, and the *News* did what it could to promote both. Like Jason Phillips's troops in the field and Ian Binnington's journalists at home, Lisa Tendrich Frank's upper-class women of Virginia's Shenandoah Valley remained steadfast in the face of disaster. Horrified though they were by the vandalism, brutality, and looting of the Union troops, they failed to lose heart. In this essay she challenges other historians studying wartime Southern women.

Several authors explore the diverse roles that race as an idea, or African Americans as a group, played in the war. Ervin L. Jordan Jr. writes of two former Virginia slaves who had fled to England, where they published accounts of their lives, stories that may have helped promote British acceptance of the Emancipation Proclamation. David G. Smith reveals how, in the 1863 raid into Pennsylvania, Lee's army engaged in capturing black civilians, and Smith explains that this extension of the war into the Yankee home front represented Southern reaction to the Emancipation Proclamation and the use of black federal troops. Marlboro Jones served in the Virginia theater as a camp servant of his Georgia master, Capt. Randal Jones, and Lucinda H. MacKethan probes beneath the surface of Marlboro's apparent fidelity to the white Joneses. Suzanne W. Jones examines the interrelationship of real circumstances and their fictional representations, particularly regarding interracial love, through Donald McCaig's *Jacob's Ladder*, a twentieth-century novel set in Virginia that reverses some conventions from nineteenth-century fiction.

In the book's final part, "After the War," the essayists survey the troubling outcomes of the war for the people of Virginia, both white and black. John M. McClure studies freedmen's education in Lexington and the leadership of agent William Coan. Like Michael Fellman earlier in these pages, McClure casts a shadow on Robert E. Lee's benign postwar image as president of Washington College in Lexington. Susanna Michele Lee—in recounting the experience of William Pattie, a white Unionist storekeeper in Warrenton—demonstrates how complexities of interpretation blurred the distinctions between secessionists and loyalists. Ambivalence and ambiguity reign in another realm as well, as Monte Hampton considers the Virginia theologian Robert L. Dabney's postwar attempt to bring together Calvinist religion, modernist ideas, and Southern culture.

The last few essays show that the same sort of Southern people of means introduced by Daniel Kilbride before the war appear chastened but proud in the days after Appomattox. Theodore C. DeLaney reveals Julia Gardiner Tyler, widow of the former president, as a woman of strong mind and will in the postwar world. Amy Feely Morsman, in an account of postwar changes in the gender roles of plantation elites, explains that upper-class gender roles changed for a time as former slaveowners adapted to postwar exigencies, but the old norms returned with the next generation. Caroline E. Janney closes the volume with an account of women taking on the formidable task of burying the thousands of Confederate dead with dignity and honor. In the impoverished town of Petersburg—scene of so much carnage in the last months of the war—the local ladies managed the effort, in Janney's view, in the absence of much money from the city or assistance from upper-class men.

Most of these essays raise questions that likely apply to much of the rest of the South or at least to the Confederate South. Janney's women engaged in an enterprise that, though local, was duplicated throughout the New South. Similarly, people from across the region—Unionist or Confederate—had to calculate their loyalties and priorities during the winter of 1860–61, sought to reconcile conflicting belief systems, attempted to keep the faith during a brutal war, tried to retrieve lost property through the Southern Claims Commission, undertook to teach freedmen's schools, had to piece their lives back together after the war, and had to figure what to make of the war, its leaders, and its outcome.

Thus we have in these pages fresh interpretations of events and figures, great and small, from General Lee to the last soldier interred in Petersburg's Blandford Churchyard. If there is one overarching theme to enclose all the essays, it is this—a reaffirmation of what Gavins Stevens declared in William Faulkner's *Requiem for a Nun:* "The past is never dead. It's not even past." On that point, if on no other, the neo-Confederates and those who watched with greater sympathy the Lincoln ceremony outside the Tredegar Museum might find common ground.

Notes

1. Michael D. Shear and Peter Whoriskey, "Lincoln Statue Heightens Old Pains: Confederacy Backers Say They'll Never Recognize Tribute," *Washington Post,* 6 April 2003; see also Bill Baskervill, "Lincoln Statue in Richmond Offends Confederate Group," *Hampton Roads News,* 27 December 2002.
2. Previous books on the general topic of Civil War Virginia include two with titles that somewhat resemble that of this book: James I. Robertson Jr., *Civil War Virginia: Battleground for a Nation* (Charlottesville, Va., 1991), and John G. Selby, *Virginians at War: The Civil War Experiences of Seven Young Confederates* (Wilmington, Del., 2002).

PART ONE

LEE

The Malleable Man

Robert E. Lee in the American Mind

EMORY M. THOMAS

Here is a passage from Stephen Vincent Benét's *John Brown's Body:*

> —And so we get the marble man again,
> The head on the Greek coin, the idol-image
> The shape who stands at Washington's left hand,
> Worshipped, uncomprehended and aloof,
> A figure lost to flesh and blood and bones,
> Frozen into legend out of life,
> A blank-verse statue—[1]

This has been the dominant image of Robert E. Lee in the popular mind—Lee as marble, rigid, and remote. Yet the "marble man" has been quite lively, or rendered so by those who fashioned and viewed Lee's image in art, as well as by many who wrote about him.

Consider the equestrian statue erected in Richmond in 1890 on what became Monument Avenue. An Ohio-based sculptor initially won the commission, and Jubal Early wrote Virginia governor Fitzhugh Lee (General Lee's nephew) that if a Yankee executed the work, he would "get together all the surviving members of the Second Corps (of Lee's army) and blow it up with dynamite." So the sculptor became Jean Antoine Mercié—appropriately from Toulon in deepest southern France, no Yankee from Ohio.[2]

Although hordes of people lauded the statue and the subject, John Mitchell Jr.—an African American member of the Richmond City Council and the editor of the *Richmond Planet*—dissented in print. "The men who talk most about the valor of Lee and the blood of the brave Confederate dead are those who never smelt powder," he wrote. And the day the statue was unveiled, Mitchell called the event a monument to a "legacy of treason and blood."[3]

Mitchell's was a lonely voice in 1890, but black criticism of Lee's veneration did not end there. In 1999 some people in Richmond built a flood wall beside the James River and planned a tourist attraction. On the wall's twenty-nine panels, promoters installed pictures of people and scenes from Richmond's past. Robert E. Lee's picture provoked outrage from Richmond City Council member Sa'ad El Amin, who termed Lee a "Hitler," a "Stalin," and demanded its removal. Here was an example of a theme: Lee = the Confederacy; the Confederacy = slavery and oppression. The furor inspired much outcry.[4]

During the spring of 2001, a portrait of Lee became a bargaining chip in what I believe was a good Cause—removing a representation of the battle flag of the Army of Northern Virginia (Lee's army) from the state flag of Georgia. In the practice of traditional Southern virtues—good manners and concern for the feelings of others—Governor Roy Barnes rammed a compromise design for a flag through the General Assembly. Then on Confederate Memorial Day (April 26), the governor unveiled a portrait of Lee restored to the capitol. The portrait was the quid for the pro quo vote of an influential state senator from South Georgia.[5]

Cast in bronze, carved in marble, or emblazoned on canvas, Robert E. Lee as icon has had a fluid history. He has stood—or, in the case of the Edward Valentine's recumbent statue in the chapel at Washington and Lee, lain—for all manner of causes in the minds of his beholders.

In the written word, as well as in icon, Lee has been more and less than he was in life. The literary monument surpassing Mercie's and Valentine's and everyone's canvases has been Douglas Southall Freeman's four volumes of *R. E. Lee: A Biography*. Freeman wrote of Lee in 1935: "Robert Lee was one of the small company of great men in whom there is no inconsistency to be explained, no enigma to be solved. What he seemed, he was—a wholly human gentleman, the essential elements of whose positive character were two and only two, simplicity and spirituality."[6] Freeman concluded his work: "There is no mystery in the coffin there in front of the windows that look to the sunrise."[7]

For a long, long time, Lee, essentially Freeman's "Lee," has been an

American hero. And this same Lee has been a secular saint below the Potomac and Ohio rivers. Yet, even in the South, the Lee paean has never been unanimous. Here, from one region or another, by writers of fiction and nonfiction, are samples of Lee counterpoint.

Allen Tate, writing in 1929 to his friend Andrew Lytle about the frustrations of writing a biography of Lee, said of Lee that he "valued his own honor more than the independence of the South. If he had taken matters in his own hands, he might have saved the situation; he was not willing to do this. It would have violated his Sunday School morality." By 1931 Tate was downright disgusted, he wrote Lytle: "The longer I've contemplated the venerable features of Lee, the more I've hated him. It is as if I had married a beautiful girl, perfect in figure, pure in all those physical attributes that seem to clothe purity of character, and then had found when she had undressed that the hidden places were corrupt and diseased."[8] Not surprisingly, Tate never completed his biography of Lee.

Gertrude Stein wrote in her *Everybody's Autobiography* (1937) that Lee was a "weak man," because he knew the Confederacy could not win and lacked the courage to say what he knew.[9]

Novelist Michael Shaara won a Pulitzer Prize in 1975 for *The Killer Angels* about the battle of Gettysburg. Shaara portrayed Lee as a confused, sad, sick, old man who seemed determined to have one more mass bloodletting before he died. The novel became the basis for the 1993 film *Gettysburg*.

I cannot leave the realm of fiction without mention of the best work of fiction about Lee, M. A. Harper's *For the Love of Robert E. Lee* (1992). In this book, the teenaged narrator says: "Try to co-opt him now, if you want to. You can't. The line has been broken. Y'all did it. You wouldn't claim him after the war. Fine. He's ours, ours alone, forever and ever, by mutual choice. We chose him and he chose us. We were *worth* choosing. So the rest of you will just have to make do with Sherman and Grant and the rest of the second-raters. We haven't had any U.S. Presidents until Johnson. We're used to being a joke. The poorest. The baddest. And we are *bad*. Yes, we're bad. But we've got Robert E. Lee, and you can't have him."[10]

In 1960, a quarter-century after Freeman published his opus, historian T. Harry Williams reexamined Lee: "Let us concede that many of the tributes to Lee are deserved. He was not all that his admirers have said of him, but he was a large part of it. But let us also note that even his most fervent admirers, when they come to evaluate him as a strategist, have to admit that his abilities were never demonstrated on a larger scale than a theater."[11]

In subsequent years, other historians analyzed Lee and his image. Thomas L. Connelly in 1977 published *The Marble Man: Robert E. Lee and His Image in American Society*. This analysis by a brilliant scholar began in earnest the revisionist critique of Lee as a soldier, saint, and human being. After devoting the bulk of his book to interpreting the Lee image, Connelly offers his version of the Lee reality:

> In truth, Lee was an extremely complex individual. Lee the man has become so intermingled with Lee the hero symbol that the real person has been obscured. Efforts to understand him, and to appraise his capabilities fairly, have been hindered by his image as a folk hero.
>
> Lee was neither serene nor simple. His life was replete with frustration, self-doubt, and a feeling of failure. All these were hidden behind his legendary reserve and his credo of duty and self-control. He was actually a troubled man, convinced that he had failed as a prewar career officer, parent, and moral individual. He suffered the hardships of an unsatisfactory marriage, long absences from his family, and chronic homesickness for his beloved Virginia. He distrusted his own conduct. The specter of family scandals in the past, his unhappy marital situation, his strong Calvinist obsession with sin—all united to make Lee fear for his self-control.[12]

And since Connelly's *Marble Man* and his and Barbara L. Bellows's *God and General Longstreet: The Lost Cause and the Southern Mind* (1982), imitators—pale, in my opinion—have flocked to Connelly's anti-Lee colors. Alan Nolan in 1991 published *Lee Considered: General Robert E. Lee and Civil War History*. About this work, I confess to have said in print: "Nolan's book reveals a spirit mean and sad, and neither of these adjectives applies to Lee."[13] Then in 2000 came Michael Fellman's *The Making of Robert E. Lee*. Like Connelly and Nolan before him, Fellman seems to me to be so much in thrall to—repelled by— the Lee legend, myth, hagiography, that he spends most of his energy and ink protesting what Lee was not rather than elucidating who Lee was.[14]

This has been necessarily a hasty sample of what artists, writers, historians, and real people have made of Robert E. Lee. Now I believe I have the obligation to say what I believe about the person. The best answer I can offer is my Lee corpus, *Robert E. Lee: A Biography* (1995) and *Robert E. Lee: An Album* (2000).[15] More briefly here, let me offer some thoughts.

I believe that Robert E. Lee was a great man. He was great (1) because of what he did, (2) because of his response to the universal quandary about freedom and control, and (3) because of what I term Lee's comic vision of life.

Lee's deeds were important. Here is Stephen Vincent Benét again:

> Yet—look at the face again—look at it well—
> This man was not repose, this man was act.
> This man who murmured "It is well that war
> Should be so terrible, if it were not
> We might become too fond of it—" and showed
> Himself, for once, completely as he lived
> In the laconic balance of that phrase;
> This man could reason, but he was a fighter,
> Skilful in every weapon of defence
> But never defending when he could assault,
> Taking enormous risks again and again,
> Never retreating while he still could strike,
> Dividing a weak force on dangerous ground
> And joining it again to beat a strong,
> Mocking at chance and all the odds of war
> With acts that looked like hairbreadth recklessness
> —We do not call them reckless, since they won.
> We do not see him reckless for the calm
> Proportion that controlled the recklessness—
> But that attacking quality was there.
> He was not mild with life or drugged with justice,
> He gripped life like a wrestler with a bull,
> Impetuously. It did not come to him

> While he stood waiting in a famous cloud,
> He went to it and took it by both horns
> And threw it down.[16]

Lee was great for the quantity and quality of his accomplishments. Here, in brief, is what he achieved.

He was initially an engineer. He graduated West Point (1829) second in his class, rechanneled the Mississippi River, opened the upper Mississippi to navigation, won the Mexican War, and captured John Brown and freed Brown's hostages.

Lee was then a warrior. He armed and organized Virginia troops; found frustration in the Kanawha Valley and on the coast of South Carolina, Georgia, and Florida; and then came to command: Seven Days, Second Manassas (Bull Run), Sharpsburg (Antietam), Fredericksburg, Chancellorsville, Gettysburg, Bristoe Station, The Wilderness, Spotsylvania, Cold Harbor, Petersburg, Appomattox.

Finally, Lee was an educator. At Washington College (later Washington and Lee University), he introduced elective courses, voluntary chapel, a law school, and a journalism school. And he replaced the myriad rules common to colleges at that time with one rule: "Every man must be a gentleman."

Here is what Lee did about freedom. He suffered from a huge birth defect—his father, "Light-Horse Harry" Lee—and the negative example of his father drove Lee to restore the family honor and pursue righteousness. I believe that Jean-Jacques Rousseau had it backward when he wrote that people are born free, but are everywhere in chains. Most of us are born in chains—slaves to custom, family, society—to whoever or whatever shapes (warps) our lives. Lee and the rest of us need to get free.

Lee acted out a paradox: to be free, he followed rules and obeyed orders. To his oldest son, Custis, Lee wrote: "I am fond of independence. It is that feeling that prompts me to come up strictly to the requirements of law & regulations. I wish neither to seek or receive indulgence from any one."[17] Lee controlled himself to liberate himself.

Lee wrote, "The great duty of life is the promotion of the happiness and welfare of our fellow men."[18] Conversely, Lee believed that sin and wrong were essentially the fruits of selfishness.

Lee was the old man who stared into the face of an infant and intoned, "Teach him to deny himself." It is easy for rigid people to associate Lee with absolutes and over-noble platitudes. But Lee lived beyond conventions and conventional wisdom. Here is what he wrote to P. G. T. Beauregard about treason:

> True patriotism sometimes requires of men to act exactly contrary, at one period, to that which it does at another, and the motive which impels them—the desire to do right—is precisely the same. The circumstances which govern their actions change; and their conduct must conform to the new order of things. History is full of illustrations of this. Washington himself is an example. At one time he fought against the French under Braddock, in the service of the King of Great Britain, at another, he fought with the French at Yorktown, under the orders of the Continental Congress of America, against him. He has not been branded by the world with reproach for this; but his course has been applauded.[19]

It may have been no accident that Confederates wore shades of gray.

An appropriate metaphor for Lee's morality is a kite, as portrayed by Wyatt Prunty:

> Vivid for the sky's emptiness,
> A bright red patch against the haze and blue,
> It soars along a shortened line, but falls
> When given run before the wind;
>
> Or like a solitary song's release,
> The kite unreels along a spool of thread,
> An outward surge over the wind,
> Flying by the force of being held.
>
> The single master of a vacant lot,
> By pulling down it rises up,
> This craft of putting fragile things aloft,
> Of letting go and holding on at once.[20]

Lee was act. Lee acted out the tension between freedom and control. Lee possessed a comic—as opposed to tragic—vision of life. To his son Custis, who was undergoing a nineteenth-century version of the sophomore slump at West Point, Lee wrote: "Shake off those gloomy feelings. Drive them away, fix your mind & pleasures upon what is before you. . . . All is bright if you will think it so. All is happy if you will make it so. Do not dream. It is too ideal, too imaginary. Dreaming by day, I mean. Live in the world you inhabit. Look upon things as they are. Take them as you find them. Make the best of them. Turn them to your advantage."[21] And Lee took his own advice. He made the best of every circumstance—personally and professionally.

Lee sought wit and excitement in the company and especially the correspondence of bright, young women. As a young bachelor, Lee had courted a young woman named Eliza Mackay. Later, after his own marriage, Lee learned that Eliza was about to marry. On her wedding day, he wrote to her, "But Miss E. how do you feel about this time? Say 12 o'clock of the day, as you see the shadows commence to fall towards the East and know that at *last* the sun will set?" Interrupted in his writing, Lee returned to his letter four days later. By this time, Eliza was married, and Lee asked: "And how did you disport yourself my child? Did you go off well, like a torpedo cracker on Christmas morning."[22]

Lee attempted to redeem awkward circumstances and bring grace. At St. Paul's Church, in Richmond, in June 1865, a very large black man first responded to the call to receive communion. Gasp. No one moved, except Lee, who walked forward and knelt beside him.[23]

At one of the worst periods of his life, in December 1863, Lee received at his headquarters a note from Lucy Minnegerode and Lou Haxall, who signed themselves "your two little friends." "We the undersigned," the girls wrote, "write this little note to you our beloved Gen. to ask a little favor of you which if it is in your power to grant we trust you will. We want Private Cary Robinson of Com. G. 6th V. Mahone's Brig. to spend his Christmas with us, and if you will grant him a furlough for this purpose we will pay you back in thanks and love and kisses."[24]

The war was going badly. Lee was suffering from what was likely an attack of angina. His wife was crippled, a son captured, a daughter-in-law dying. Moreover, Lee had lost almost all the wealth he ever possessed or controlled. Yet in timely manner, with the warmest of hearts, he responded to his "two little friends":

> I rec'd the morning I left camp your joint request for permission to Mr. Cary Robinson to visit you on Xmas, and gave authority for his

doing so, provided circumstances permitted. Deeply sympathizing with him in his recent affliction it gave me great pleasure to extend to him the opportunity of seeing you, but I fear I was influenced by the *bribe* held out to me, and will punish myself by not going to claim the thanks and love and kisses promised me. You know the self denial this will cost me. I fear too I shall be obliged to submit your letter to Congress, that our Legislators may know the temptations to which poor soldiers are exposed, and in their wisdom devise some means of counteracting its influence. They may know that bribery and corruption is stalking boldly over the land, but may not be aware that the fairest and sweetest are engaged in its practice.[25]

Robert E. Lee offers ample evidence that the human condition is flawed. By the standards of his time, as well as the present time, Lee falls short of perfection. But who does not? Lee forged greatness from the human condition. He achieved great feats. He struggled nobly in that universal tension between control and freedom. And he responded to the challenges and failures in his life with grace and good humor. Lee's life was important in his time; his story offers inspiration in our time.

Notes

"The Kite" by Wyatt Prunty, *The Times Between*, ©1982 Wyatt Prunty, reprinted with permission of The Johns Hopkins University Press.

1. Stephen Vincent Benét, *John Brown's Body* (New York, 1928), 171.
2. The story and the quotation are from Virginius Dabney, *The Last Review: The Confederate Reunion, Richmond, 1932* (Chapel Hill, N.C., 1984), 7.
3. Ibid. See also Ann Field Alexander, *Race Man: The Rise and Fall of the "Fighting Editor" John Mitchell Jr.* (Charlottesville, Va., 2002), 39, 208.
4. See *Washington Post*, 18 June 1999, A40; *Roanoke Times*, 20 June 1999, A1, 4; *Richmond Free Press*, 17–19 June 1999, A11; *Richmond Times-Dispatch*, 4 June 1999, A1, 17.
5. *Atlanta Journal Constitution*, 27 April 2001, D1, 5.
6. Douglas Southall Freeman, *R. E. Lee: A Biography* (New York, 1934–35), 4:494.
7. Ibid, 505.
8. Tate to Lytle, 1 April 1929, and Tate to Lytle, 16 July 1931, in *The Lytle-Tate Letters: The Correspondence of Andrew Lytle and Allen Tate*, eds. Thomas Daniel Young and Elizabeth Sarcone (Jackson, Miss., 1987), 21, 46.
9. Gertrude Stein, *Everybody's Autobiography* (London, 1938), 213–14.
10. M. A. Harper, *For the Love of Robert E. Lee* (New York, 1992), 312.

11. T. Harry Williams, "The Military Leadership of North and South," in *Why the North Won the Civil War*, ed. David Donald (Baton Rouge, La., 1960), 39.

12. Thomas L. Connelly, *The Marble Man: Robert E. Lee and His Image in American Society* (New York, 1977), xiv.

13. Alan T. Nolan, *Lee Considered: General Robert E. Lee and Civil War History* (Chapel Hill, N.C., 1991); my comments in "Rebellion and Conventional Warfare," in *Writing the Civil War: The Quest to Understand*, eds. James M. McPherson and William J. Cooper Jr. (Columbia, S.C., 1998), 55.

14. Michael Fellman, *The Making of Robert E. Lee* (New York, 2000).

15. Emory M. Thomas, *Robert E. Lee: A Biography* (New York, 1995), and *Robert E. Lee: An Album* (New York, 2000).

16. Benét, *John Brown's Body*, 173.

17. Lee to Custis Lee, 22 June 1851, U.S. Military Academy Library and Archives, West Point, New York.

18. Material in the rear of Lee's diary, VHS.

19. Lee to Beauregard, 3 October 1865, in J. William Jones, *Life and Letters of Robert Edward Lee, Soldier and Man* (Washington, D.C., 1906), 390.

20. Wyatt Prunty, *The Times Between*, 3, "The Kite."

21. Lee to Custis Lee, 28 March 1852, Robert E. Lee Papers, VHS.

22. Lee to Eliza Mackay Stiles, quoted in Freeman, *Lee* 1:113–14.

23. T. L. Broun, "Negro Communed at St. Paul's Church," *Confederate Veteran* 13 (1905): 360.

24. Lucy Minnegerode and Lou Haxall to Lee, n.d., quoted in Thomas, *Lee: A Biography*, 315–16.

25. Lee to Lou and Lucy, Richmond, 14 December 1863, ibid., 316.

Robert E. Lee

Myth and Man

MICHAEL FELLMAN

"'Tell Hill he *must* come up. Strike the tent,' he said, and spoke no more.'" Douglas Southall Freeman took these lines uncritically from Col. William Preston Johnston's purportedly eyewitness account of the 1870 deathbed scene of President Robert E. Lee of Washington College. These were soul-stirring final words, but they would have been a physiological impossibility. Writing in the *Virginia Magazine of History and Biography* in 1990, five distinguished neurologists sifted all available evidence left by those closest to the deathbed. They concluded that, for the last two weeks of his life, following his massive stroke, Lee could utter only the occasional monosyllable, suffering as he did from abulia—literally absence of the will.[1]

This touching scene, on which generations of Southern school children were raised, arose, in fact, from the need of many white Southern leaders and ordinary citizens to believe that Robert E. Lee's death had to be beautiful and transcendent, because he was the very personification of the Southern nation, the embodiment of unbending Southern nationalism. This was the only acceptable style of death for the peerless leader.

By similar mythic necessity, many have wanted to believe that immediately after the war, when a black man had the effrontery to come down to the front of the church to take communion at St. Paul's Episcopal Church in Richmond, Robert E. Lee came down the aisle to share the flesh and the blood of Christ with him, thus demonstrating biracial peace. This story derives from two very dubious brief passages, written in the popular press in 1905, forty years after the supposed event. And even according to them, Lee might have been shaming the black man rather than accepting him. But the demands of legend have overwhelmed the critical capacities of scholars who have retailed the story as gospel.[2]

Concerning Lee's transformation from a human to the chief Confederate monument, Thomas L. Connelly wrote in his brilliant analysis of the posthumous Lee legend, *The Marble Man:* "The ultimate rationale of this pure nation was the character of Robert E. Lee. The Lost Cause argument stated that any society which produced a man of such splendid character, must be right."[3] Not only did this beatification transpose Lee into sainthood, but it also made his a most *political* sainthood. This essay explores two aspects of that transformation. One aspect is the historical Lee's actual participation in the early, formative stages of the victorious postwar, post-Confederate nationalist movement that destroyed Reconstruction and recreated white supremacy as a segregationist caste system, one that would last nearly one hundred years. The other aspect is the posthumous uses made by others of Lee's heritage, transforming him into an extremely "living" and useful historical monument, precisely by denying his human qualities in the name of the paragon, the usable paragon of all the genteel virtues.

In 1868 the historical Lee had been drawn into the Democratic presidential campaign. William S. Rosecrans, who was deputized to White Sulphur Springs, where Lee summered with other ex-Confederate bigwigs, induced Alexander H. H. Stuart, the leading Virginia backroom politician of his day, to draft a campaign letter. Lee willingly affixed his name as head signatory, and over thirty others then added their signatures. The Democratic position was that the most conservative possible group of older Southern leaders could and should be trusted with the restoration of power as the means to end Reconstruction. Traditional paternalism could be trusted, the letter asserted. "The idea that the Southern people are hostile to the negroes and would oppress them, if it were in their power to do so, is entirely unfounded. They have grown up in our midst, and we have been accustomed from childhood to look upon them with kindness."[4]

Not just idealism characterized white paternalism, however. In view of the practical need for black labor, the letter went on, "self-interest, if there were no higher motive, would therefore prompt the whites to protect blacks." And only white domination could form the basis of this interested and kind paternalism: "It is true that the people of the South, in common with a large majority of the people of the North and West, are, for obvious reasons, inflexibly opposed to any system of laws that would place the political power of the country in the hands of the negro race." This rigid opposition, the letter explained, stemmed not from "any enmity"—any deep-seated race hatred—but from a "deep-seated conviction" that blacks lacked the "necessary intelligence to make them safe repositories of political power. They would inevitably become the victims of demagogues who for selfish purposes would mislead them into serious injury of the public." Southern whites wanted peace and the restoration of the Union—"relief from oppressive misrule"—based on a return of what these gentlemen called the "birth-right of every American," that is to say the vote for disenfranchised ex-Confederates as for every other white man. After restoration, later called Redemption, the natural white ruling class would "treat the negro populations with kindness and humanity."[5]

The letter's language was moderate; the politics were not. White paternalism was to be a free grant from above, rather than a negotiated compromise resulting from any kind of power sharing with blacks. By 1877, growing frustrated and bored with Reconstruction, and as a means to resolve the hung election of 1876, the Republicans would agree with the essential terms of this proposal, and so Reconstruction ended on the Redeemers' terms.

After the war, Lee was close to the two leaders of Redemption in Virginia, Alexander H. H. Stuart and James B. Baldwin, both of whom lived in Staunton, just forty miles up the road from Lexington, where Lee resided after the war. Lee was a member of the conservative portion of the self-named Conservative coalition of ex-Whigs and Democrats that formed in Virginia in the late 1860s. At the moderate end was William Mahone, whose forces urged the acceptance of black suffrage as grounds for the early reclaiming of home rule. Adding an equivalent claim for the restoration of the vote to ex-Confederates, conservatives accepted black suffrage, and even opposed the nomination of a too-overt white racist for the governorship. Horace Greeley then brokered the deal with President U. S. Grant, and Virginia reentered the Union in 1870 without the full experience of a Reconstruction government.

Some historians have argued that Virginia experienced Reconstruction later than other former Confederate states, after the 1879 rise to state control of the Readjuster Movement. William Mahone had been squeezed out of power by the Conservative coalition by the Bourbons to his right, including Lee's closest associates. They insisted on paying off Virginia's prewar debts (unpaid during the war) in full, and to do so starved public education, especially for blacks, and they required payment of a poll tax as a condition of voting. When the Readjusters gained control of the state government, they cut the linkage of the poll tax to the vote, thus ending it as a disfranchising device; funded education for blacks, who had voted for them; and slashed the state debt; while not truly sharing power with African Americans.[6] *This* was Southern white moderation.

In this political formation, Lee was a conservative, not a moderate. Before his death, he had explicitly predicted that, once back in power, whites would squeeze blacks out of any and all meaningful political participation, and so they did. By the 1883 elections, the conservatives regrouped and drove Mahone and white moderation from power for the remainder of the nineteenth century and well into the twentieth.

In private, after the war, the publicly bland Lee was bitter in his states' rights Southern nationalism. He was most open with his Parisian nephew, Edward Lee Childe, a real favorite of his, perhaps because Childe was at a safe, transatlantic distance. To Childe, Lee sometimes expressed what could only be considered angry and anti-democratic anti-Americanism in the form the Republicans were taking the nation. "The tendency seems to be one vast Government, sure to become aggressive abroad & despotic at home," Lee wrote in 1867, "and I fear it will follow that road which history tells us such Republics have trod, might is believed to be right & the popular clamor the voice of God. . . . The greatest danger is the subversion of the old form of government and the substitution in its place of a great consolidated central power [that will] trample upon the reserved rights of the states & in time annihilate the Constitution."[7]

As well as being fundamentally opposed to postwar American nationalism, Lee was often antiblack. For example, in 1868 he wrote to his youngest son, Robert E. Lee Jr., "you will never prosper with the blacks, and it is abhorrent to a reflecting mind to be supporting and cherishing those who are plotting & working for your injury, and all of whose sympathies and associations are antagonistic to yours. . . . Our material, social and political interests are naturally with the whites."[8] In the late 1860s, Lee pushed for black deportation and white immigration, as did many Virginia planters and industrialists, hoping for what one historian has called the immigration panacea. But in 1868, of 213,000 predominantly northern and western European immigrants to the United States, exactly 713 moved to Virginia.[9] Few Europeans wanted to hazard settling in the impoverished and violent postwar South. And black Southerners did not simply go away either. Men like Lee, who wished they would, never formulated a plan for voluntary or forced black migration, but the wish was there that they would simply depart.

Thus, after the war, Lee was never apolitical. He participated actively in the rebirth of Southern white nationalism, albeit in the *public* role of the austere senior statesman above the fray. But even better political uses of him by this cause could be made after his death, when the story was reformulated to insist that Lee had been entirely above politics. Politics are a mess, politicians are dogs, and, contrarily, the expression of supposedly eternal values is central for political movements, particularly revolutionary or counterrevolutionary ones. As Thomas Connelly has written, a pure man purified the Lost Cause. For the cult of Lee, the best text is Edward V. Valentine's 1883 white marble statue of Lee at the burial shrine in Lexington, lying not dead but asleep on the field of eternal battle, booted and with a sword at his side, in full Confederate uniform, forever ready to awaken and defend his people.

Two more texts, both taken from a public meeting in Richmond, twelve days after his death, demonstrate how quickly Lee was turned into a demigod. (By the way, Lee was a reserved man and would have detested this adulatory oratory.) Jubal T. Early, perhaps the leading ex-Confederate propagandist of the Lost Cause, strode to the platform and declared: Lee's "fame belongs to the world and to history, and [a] sacred duty devolves upon those whom, in defense of a cause he believed to be just, and to which he remained true to the latest moment of his life, and led so often to battle," to honor him appropriately. "We owe it to our fallen comrades, to ourselves, and to posterity, by some suitable and lasting memorial, to manifest to the world, for all time to come, that we were not unworthy to be led by our immortal chief, and [are] not now ashamed by the principles for which Lee fought." And then it was Jefferson Davis's turn to speak. More important than Lee's brilliant career, said Davis, were "his immortal qualities that rose to the height of his genius." Among these was "self-denial—always intent on the one idea of duty—self-control." Davis concluded: "This good citizen, this gallant soldier, this great general, this true patriot, had yet a higher praise than this—he was a true Christian."[10]

Here was light itself, and the destruction of Reconstruction had both light and dark sides, inextricably bound together in an understood if unstated political dialectic. There was the paramilitary, or terrorist, branch and the legitimist branch, which worked together by inference—mutually understood inference (and sometimes more overtly)—to achieve a common goal, power. The legitimist branch, run by gentlemen of station and honor, promised kind paternalism once white power was secured (secured by any means necessary; *that* was the inference). The redeemed regime would not be biracial, but top down in its protection of blacks on the part of unchallenged white authority. This kinder side of redemption was not untrue, as these men meant what they said, but it was always reinforced, whenever necessary, by the dark side, by force, whether in everyday acts of discrimination or in threats, or in various forms of violence, culminating in lynching, an increasingly common practice in the post-Reconstruction South.

However, *deniability* remained all-important, both for psychological reasons and for the political need to maintain the aura of justice. Others—trashy whites—did the lynching, while good whites would always be kind to blacks if only left alone to be so. This combination of light and dark was to remain true well into my lifetime, and I am not that old. Only black action and outside pressure ended segregation—it did not wither of itself. Left to their own devices, Southern white liberals—and more-conservative paternalists—forever failed to escape the embrace of Southern white reaction, failed to establish a moderate biracial alternative.

This was a Southern nationalist movement, like many other separatist movements, and yet to a considerable degree it became American and not just Southern. This can be seen, for example, in the 1884 election of Grover Cleveland, an understudied event. This first Democratic president elected since 1856 brought many ex-Confederates into powerful positions in his inner circle of advisers, his cabinet, and the Supreme Court, as they had already regained immense power in Congress. By 1896 the Supreme Court would legitimate formal segregation, and in 1898 a splendid little war reunited Southern and Northern warriors in a vigorous new American imperialism. Protestant Northerners, afraid of waves of Jewish and Catholic immigrants, of labor strife, of wild urbanization, saw real virtue in the modes of Southern white rule over their lower orders, and made more overt alliance with the Bourbons.[11]

In this process, Lee was also nationalized. Men on both sides of the Civil War, the argument ran, had been honorable, brave, and true to their beliefs, and Lee had been the first among this vast brigade, peaceful, always conciliatory, disinterested, duty-bound, noble—in sum, the pure American hero after all. This deracination of Lee from his historical context of rebellion and resistance was all mythic, all historically inaccurate, and all ideologically indispensable. Not coincidentally, the height of the Lee cult, roughly 1890 to 1930, was also the nadir of race relations and the black experience in postslavery America.

Finally, this ideologically useful Lee was most impressive when wrapped in the myth of the tragic Lee—according to which he had sacrificed all save honor for the defense of slavery and for secession, in neither of which he believed. Duty overcame personal judgment, this argument goes, as if this would have been a virtue. In *The Making of Robert E. Lee*, I have analyzed Lee's single serious statement on slavery, made in 1856, which I found to be old-fashioned for its day, an argument defending slavery as a necessary evil, as opposed to the argument that slavery was a positive good, the more radical and more common late-antebellum proslavery position. Someday, slavery would be extinguished, according to Lee, but God moved slowly: "While we see the course of the final abolition of human slavery is onward, & we give it the aid of our prayers & all justifiable means in our power, we must leave the progress as well as the result in His hands who sees the end; who chooses to work by slow influences; and with whom two thousand years are but as a single day."[12]

Such fatalism, such inevitable and almost infinite postponement of abolition, was a proslavery position, not antislavery in the context of the United States in 1856. Moreover, when push came to shove, along with the rest of the Virginia gentry class, Lee went without doubt, hesitation, or later regret with those of his blood and marrow, with Virginia, the South, the plantation class, the white race. The bolder and harsher leaders of antebellum Southernism, the fire-eaters, had banged the drum in 1861, and then the softer and more genteel gentlemen marched into war bound together with them. So it would be during the destruction of Reconstruction, with the gallant Lee posthumously still turned to the task, as the chief and fully disembodied spiritual avatar of Southern white-supremacist nationalism.

Notes

1. William Preston Johnson, "Death of General Lee," in *Personal Reminiscences of General Robert E. Lee*, ed. J. William Jones (New York, 1875), 451; Douglas Southall Freeman, *R. E. Lee* (New York, 1934–35), 4:492; Marvin P. Rozear, E. Wayne Massey, Jennifer Horner, Erin Foley, and Joseph C. Greenfield Jr., "R. E. Lee's Stroke," *VMHB* 97 (April 1990): 291–308.

2. Col. T. L. Broun, of Charleston, West Virginia, as quoted in the *Richmond Times-Dispatch*, 16 April 1905, and the *Confederate Veteran* 13 (August 1905): 360. Colonel Broun thought Lee's act (assuming it did take place) was conducted "as if the negro had not been present. It was a grand exhibition of superiority shown by a true Christian and great soldier under the most trying and offensive circumstances." It is revealing to compare the white supremacist original with Emory Thomas's romantic interpretation of this source: "Another person arose from the pew and . . . knelt near the black man and so redeemed the circumstance. This grace-bringer, of course, was Lee," whose "actions were far more eloquent than anything he spoke or wrote" (*Robert E. Lee: A Biography* [New York, 1995], 372). Readers are urged to consult the documents from 1905, which appear in the appendix to this volume.

3. Thomas L. Connelly, *The Marble Man: Robert E. Lee and His Image in American Society* (Baton Rouge, La., 1977), 94.

4. Lee to William S. Rosecrans, 26 August 1868, Robert E. Lee Papers, VHS.

5. Ibid.
6. For postwar Virginia politics, see Michael Fellman, *The Making of Robert E. Lee* (New York: Random House, 2000), 264–94; Jack P. Maddex Jr., *The Virginia Conservatives, 1867–1879* (Chapel Hill, N.C., 1979); Maddex, "Virginia: The Persistence of Centrist Hegemony," in *Reconstruction and Redemption in the South*, ed. Otto H. Olsen (Baton Rouge, La., 1980), 113–55; and Richard Lowe, *Republicans and Reconstruction in Virginia, 1856–70* (Charlottesville, Va., 1991). For Mahone, see Jane Dailey, *Before Jim Crow: The Politics of Race in Postemancipation Virginia* (Chapel Hill, N.C., 2000), and the still valuable Nelson M. Blake, *William Mahone of Virginia: Soldier and Political Insurgent* (Richmond, 1935).
7. Lee to Edward Lee Childe, 5 January 1867, Lee Papers, Jesse Ball Dupont Library, Stratford Hall Plantation, Stratford, Virginia.
8. Lee to Robert E. Lee Jr., 12 March 1868, quoted in *The Recollections and Letters of Robert E. Lee*, ed. Robert E. Lee Jr. (1904; rept. New York, n.d.), 306.
9. Maddex, *Virginia Conservatives*, 178–83.
10. Addresses of J. A. Early and Jefferson Davis to the Surviving Officers of the Army of Northern Virginia, Lynchburg, 24 October 1870, in Jones, *Reminiscences*, 334, 340–41.
11. This discussion of the destruction of Reconstruction and the triumph of white supremacy as the culmination of the era of the Civil War is fleshed out in Michael Fellman, Lesley J. Gordon, and Daniel E. Sutherland, *"This Terrible War": The Civil War and Its Aftermath* (New York, 2002), 346–82.
12. Fellman, *Making of Robert E. Lee*, 72–74. For the full text of this letter from Lee to his wife, Mary Custis Lee, 27 December 1856, see Freeman, *Lee* 1:371–73.

Robert E. Lee and the Concept of Honor

BERTRAM WYATT-BROWN

For generations General Lee epitomized the white South's devotion to the principles of honor. As early as 1868, three years after the end of the war, Gen. Jubal Early, C.S.A., declaimed: "Our beloved chief stands, like some lofty column which rears its head among the highest, in grandeur, simple, pure and sublime, needing no borrowed luster." Nor, in some minds, has his reputation since dimmed or become tarnished. A recently published book has it that Lee and his partner in war, Stonewall Jackson, "epitomized the virtues of duty, valor and honor that patriotic Americans hold dear"—even if their secessionist cause would have tragically crippled the future of the American states. Attorney General John Ashcroft has proclaimed Lee a "patriot" to be forever venerated—else "we'll be taught that [Lee and other Confederates] were giving their lives, subscribing their sacred fortunes and their honor to some perverted agenda." As these convictions indicate, for so many whites reared in the South, Lee still seems wrapped in a cloak of pure dignity.[1]

Yet, in scholarly circles, Lee has lately undergone the trials of revisionism that so many of the famous dead have experienced. Thomas Connelly's *The Marble Man*, Alan Nolan's *Lee Considered*, William Piston's study of Longstreet, *Lee's Tarnished Lieutenant*, Michael Fellman's provocative *The Making of Robert E. Lee*, and Emory Thomas's biography have all chipped away at the notion of Lee as pure hero. My purpose is not to challenge these healthy efforts to humanize him but to argue that the mythic Lee should not entirely disappear. Beneath the level of idolatry lay the reality of greatness itself. So long as honor retained its value in Southern and—to some degree—in national life,

Robert Edward Lee exemplified the best aspects of a code that also encompassed, alas, some very deplorable notions and prejudices.

The ethic of honor was a code that nineteenth-century American society, particularly in the slave states, understood and practiced. Yet, it no longer has the intensity and centrality of meaning that it did when everyone knew what a lady and a gentleman were supposed to be and how they should comport themselves. Now those terms are not only out of fashion, but they are also used in derision. Of course, we still apply the concept in specific instances. Honor may refer to a judge, for example: "His Honor." It can signify the acceptance of an invitation or a bank check. Honor and its opposite, shame, have other uses too. Clubs like the U.S. Senate can expel members—an occurrence that ought to happen more often than it does—for bringing "dishonor" on the body. Women may try in vain to enter a military college when men think that their honor would be violated by the women's presumption. Yet, how trivial these examples are in comparison with the almost pervasive use of honor, gentility, respectability, and similar moral designations in the middle of the nineteenth century. In that period, honor consisted of one's sense of identity and rank in society. The claimant to honor sought social approval to reinforce a pride of place. Therefore, appearances meant everything. Repression of the unpleasant or unflattering became a key to social discourse and self-evaluation.[2]

This idea of honor's dimensions is pertinent in many ways to General Lee as well as to most of his Southern contemporaries, yet we must also consider a corollary to it, the role of grace. In combining grace and honor, we need not remount the old general on his pedestal. At the same time, Lee ought not to be stripped of his rank among the great men of his day. Grace might be called the sacred side of honor. Honor in this sense grows into something more precious to the claimant than his life. As two anthropologists have written, "Rather death than dishonor!" was "the ideal expression of this sentiment, whether on the battlefield or in the boudoir."[3] Like chastity, another old-fashioned idea, grace is alien to our culture. What leading figure in the headlines today can claim an abundance of grace?

In traditional fashion—after all, the Old South was a patriarchal society—Lee inherited his concept of honor from his father. We cannot appreciate Lee's character without examining the relationship of the son to his father. Robert Edward Lee was the son of an honorable gentleman, Henry "Light-Horse Harry" Lee, who emerged from the American Revolution a hero, yet was also a tragic figure. Born of distinguished Virginia lineage, the elder Lee had left his Princeton studies to serve in George Washington's army at the outbreak of the Revolution, but he achieved his fame under Gen. Nathanael Greene in the Southern campaigns against Gen. George Cornwallis. He had previously refused Washington's offer to make him his aide-de-camp, declaring: "I am wedded to my sword," and, he went on, "my secondary object . . . is military reputation," with hope of deserving "your Excellency's patronage" as "a stimulus to glory, second to none in power of the many that operate upon my soul." Expressing himself in this way, Lee embodied the highest aims of military honor—battle daring for the sake of immortal fame. The sentiment may sound romantic in the Byronic sense. Its origins, however, may be found in the glorifications of martial valor in Homer, Thucydides, Virgil, or Beowulf. In other words, the kind of honor that Henry Lee understood harkened back to the masculine universalities that had their beginnings in premodern times. As Xenophon expressed the ideal, "And when their fated end comes, they do not lie forgotten and without honor, but they are remembered and flourish eternally in men's praises."[4]

After the Revolutionary War, Henry Lee's first marriage was to his cousin Matilda Lee. Just before she died, she had encumbered her estate in 1790 with a trust for their only son (also named Henry). That decision protected it from her husband's creditors, of whom there were already all too many. Waving aside his accumulation of debts, as high-living governor of his state, "Light-Horse Harry" then married the aristocratic Ann Hill Carter, heir to 25,000 acres surrounding the great house Shirley on the north bank of the James River below Richmond. Charles Carter, her wealthy father, had objected to the union. Her suitor was seventeen years his intended's senior. Another impediment was his pro-French politics. General Lee could hardly bring his age closer to Ann's twenty years, but he did repudiate his radical Revolutionary views, and Charles Carter permitted the marriage to go forward.[5]

Like Robert Morris, Alexander Hamilton, and other notables of the day, General Lee recklessly speculated in landholding companies and eventually lost much of his wife's estate, not to mention his own. Morris, himself bankrupted, owed Lee $40,000 and never paid back a penny. Lee's handling of these financial troubles, far from indicating a feckless irresponsibility, demonstrated his adherence to the code of honor. Irate creditors had General Lee jailed in 1809, yet his decision to spend months in prison was his sole means to hold his land. Otherwise, by Virginia law, he would have had to declare insolvency and would thereby have lost it all through trusteeship and sheriff's sale— to the economic ruination and lost social standing of his dependents. At one point, he confessed that he had had to mortgage some 19,000 acres in southwestern Virginia to "pay," he noted, "certain debts wherein my honor was concerned."[6] In a sense, he sacrificed his own dignity, well-being, and even freedom for the sake of his family. The Revolutionary War hero did everything he could to hold as much land as possible in trust to assure the fiscal safety of his family. That insistence upon putting family and kinfolk first and foremost was a cardinal principle of his son Robert many years later.[7] Neither before nor after "Light-Horse Harry" Lee's death were his wife and children ever destitute at any time, though inevitably reduced in circumstance from the high standing once enjoyed.[8]

The threat of dishonor dogged Lee in a way that his most famous son happily never had to confront. In 1812 a Jeffersonian mob in Baltimore beat the fiery Virginia Federalist nearly to death. One rioter stabbed him twice in the face, and another tried to remove his nose with a knife. To pull or disfigure a man's nose at the time was considered the height of disgrace, a visible mark to symbolize a figurative castration. Humiliated, depressed, half-blinded, and penniless, Lee fled from Virginia to the West Indies to escape the pity and embarrassment of friends and the pursuit of creditors. Six years later, while on his way back to his wife and family, he died from the old Baltimore wounds. His youngest son, Robert, was six when he last saw his father and only eleven when his "brilliant, lovable, and unfortunate father," as Robert E. Lee biographer Douglas Southall Freeman wrote, departed this life in 1818.[9]

Before he died, Harry Lee had given young Robert no canny moral advice, either in person or by letter. Although his departure from his family prevented him from beginning a close tie with his youngest son, Harry Lee did leave the future general an ethical legacy. It consisted of his memoir, written in the Spotsylvania County jail in 1810 and published as *Memoirs of the War of Independence in the Southern Department of the United States*. We know that his story of daring exploits, fierce fighting, and the tragedy of battle was often in Robert Lee's thoughts. Only two years before his own death, Lee, then president of Washington College, had his father's account republished.[10]

Robert Lee certainly lived up to the prescriptions that his father could not wholly match himself. But Emory Thomas, Lee's impressive recent biographer, goes much too far when he asserts: "To redeem Light-Horse Harry Lee's misdeeds and restore the family fame, Robert Lee would become his father's hero."[11] Instead, the son honored the father. He was not restoring but upholding a family tradition of valor and duty: worthy father, worthy son. Yet, much credit must be given to Ann Hill Carter Lee, who reared her children for the most part without the aid of her wayward husband.

One might have expected Robert Lee to be driven into deep depressions in light of the early loss of his father and the decline of the once-powerful family to a lower social standing. That reaction often befalls orphaned young boys.[12] If he were such a victim of gloom, he would have found himself in the company of some important contemporaries. Suffering in varying degrees from chronic depression were motherless Abraham Lincoln, near alcoholic U. S. Grant, and orphan William Tecumseh Sherman. And on Lee's side of the battle lines, Jefferson Davis, his commander in chief, who lost his father when the boy was in his teens, Braxton Bragg, John Bell Hood, Richard Ewell, Robert Toombs, and Lee's right arm, Stonewall Jackson, all were victims of what fellow depressive Winston Churchill used to call "the Black Dog."[13]

Lee, though, never fell into deep despondency. Indeed, his equanimity seems remarkable given the strains that his desperate undertakings to keep the Confederacy alive inevitably entailed. At the battle of Antietam, Lee was coolness personified. At 3 o'clock, on September 17, 1862, the Federals were about to break through on the Rebel right. Having found a good position to watch the unfolding battle, Lee asked a passing lieutenant to turn his telescope on a column barely visible but moving rapidly. "What troops are those?" Lee asked. Young John Ramsay replied, "They are flying the Virginia and Confederate flags." According to Freeman's rendition, "Lee did not move a muscle, though the words spelled salvation. 'It is A. P. Hill from Harpers Ferry,' he said quietly."[14] If the loss of his father—normally a disruptive, even traumatic, event for small boys—failed to result in unrequited grief, he may have been what psychologists call "the invulnerable child."[15] That term identifies a young victim who barely shows late signs of the traumas but rises above them. Some kind of thick carapace almost impossible to penetrate covers the inner wound. One must wonder if Lee hid such inner doubts more successfully than most, as Thomas Connelly and others claim. Or was there a genuine simplicity and directness that Douglas Southall Freeman celebrates?[16] In any event, Lee achieved a balance of temper that his father and most of Robert Lee's contemporaries could not match.

In contrast to Henry Lee, Robert developed a sense of prudence and practicality in all things; he loved order and moderation as if he had cast himself in the image of the emperor Marcus Aurelius, whose *Meditations* laid out the prescriptions of the Stoic temperament. Yet, his father represented a daring, a willingness to risk much, even in defiance of the gods, and a sense of honorable noblesse oblige. Emory Thomas remarks, after recounting the losses at Gettysburg and Lee's own declining health, that the general "continued capable of exhibiting grace under all but overwhelming pressure."[17]

The critic might challenge these flattering conclusions. One could ask why, then, did Lee resign his commission in the Federal army to fight the Union that his father had fought so bravely to create? It could be said that, when he took up arms against an army that President Abraham Lincoln and Gen. Winfield Scott offered him to lead, his decision surely betrayed his oath of allegiance to uphold the Constitution. In treating Lee's resignation from the Federal army, historian Alan Nolan uses my interpretation of honor to charge him with a "self-serving" and slippery sense of the ethic. I am reported to have proposed that honor was "self-regarding in character." Nolan applies that state of mind to Lee so that he is alleged to have made his adherence to honor merely "a convenient label . . . for what he wanted to do or had already done. Lee's honor," Nolan continues, "was therefore on occasion simply rhetorical, a matter of saying the magic word, a self-fulfilling incantation. . . . Lee was honorable," Nolan argues, "because he said so."[18]

But self-regard is not invariably immoral; it can mean self-possession, a quality of self-confidence—knowing exactly who you are to yourself and to others. In the most remarkable way, Lee had so little doubt about his identity that he inspired awe by the very natural, graceful manner of his speech, bearing, and modestly asserted assumption of leadership. Consider the circumstances of his decision in 1861 to resign his career and accept whatever role Providence and the authorities in Virginia might have prepared for him. He had to act quickly, because he did not wish to resign when given orders that he could not conscientiously fulfill. All the interviews with Winfield Scott and Lee's friend Francis Preston Blair took place when Lee had received no command save to leave his military station in Texas and hasten to Washington. He waited almost until the Ordinance of Secession in Virginia had been passed by referendum before leaving the army, not out of some underhanded subterfuge or Hamlet-like indecision, but simply, as he wrote a relative, "to save me from such a position and to prevent the necessity of resigning under orders." In modern parlance, he thus became a free agent. Yet, as he put it, he had "no desire ever again to draw my sword . . . save in defense of my native State."[19]

The decision to join the Confederacy had everything to do with Lee's concept of honor. By its standards, he had no choice. "If blood means anything," wrote Douglas Freeman, Lee "was entitled to be what he fundamentally was, a gentleman." Without taking account of his tie to the ancient code, his decision to join the Confederacy would be inexplicable. The firmness of his belief in the ethic was evident from his moral instructions to his children in the 1850s. "Honor and fame are all that men should aspire to," Lee had asserted. With steady application and valor, "they will at last be won," he wrote his son Custis in 1851. "Hold yourself above every mean action. Be strictly honorable in every act, and be not ashamed to do right." Lee was determined that his youngsters should grow in grace and Stoic rectitude. Though often absent from home, he remained solicitous about them, combining the patriarchal tradition with an endearing playfulness. Robert Jr., for instance, reminisced that his father "gave me my first sled, and sometimes used to come out where we boys were coasting to look on," and he allowed the children an intimacy not altogether common in that day of austere patriarchy. He even let the little ones "climb into bed in the morning and lie close to him, listening while he talked to us in his bright, entertaining way."[20]

Honor meant much in Robert Lee's household, but slavery little. Like so many in the Virginia upper class, including his father's adversary, Thomas Jefferson, Lee entertained strong doubts about the morality and suitability of slavery, but such opinions were not ideals to be acted upon. Much more important to him than the fate of slavery was the obligation to uphold the traditions of his class, community, and state. The tradition of honor imposed that duty, and Lee followed it. "I prize the Union very highly," he wrote in the last days before secession, "& know of no personal sacrifice that I would not make to preserve it, save that of honour."[21]

Indeed, that same sense of honor cannot be separated from the principle (as it then was considered) of white superiority and black subordination. That arrangement seemed to nearly all white Southerners as ordained by God, who in his wisdom had selected whites to masterhood and blacks to perpetual bondage. Lee must bear the moral stigma of that close connection between his concept of honor and his comfort in slaveholding and pride of color. In July 1864 Lee did not react to the massacre of black prisoners of war after the Union disaster at the Crater in the battle of Petersburg. The bloody, heart-wrenching scene had to have become known to the commanding general, but he spoke not a word about the murder of unarmed African Americans.[22] Honor can turn a blind eye when the subject is thought to be beneath recognition.

With regard to Lee's racial attitudes, myths and uncertain memories have created some historical confusion. In June 1865 the defeated general attended a service at St. Paul's Episcopal Church in Richmond. Also present was Col. T. L. Broun, C.S.A., of Charleston, West Virginia. According to the colonel's recollections, published in 1905, a tall, dignified, and impeccably dressed black man "with an air of military authority" went up to the chancel to receive the sacraments. Everyone else in the congregation sat dumbfounded and immobile—the communicants were shocked, as Colonel Broun recalled, "being deeply chagrined at this attempt of the Federal authorities, to offensively humiliate them during their most devoted church services." Lee rose from his pew, walked to the communion rail, and knelt not far from the black worshiper. All the others in the congregation, including Broun, followed his example. "By this action of General Lee, the services were concluded, as if the negro had not been present. It was a grand exhibition of superiority shown by a true Christian and great soldier under the most trying offensive circumstances."[23]

Of course, that might have been a reading that better conformed to the Jim Crow era of 1905. A charitable version would claim that Lee may have meant a reconciliation between officers of the two sides, regardless of color. We do not know if the black communicant was given the Eucharist or simply passed over, or if Lee showed any gesture of Christian welcome after the service. Colonel Broun's interpretation, sadly, seems the most likely. For Lee, gentleman and Virginian, the proper course was to diffuse a fragile and potentially dangerous situation, not without recognizing the dictates of white honor.

As the incident at the church and the silence at Petersburg demonstrate, Lee was a more complicated figure than his image as an icon of the postwar South's Lost Cause legend suggests. Actually, he was utterly simple in choosing his destiny. Two interrelated factors, and they alone, explained his decision to resign his commission, return to Virginia, and accept appointment under the new government. He wrote Anne Marshall, his sister, about one of them: "I have not been able to make up my mind to raise my hand against my relatives, my children, my home."[24]

From earliest times in Western civilization, the cardinal principle of honor was familial loyalty and defense. Who else in a transient and chronically violent world could one trust save one's kinspeople? To war against one's own family was a violation of law. Unwritten and often unspoken, that law of survival superseded all other claims. To Lee, as to nearly all Confederates, the commandment to protect and promote family interests could not be violated. It helped to drive the

Upper South out of the Union. Who did not have kindred farther south? In time, a sense of abstract nationality, transcending family and friends, might have been constructed upon the secession effort, but certainly not in 1861. Rather, the archaically familial and social concepts of honor and sense of insult and pride superseded notions of a truly separate nation. As William W. Freehling cogently argues, the South was riven with fatal dissensions.[25]

The second reason for Lee's secessionism was equally a matter of conscience—one arising from the primal code as much as from Christian heritage. As Mrs. Lee wrote a friend, "My husband has wept tears of blood over this terrible war, but as a man of honor and a Virginian, he must follow the destiny of his State."[26] The Old Dominion was not an abstraction in Lee's mind. Inextricably it was bound up with the life and heritage of the Lees, Carters, Marshalls, and other clans with which he was associated, the living and the dead. Lee had no choice in the matter.

Culturally, morally, spiritually, Lee was compelled to forsake the Union. On this count he is sometimes accused of a narrowness of vision, but the complaint itself is parochial. Lee could not escape a momentous choice: he was compelled to fight either for or against his kin. The Lees, after all, were connected with just about everybody of high standing in Virginia. The option simply to exile himself would not have crossed his mind. By any standard, that was the coward's way out, a rejection of what Lee's God had set before him as moral choice. "I should like to retire to private life, if I could be with you and the children, but if I can be of any service to the State or her cause I must continue," Lee wrote his wife in early June 1861 from Richmond. "May God guard and bless you . . . and our suffering country, and enable me to perform my duty."[27]

Obligations to family and to his code were so important that Lee never really felt that a promise of ultimate success had to figure into his joining the Confederacy. How alien it is to our way of thinking that someone could devote his life to a cause that he really thought was doomed from the start. Honor, though, may require dedication to a predictably vain struggle. In military circles, moreover, such action in the face of impending disaster is not unusual, even as it makes the will to fight against the fates more desperate. As often happens, war is not "a rational pursuit of political goals," as political scientist Avner Offer notes, "but a gesture of defiance, taken, like the duel, against the odds."[28] So it was in Lee's perspective. So it has been in other instances.

Consider the attitude of the Austrian and German generals on the eve of war in 1914. Prussian generals Helmuth von Moltke and Erich von Falkenhayn, together with Franz Conrad von Hötzendorf, chief of staff of the Austro-Hungarian army, were certain that the politicians were foolishly promising their constituents a quick and easy triumph. But all three, having long promoted the duel as a means to strengthen officer corps morale, shared a common faith in martial honor, come what may. Von Moltke wrote gloomily on July 29, 1914, that the conflict soon to begin "will annihilate the civilization of almost the whole of Europe for decades to come." But, like Lee, he considered it a matter of honor and duty to enter the fray and prove his loyalty to his kindred and country. Likewise, five days later von Falkenhayn predicted: "Even if this [war] drives us into ruin, it will be worthwhile." General Conrad, in Vienna, realized that his emperor, Franz Josef, also doubted success. Nonetheless, in the name of honor, the aged ruler had exclaimed, "If the Monarchy is doomed to perish, let it at least perish decorously," that is, with dignity, and Conrad, himself a pessimist, heartily agreed. As the historian Donald Kagan has pointed out, wars are not always rationally undertaken but may well be the consequence of pride, honor, and loyalties that override practical assessment of the result.[29]

General Lee belonged to that select cadre of men that install honor ahead of all else, including victory. One of the outstanding features of Emory Thomas's biography is his stress on Lee's recognition of Confederate fragility—the tenuousness of the whole experiment from first to last. Not for a moment did such a grim view of the future affect Lee's generalship and loyalty. Douglas Freeman caught Lee's remarkable blending of dignity, passion, and sorrow when he described how Lee responded to General Imboden's sympathetic remark after both had witnessed Pickett's charge at Gettysburg. Imboden had found Lee next to Traveler standing in the dark, profoundly silent. "'General, it has been a hard day on you.' 'Yes, it has been a sad day for us,'" Lee answered mournfully. Then, as if having just undergone an epiphany, he exclaimed with passion: "I never saw troops behave more magnificently than Pickett's division of Virginians did today in that grand charge upon the enemy. And if they had been supported as they were to have been—but for some reason not yet fully explained to me, were not—we would have held the position and the day would have been ours." A pause followed. Then Lee sighed, "Too bad! Too bad! Oh, too bad!"[30]

Lee's sense of grace, no less a part of the man than his dedication to Stoic honor, was apparent in another way: his preference for the avoidance of personal confrontations or angry scenes. He relied instead on his commanding presence to establish respect. The code of honor might be said to provide two ways for men to handle differences and rivalries. The first is the familiar one of violence—the infuriated response to alleged insult. Politicians like Alexander Hamilton, Aaron Burr, and Andrew Jackson, as well as such duelists as Confederate senator Louis Wigfall of Texas from Lee's generation, satisfied their demands for vindication on the field of honor. Lee never would have adopted that course. Instead, like such notables as Thomas Jefferson, James Madison, and John Marshall, he adopted a mode of gentility, a punctilious silence, and a form of diplomatic speech that precluded intemperate impulses. Lee's success as a general was attributable in part to this consensual approach to matters. He had long been famous for his insistence on a voluntary style of leadership. He encouraged an independence of will in those generals whom he thought, sometimes wrongly, trustworthy to carry out orders. He tended, however, to couch his orders in the polite fashion of wishes rather than as incontestable commands. Sometimes that mode led to misapprehensions.

These illustrations may partially capture the more glorious and benign aspects of the honor code. Yet honor is a very ambiguous concept. It has a darker, crueler side that displays an indifference to suffering and death of those not caparisoned in the robes of honor. Like most other codes of ethics, including Christian strictures, it can easily be made a source of rationalization and manipulation. An act called honorable may seem to violate the very core of principle. For instance, after the Confederate victory on June 3, 1864, in the Cold Harbor campaign, U. S. Grant proposed to dispense with the usual protocols so that his troops could remove the wounded and bury the dead on the battlefield. Ordinarily a flag of truce would signal the momentary lull, but Grant wanted the litter bearers to proceed at once to their tasks. All the wounded Union troops were behind Confederate lines, but no Rebels were left on Union turf. So, with nothing to gain from the transaction, Lee refused. He claimed that a flag of truce must be carried as custom required. Grant's felt his dignity affronted, and the verbal skirmish persisted for four days. Grant finally gave way and had the traditional white flag paraded. By then, only two Union soldiers were found still alive.[31]

Had Lee acted honorably in his insistence on following the rules of war? Certainly; the fault was Grant's. He had tried and failed to gain a moral advantage. Although having lost the battle, he sought to win the truce. Lee's sense of honor demanded that the defeated party should not claim equality or superiority in such a transaction. By the lights of the day, by the rules of his lifelong profession, he was fully justified. Yet his rigidity betokened a lack of mercy. Such punctiliousness as the incident revealed suggests that Lee had a colder side to his nature than his often-winning sense of humor, and warmth of feeling for those he knew well, seemed to portend.

The tables turned when Lee tried to surrender in April 1865. For a while, Grant could not be found and was, perhaps deliberately, a half-hour late in arriving at the Appomattox Court House. It was a subtle form of asserting authority over the surrendering foe. Grant knew how to return the unpleasantness Lee had exhibited at Cold Harbor.

Despite these lapses, if such they were, Lee's Stoic temperament, that is, his combining of grace and honor, remains his most outstanding feature. Perhaps the tragedy of his father's career so many years before had prepared the Civil War general to adopt that pagan, tragic outlook that Emperor Marcus Aurelius had used long ago: expect nothing but what the gods decree, for good or ill defeat. Be satisfied solely in the most conscientious performance of duty imaginable.[32]

Of course, Lee was no saint. He fervently entertained many of the prejudices, racial and otherwise, that his fellow white Virginians held—with which the nation still grapples. He never understood, for instance, the humanity or bravery of the black troops who, in fighting his forces at the Crater, suffered enormous casualties. Toward the end of the war, the once-unflappable general's self-discipline unraveled in the face of the inevitable surrender that lay ahead. He grew testy. He lashed out at his staff with petty complaints. Sometimes he indulged in bitter sarcasm. He told Senator Benjamin Hill that the Confederates had made a colossal mistake at the very start. Hill asked what that error was. Lee replied, "Why, sir, in the beginning we appointed all our worst generals to command the armies, and all our best generals to edit the newspapers." He reminded Hill that he had put all his professional skill into his plans, thinking them nearly "perfect," only to discover afterwards that somehow defects had tarnished the result. Lee had even wondered, he told Hill, why he had not seen the problems earlier. But then, he exclaimed, "When it was all over, I found by reading a newspaper that these best editor-generals saw all the defects plainly from the start. Unfortunately, they did not communicate their knowledge to me until it was too late."[33]

Throughout his life, General Lee exhibited virtues that momentary transgressions did not stain. He possessed a gravitas that we have not seen in high places since the death of George C. Marshall, his worthy descendant. At the same time, the kind of conservatism and sense of white hegemony that Lee exemplified and lived by would scarcely add to his stature today. We can admire his style of leadership, his sense of noblesse oblige and courtesy, his fundamental integrity, but not the cause for which he led so many fellow Virginians to their death, and not the rationale by which he justified a tragic decision to rebel against his country. More than anyone else, his brilliant generalship led to the inexorable ruination of the very land he was defending. Ironically, Lee helped to solve the great issue of American freedom versus American slavery. He did so by forcing a prolongation of a war that ended in black emancipation and the construction of a new and more liberated republic. That was, it could be said, his most honorable contribution, unwelcome though it was to his fellow white Virginians and, it seems, unwelcome though it is to those who still mourn the Confederacy's defeat.

Notes

1. Early quoted in Gaines M. Foster, *Ghosts of the Confederacy: Defeat, the Lost Cause, and the Emergence of the New South, 1865 to 1913* (New York, 1987), 59; James I. Robertson Jr., *Jackson & Lee: Legends in Gray* (Nashville, Tenn., 1995), 9, cited by Gary W. Gallagher, "Jubal A. Early, the Lost Cause, and Civil War

History: A Persistent Legacy," *The Myth of the Lost Cause and Civil War History*, eds. Gary W. Gallagher and Alan T. Nolan (Bloomington, Ind., 2000), 51; John Ashcroft is quoted in Roy Blount Jr., *Robert E. Lee* (New York, 2003), 3.

2. Robert Nisbett and D. Cohen, *The Culture of Honor: The Psychology of Violence in the South* (Boulder, Colo., 1996); Bertram Wyatt-Brown, *Southern Honor: Ethics and Behavior in the Old South* (New York, 1982); John G. Peristiany, *Honor and Shame in Mediterranean Societies* (Chicago, 1966); Bertram Wyatt-Brown, "Honor's History across the Academy," *Historically Speaking* 3 (June 2002): 13–15.

3. John G. Peristiany and Julian Pitt-Rivers, eds., *Honor and Grace in Anthropology* (Cambridge, 1992), 2.

4. Quoted in Burton J. Hendrick, *The Lees of Virginia: A Biography of a Family* (Boston, 1935), 336; Xenophon quoted in Wyatt-Brown, *Southern Honor*, 36; Donald Kagan, *The Peloponnesian War* (New York, 2003), 57. See also Moses I. Finley, *The World of Odysseus* (New York, 1951); Donald Kagan, "Honor, Interest, and the Nation-State," in *Honor among Nations: Intangible Interests and Foreign Policy*, ed. Elliott Abrams (Washington, D.C., 1998), 2–3.

5. Douglas Southall Freeman, *Lee: An Abridgement in One Volume*, ed. Richard Harwell (New York, 1961), 4, 5–6.

6. Henry Lee to John Nicholas, 19 October 1796, in Henry Lee Papers, 1794–1813, Library of Virginia, Richmond. (I thank Glenn Crothers, University of Florida, for supplying me with this documentation.)

7. Timothy Harrington to Henry Lee, 21 September 1808, deed between McCarty Fitzhugh and Henry Lee, 10 December 1809, Henry Lee to Bernard Carter, 21 January, 7 March 1810, deed between Henry Lee and Bernard Carter, 5 March 1810, Henry Lee to Bernard Carter, 22 April 1813: "You cannot I think neglect a body of land so important to yr. children [Henry Lee's grandchildren], especially if I shd. aid you in releasing it from all liens," Henry Lee Papers, Library of Virginia.

8. T. Michael Miller, "An Analysis of Light Horse Lee's Financial and Real Estate Transactions" (unpublished paper, 1990), 59–60 (kindly supplied by Glenn Crothers).

9. Emory M. Thomas, *Robert E. Lee: A Biography* (New York, 1995), 23, 36–37; Freeman, *Lee*, 4.

10. Henry Lee, *Memoirs of the War of Independence in the Southern Department of the United States*, ed. Robert E. Lee (New York, 1870).

11. Thomas, *Lee*, 256.

12. Alistair Munro, "Parental Deprivation in Depressive Patients," *British Journal of Psychiatry* 112 (1966): 443–57; Munro, "Some Familial and Social factors in Depressive Illness," ibid. 112 (1966): 429–41; E. James Anthony, "Psychoanalysis and Environment," in *The Course of Life*, vol. 6, *Late Adulthood*, eds. George H. Pollock and Stanley I. Greenspan (Madison, Conn., 1993), 261–310.

13. Jean Edward Smith, *Grant* (New York, 2001); Michael Fellman, *Citizen Sherman: A Life of William Tecumseh Sherman* (New York, 1995); Michael Burlingame, *The Inner World of Abraham Lincoln* (Urbana, Ill., 1994); (on Ruffin) Bertram Wyatt-Brown, *Hearts of Darkness: Wellsprings of a Southern Literary Tradition* (Baton Rouge, La., 2003), 47–56; Grady McWhiney, *Braxton Bragg and Confederate Defeat* (Tuscaloosa, Ala., 1991); William Y. Thompson, *Robert Toombs of Georgia* (Baton Rouge, La., 1966); William C. Davis, *Jefferson Davis: The Man and His Hour* (New York, 1991); Byron Farwell, *Stonewall: A Biography of General Thomas J. Jackson* (New York, 1992); Anthony Storr, *Churchill's Black Dog, Kafka's Mice, and Other Phenomena of the Human Mind* (New York, 1988).

14. Freeman, *Lee*, 261.

15. See the citations in note 12; the quotation is from Anthony, "Psychoanalysis and Environment," 304. (I owe this citation to Anne Wyatt-Brown, who called my attention to its relevance.)

16. Thomas L. Connelly, *The Marble Man: Robert E. Lee and His Image in American Society* (New York, 1971); Alan T. Nolan, *Lee Considered: General Robert E. Lee and Civil War History* (Chapel Hill, N.C., 1991); Freeman, *Lee.*

17. Thomas, *Lee*, 315.

18. Nolan, *Lee Considered*, 55–56.

19. Robert E. Lee to Reverdy Johnson, 25 February 1868, Robert E. Lee to Smith Lee, 20 April 1861, in Captain Robert E. Lee, *Recollections and Letters of General Robert E. Lee* (New York, 1924), 26–27.

20. Lee, *Recollections*, 8, 9, 13; Lee to Custis Lee, 4 May 1851, in J. William Jones, *Life and Letters of Robert E. Lee, Soldier and Man* (New York, 1906), 72.

21. Quoted in Thomas, *Lee*, 186.

22. Lee, *Recollections*, 341–42.

23. "Negro Communed at St. Paul's Church," *Richmond Times-Dispatch*, 16 April 1905, 5, and *Confederate Veteran* 13 (August 1905): 360. (I owe these crucial references to Philip J. Schwarz, Virginia Commonwealth University.) Cf. Thomas, *Lee*, 372. And see the 1905 publications in the appendix to this book.

24. Lee, *Recollections*, 26.

25. For instance, many people in the South, particularly in the mountain regions—finding the honorable course to be a parochial repudiation of Confederate centralism—despised a war that benefited only the rich slaveholder (Freehling, *The South vs. the South: How Anti-Confederate Southerners Shaped the Course of the Civil War* [New York, 2001]).

26. Lee, *Recollections*, 35.

27. Lee to Mary Custis Lee, 9 June 1861, in Lee, *Recollections*, 35.

28. Avner Offer, "Going to War in 1914: A Matter of Honor?" *Politics and Society* 23 (June 1995): 213–41, quotation at 221–22.

29. The quotations and general argument about pessimism, honor, and warfare are in Avner Offer, "Going to War in 1914." See also Kevin McAleer, *Dueling: The*

Cult of Honor in Fin-de-Siècle Germany (Princeton, N.J., 1994), 40, 109, 110–11, 114, 164; "Donald Kagan on National Honor," a conference paper entitled "Intangible Interests and U.S. Foreign Policy" (1996), at http://www.cs.utexas.edu/ users/vi/notes/kagan.html.

30. Freeman, *Lee*, 341.

31. Thomas, *Lee*, 335.

32. Quoted in Blount, *Lee*, 136.

33. Thomas, *Lee*, 352.

A Man of Constant Sorrow

The Enduring Enigma of Robert E. Lee

CHARLES JOYNER

> I am a man of constant sorrow,
> I've seen trouble all my days
> —traditional folk song, as sung by Ralph Stanley

There is a mythic quality to America's Civil War era. When Robert Penn Warren calls it "our Homeric period" and Charles Roland titles his military history *An American Iliad*, they are only acknowledging an aura that is already palpable. Recently the historian Charles Dew, an authority on Virginia's role in the war, drove me down the broad expanse of Richmond's Monument Avenue, past the statues of such fabled Confederate heroes as Robert E. Lee, Stonewall Jackson, and Jefferson Davis, stretching sixty feet toward heaven. The sight is breathtaking, especially so when one reflects that of all the cities in the world, only Richmond and Atlanta—with its nine-story bas-reliefs of Lee, Jackson, and Davis chiseled into Stone Mountain—share the distinction of erecting such icons to leaders of a failed rebellion *within* the nation they rebelled against.

Another of Richmond's monuments to Robert E. Lee is Douglas Southall Freeman's four-volume biography, so influential in shaping the symbolism of the "good, gray general with kindly eyes." I doubt that Dr. Freeman would share my sense of General Lee as an enduring enigma. Certainly Lee posed no enigma to him. Lee was "a great and simple person," he wrote. "What he seemed, he was—a wholly human gentleman, the essential elements of whose positive character were two and only two, simplicity and spirituality." The Robert E. Lee of Freeman's biography was a Christian gentleman, devoted to honor and duty and opposed to both slavery and secession. One might call him a rebel without a cause.[1]

To say that Freeman's biography was well received is to understate. It not only won the journalists' Pulitzer Prize but also received high praise from professional historians. James I. Robertson Jr. declared it "the greatest piece of biographical writing in American literature."[2] Yet, there remain paradoxes in Lee's character and psyche that would seem to demand more complex answers than a litany of simplicity and spirituality.

Freeman's Lee was a Christian gentleman, and Shelby Foote recalls, "In my day, and I think still to a considerable degree, Robert E. Lee was a Christ figure, without sin." It is true that the actual Lee rejected his father's eighteenth-century rationalism and went through the motions of Anglican devotion. But he always seemed to find the church more endurable behind rows of Roman columns. Walker Percy suggests that Lee was less Christian than Stoic, riding into Chancellorsville with Epictetus in his pocket, embracing a philosophy of endurance rather than a gospel of hope. With neither fear of death nor hope of heaven, he saw man's chief end not to avoid the punishments and reap the rewards of the hereafter but as self-discipline, as the preservation of one's own "integrity and dignity" (as Marcus Aurelius put it) for its own sake.[3]

"Lee was neither serene nor simple," declares Thomas L. Connelly, in his book *The Marble Man*, the first major challenge to Freeman's interpretation. According to Connelly, Lee's "life was replete with frustration, self-doubt, and a feeling of failure. All these were hidden behind his legendary reserve and his credo of duty and self-control. He was actually a troubled man, convinced that he had failed as a prewar career officer, [as a] parent, and [as a] moral individual." The attorney Alan Nolan, in his *Lee Considered*, intensifies Connelly's criticisms into a forceful indictment. Lee biographer Emory Thomas agrees that Lee's strained marriage prompted flirtations with other women, that his prolonged absences from home hampered his efforts to be a good father, and that he did not share his inner self even with his wife and children. But Thomas doubts that Robert E. Lee was much given to questioning his own judgment on such matters.[4]

The historian Bertram Wyatt-Brown, in his studies of the pattern of "mourning, depression, and their sometime consort, mania" running through the field of Southern letters, notes the profound effects on children of losing a parent in childhood. Robert E. Lee's father— the fabled "Light-Horse Harry" of the American Revolution—not only dishonored his family with reckless debts but also deserted them when his son was but a child. It would have been surprising if the sensitive boy had *not* experienced a profound sense of loss. Confronted with an embarrassing lag between expectations and circumstances, Robert E. Lee was faced with the chore of reconciling ideals with practice, with achieving a rationalization. "When such adversities occur early in life," writes Wyatt-Brown, "the child has no adequate means for dealing with feelings of anger, guilt, and sense of betrayal." Connelly believed that the young Lee drove his grief and guilt deep into himself, hiding it beneath ideals of duty and self-control. Connelly also emphasized strong connections between Lee's tormented "inner self" and his audacious and aggressive combativeness as a general. Driven by a persistent sense of failure, he felt a need to act boldly to prove to others that he was not a failure.[5]

Eudora Welty, in her classic essay "Place in Fiction," offers a useful perspective for understanding Lee in the concept of "place." Her "sense of place" is not something spatial, but a dramatic dimension of life, a "primary proving ground" endowed with sensory experience and charged with complex emotions, manifesting the profound psychological and existential attachments of human beings to particular places. What did a "sense of place"—in Lee's case, Virginia—mean to him personally? Freeman argued that Lee's nativity as a Virginian was fundamental to his character and actions. While Freeman's own nativity as a Virginian seems no less fundamental to his character—and interpretations—than Lee's, in this case his interpretation is convincing. Most of Lee's thoughts and decisions do appear to have been motivated by the struggle for mastery in Virginia. Lee and Virginia sustained each other, and it is difficult to explain or even understand one without the other.[6]

But it was not Lee's "unwillingness to look beyond Virginia" that was his greatest weakness as a military commander, as some have argued. He learned early in the war that his chances of success were enhanced if he fought, in historian William W. Freehling's phrase, "on friendlier terrain." It was his inability to win *except* in Virginia that was the problem. His disastrous efforts to move the physical devastation of war away from Virginia's ravaged farms by invading Maryland in 1862 and Pennsylvania in 1863 were as rooted in his sense of place as in any Celtic compulsion to attack and die. Lee's identification with Virginia, his home place, his Native Ground, is unmistakable. No one loved it more, and yet no Virginian contributed more to its physical destruction.[7]

According to Freeman, Lee preferred the preservation of the Union to secession; yet he led the army of the secessionists in a war that had he won would have destroyed the American union. Freeman's Lee preferred peace to violence, yet he spent more than thirty-five years as a professional soldier, and to the soldier violence is organic and unavoidable. He was a general—who sent "boys who had fought the Gallic Wars" by conjugating Latin verbs to be conjugated themselves into death, "the ultimate future perfect tense."[8] According to Richard Weaver, "when that army went down in defeat, the last barrier to the secular spirit of science, materialism, and pragmatism was swept away." But when Robert E. Lee sent bright-eyed beardless boys up to their deaths by the scores of thousands, what was *his* responsibility for the devaluation of their lives from being into nothingness? Which side was he on in the struggle against the devaluation of human life in the Western World?[9]

Lee was considered "one of the truly gifted [military] commanders of all time," perhaps "the greatest soldier who ever spoke the English language," yet he lost the Lost Cause—quite decisively. No one has asked the obvious question more pointedly than C. Vann Woodward. "If Marse Robert was all that noble and intrepid, if Stonewall was all that indomitable and fast on his feet, if Jeb Stuart was all that gallant and dashing, and if God was on our side, then why the hell did we *lose* that war?"[10]

According to biographer Michael Fellman, Lee fell into a dismal, gloomy, and despondent period after his defeat at Gettysburg, becoming intensely discouraged and occasionally even hopeless about prospects for Confederate success. This state of mind continued sporadically until the end of the war. As early as the spring of 1864, he had come to feel that "if defeated, nothing will be left for us to live for." By early April 1865, Lee had concluded that the war had degenerated what he called the "moral condition" of his army to the point that it was no longer capable of "the boldness and decision" it had shown in the past. "From what I have seen and learned," he reported, "the country east of the Mississippi is morally and physically unable to maintain the contest." It was soon after that he said to his aides, "How easily I could be rid of this, and be at rest. I have only to ride along the line and all will be over."[11]

Since taking command of the Army of Northern Virginia three years earlier, he had demonstrated his military brilliance by winning battle after battle, with frightful loss of life, until he no longer had enough men to fight. At Sayler's Creek on April 6, he asked, "My God has the army been dissolved?" Those troops, "Lee's Miserables," had followed him under almost incredible privation and physical hardships. They were as committed to a sense of place as their commander was. They loved the land with an intense love "engendered by personal suffering and sacrifice." They had watered the land with their blood and "manured it with their dead," some "with their own limbs." They had sealed their love of the land with "the great seal of pain and hunger and sweat." Now they were withering "under almost daily sniping by enemy sharpshooters," a new way of fighting that had "the chill of murder" about it, pushed beyond endurance by sickness and disease and death.[12]

It would be Lee's moment of truth. Pondering at last the future of the men who had followed him so faithfully during four long years of arduous service, putting finally the interests of the South and its people before those of the Confederacy, or even his own fate, Lee decided "there is nothing left for me to do but to go and see General Grant." Lee's decision to surrender the Army of Northern Virginia could not have been an easy one. Throughout history leaders of failed rebellions have been forced to endure public shame and dire punishments. He faced the likely prospect of long imprisonment. Some Northern newspapers were demanding that he be hanged. And he surely knew it. He arrived at the campfire for his usual predawn staff meeting on April 9, 1865, resplendent in a new uniform with a red sash and white linen, long gray buckskin gauntlets, spit-shined boots stitched at the top with red silk, and a jeweled saber. To his astonished aides, he explained, "I have probably to be General Grant's prisoner, and thought I must make my best appearance."[13] The temptation to authorize guerrilla warfare, thus keeping the Confederacy alive, must have been powerful. But whatever the personal consequences, the time had come to furl the flag, as it would soon come to strike the tent.

Myth and legend, as well as irrefutable fact, swirled about these climactic moments of the war. Tom Hester claimed to have seen Lee and Grant arrive at Appomattox. A Virginia free black, he told Virginia Writers Project interviewer Susie Byrd that

> Gen'ral Lee tipped his hat fust, an' den Gen'ral Grant tipped hissen. Gen'ral Lee got offen his horse an' Gen'ral Grant got offen hissen. Gen'ral Lee got on a new uniform wid gold braid an' lots of buttons, but Gen'ral Grant got on an old blue coat dat's so dirty it look black. Dey stood dere talkin' 'bout half an hour, an dey shake hands an' us what was watchin' know dat Lee done give up. Den Gen'ral Lee got on his horse an' Gen'ral Grant got on hissen, an' Gen'ral Lee tipped his hat, an' Gen'ral Grant tipped hissen, an' Gen'ral Lee rode over to de rebel side, an' Gen'ral Grant rode over to our side, an' de war was over.[14]

Union general Joshua Chamberlain wrote a moving description of watching the units of the Army of Northern Virginia stack arms for the final time. These were the enemy he had faced so often in bloody combat, "men whom neither toils and sufferings, nor the fact of death, nor disaster, nor hopelessness could bend from their resolve." They stood "before us now, thin, worn, and famished," he wrote, "but erect, and with eyes looking level into ours, waking memories that bound us together as no other bond. Was such manhood not to be welcomed back into a Union so tested and assured?" Each division in turn would halt, "fix bayonets, stack arms; then, hesitatingly, remove cartridge-boxes and lay them down," he wrote. "Lastly, reluctantly, with agony of expression, they tenderly fold their flags, battle-worn and torn, blood-stained, heart-holding colors, and lay them down; some frenziedly rushing from the ranks, kneeling over them, clinging to them, pressing them to their lips with burning tears. And only the Flag of the Union greets the sky!" Seeing them now, "so thin, so pale, purged of the mortal—as if knowing pain or joy no more," Chamberlain was moved to ask, "How could we help falling on our knees, all of us together, and praying God to pity and forgive us all!"[15]

Robert E. Lee's decision to surrender may be a better measure of his greatness than any of his battlefield victories. What was lost at Appomattox—the dream of Southern independence—was heartbreaking to many who had poured out their blood and their treasure in its pursuit. But what was gained—the possibility of American unity, the possibility of truly *United* States—was in the end more important. And each of us with a Confederate ancestor still alive at the end of the war may owe our very existence to Robert E. Lee's courageous decision that day.

The real "Lost Cause" was not the war but the "synthesis of defeat," the need—at least among those on the losing side—to come to terms with what a Confederate woman called "the sudden collapse of our tried and trusted General Lee and his army," an urge to understand that became a "rage to explain" (perhaps especially to ourselves) the shame of failure in an ethic that valued the honor of success. When news of the transaction at Appomattox reached the South Carolina diarist Mary Chesnut, she asked herself, "Did we lose by imbecility or because one man cannot fight ten for more than four years?"[16]

Southern literature may be more helpful than the platoon of historians that have addressed the problem of why the Confederacy lost the war. Miss Rosa Coldfield in William Faulkner's *Absalom, Absalom!* explains that we entrusted "our . . . future hopes and past pride" to "men with valor and strength but without pity or honor. Is it any wonder that Heaven saw fit to let us lose?"[17]

Freeman's Lee was devoted to honor and duty. "The curse of shame and the oath of honor" reflect "a particularly important aspect" of the honor ethic, notes Bertram Wyatt-Brown, the leading scholar of Southern honor. One took oaths "at risk of forfeiting the oath-taker's honor and reputation." When I was inducted into the United States Army in 1958, I took a solemn oath to "defend the United States of America against all enemies, domestic and foreign." I considered it, and I still consider it, a lifelong obligation of honor. Robert E. Lee took the same oath at West Point when he received his commission as a lieutenant, and in 1861 he not only broke it but went on to lead the

army of the domestic enemies in a bloody war against the United
States.[18]

Lee biographer Emory Thomas argues that honor compelled Lee
to follow his beloved Virginia out of the Union. He does not attempt
to explain why Lee's sacred oath of honor did not compel him to remain loyal to the Union, as did nearly half a million other Southerners, including his fellow Virginians George H. Thomas and James R.
Terrill, the Tennessean David G. Farragut, and the South Carolinian
Percival Drayton, all of whom became top commanders of the United
States army and naval forces. As historian William Freehling notes,
450,000 Southerners fought for the United States, one Southerner
wearing Union blue for every two wearing Confederate gray. "Thus,"
he writes, "a Southerner replaced every Northerner killed in the
Union army, with enough Southern anti-Confederate soldiers left
over to outnumber Robert E. Lee's main army."[19] It would be easier to
believe that Robert E. Lee opposed secession if he had not seceded.

After Appomattox, it is not surprising that once again Robert E.
Lee experienced a profound sense of loss. Once again he faced an embarrassing lag between ideals and circumstances. Once again it became his chore to reconcile ideals with practice, to achieve a rationalization. As a Stoic he should, of course, have fallen on his sword—like
a defeated Roman general—in the ultimate act of self-deconstruction.
However tempting such a resolution may have been to his Stoic side,
it was abhorrent to other elements of his character. However hetero-
dox his Christianity, suicide was a sin. And his sense of place and his
devotion to duty combined in the recognition—as he wrote a friend
after the war—that "the South required the presence of her sons more
than . . . at any former part of her history, to sustain and restore her."
The problem was that by then there were so few of her sons left.[20]

James McBride Dabbs used to tell the story of a Southern mother
who wrote her son after Appomattox, "Don't be shamed by losin'. You
fit better'n you knowed how. And if Old Abe's folks offer you a mule,
take it and come on home. It ain't too late to get a crop in the ground."
Now that was the courage to be where you are, the same courage
demonstrated by Robert E. Lee in his decision to surrender regardless
of personal considerations. Similarly, an upcountry South Carolina
diarist wrote: "Perhaps it is for the best. At least, I am relieved from
the army at present. . . . I am now going to work insted of to the war. I

think I will like it the best." Flannery O'Connor wrote: "The novelist is required to open his eyes on the world around him and look. If what he sees is not highly edifying, he is still required to look."[21] That is what Robert E. Lee did after Appomattox. Perhaps the greatest victory of Lee's career was his heroic effort following the war to hold depression at bay and "do his duty."

And yet it is necessary to close on an unsettling note. In 1866 Robert E. Lee testified before a congressional subcommittee, "I have always been in favor of emancipation—gradual emancipation." And in a postwar interview he declared, "So far from engaging in a war to perpetuate slavery, I am rejoiced that slavery is abolished. I believe it will be greatly for the interests of the South. So fully am I satisfied of this, in regards to Virginia especially, that I would cheerfully have lost all I have lost by the war and have suffered all I have suffered, to have this object attained."[22] No one has been able to explain what he could have meant by that statement. Was he trying to tell the Congress—and us—that he had led the army of the slave states against the army of the free states *in order* that the slaves might be *freed*? Are we to believe that Robert E. Lee, who graduated from West Point with high honors, was *unaware* that the Confederacy for which he fought so long and so valiantly was created to *prevent* the abolition of slavery and was dedicated to frustrating all efforts "to have this object attained"?

There remains a disquieting complexity in the character of Robert E. Lee, a haunting psychological ambivalence between "counterpointed . . . opposite potentialities" that still eludes the best efforts of our best historians. For they have discovered "no possibility of eliminating the contradictions and inconsistencies. They are fundamental." Lee's story must be told in "a language of argument, not a chorus of harmony."[23] The enigma of Robert E. Lee still endures. And that may be the most disquieting complexity of all.

Notes

1. Douglas Southall Freeman, *R. E. Lee: A Biography* (New York, 1934–35), 1:ix, 4:494.
2. James I. Robertson Jr., "The Continuing War," *CWH* 7 (December 1961): 443.
3. Shelby Foote, interviewed by Tony Horwitz, in his *Confederates in the Attic* (New York, 1998), 156; Walker Percy, "Stoicism in the South," *Commonweal*, 6 July 1956, 343; Marcus Aurelius, *Meditations*, 10:9. See also the discussion of

Lee's stoicism in James McBride Dabbs, *Who Speaks for the South?* (New York, 1964), 119–29.

4. Thomas L. Connelly, *The Marble Man: Robert E. Lee and His Image in American Society* (New York, 1977), xiv; Paul C. Nagel, *The Lees of Virginia: Seven Generations of an American Family* (New York, 1990), 161–85; Alan T. Nolan, *Lee Considered: General Robert E. Lee and Civil War History* (Chapel Hill, N.C., 1991); Emory Thomas, *Robert E. Lee: A Biography* (New York, 1995), 70–74, 149–72, 218; and his "The Lee Marriage," in *Intimate Strategies of the Civil War: Military Commanders and their Wives*, eds. Carol K. Bleser and Lesley J. Gordon (New York, 2001), 32–48.

5. Bertram Wyatt-Brown, *Hearts of Darkness* (Baton Rouge, La., 2003), esp. xxi, 70–71. The quotations are from his "The Desperate Imagination: Writers and Melancholy in the Modern American South," in *Southern Writers and Their Worlds*, eds. Christopher Morris and Steven G. Reinhardt (College Station, Tex., 1996), 58, 61; Connelly, *The Marble Man*, 6–10, 158, 165, 169–76, 180. Thomas, in his *Lee*, points out that "Light-Horse Harry" became a cautionary role model to his son. Readers may note literary allusions to C. Vann Woodward here and in the paragraph preceding note 20. These are deliberate.

6. Eudora Welty, "Place in Fiction," in her *The Eye of the Story: Selected Essays and Reviews* (New York, 1978), 129. As Walker Percy wrote of Miss Welty and Jackson, Mississippi, "One is in a bad way without the other" ("Eudora Welty in Jackson," *Signposts in a Strange Land* [New York, 1991], 223).

7. Lee's preoccupation with the war in Virginia," writes T. Harry Williams, "constituted a tragic command limitation in a modern war" ("The Military Leadership of North and South," in *Why the North Won the Civil War*, ed. David Donald [Baton Rouge, La., 1960], 48.) Freehling's quote is from his *The South vs. the South: How Anti-Confederate Southerners Shaped the Course of the Civil War* (New York, 2001), 56. "Celtic compulsion to attack and die" alludes to the argument of Grady McWhiney and Perry D. Jamieson that Lee and other Confederate generals possessed such a suicidal penchant for the offensive that they squandered their opportunities and armies in pointless and unwarranted offensives and counteroffensives. McWhiney and Jamieson attribute this propensity to the South's putative Celtic heritage (*Attack and Die: Civil War Military Tactics and the Southern Heritage* [Tuscaloosa, Ala., 1982]).

8. The allusions are to Andrew Hudgins's poem, "The Cult of the Lost Cause." I am grateful to J. William F. Holliday for bringing his work to my attention.

9. Richard Weaver, "The Older Religiousness of the South," *Sewanee Review* 51 (1943), reprinted in *The Southern Essays of Richard Weaver*, eds. George M. Curtis III and James J. Thompson (Indianapolis, 1987), 146. Sending "bright-eyed beardless boys up to their deaths" is an allusion to Donald Davidson's widely anthologized poem, "Lee in the Mountains," in his *Lee in the Mountains and Other Poems* (New York, 1949), 1–6.

10. Robert Edward Lee," in *Encyclopedia Americana*, 1989 ed., quoted in Nolan, *Lee*

Considered, 59; C. Vann Woodward, *The Future of the Past* (New York, 1989), 187.

11. Michael Fellman, *The Making of Robert E. Lee* (New York, 2000), 165; Lee, quoted in Freeman, *Lee* 3: 268; Lee, quoted in Wyatt-Brown, *Shaping of Southern Culture*, 240; Lee, quoted in *The Wartime Papers of R. E. Lee*, ed. Clifford Dowdey and Louis H. Manarin (Boston, 1961), 938–39. Emory Thomas argues (in *Lee*, 287–88) that Lee's joy over the victory at Chancellorsville and his sorrow over the loss of Stonewall Jackson were but fleeting emotions.

12. Lee, quoted in Freeman, *Lee* 4:84. The other quotes are from W. J. Cash, *The Mind of the South* (New York, 1941), 104. See also J. Tracy Power, *Lee's Miserables: Life in the Army of Northern Virginia from the Wilderness to Appomattox* (Chapel Hill, N.C., 1998), 117; Drew Gilpin Faust, "The Civil War Soldier and the Art of Dying," *JSH* 67 (February 2001): 3–38. Connelly and other critics have argued that Lee's fixation on strategic offensives was imprudent and senselessly squandered the Confederacy's terribly outnumbered troops. Steven E. Woodworth is critical of Jefferson Davis for his failure to curb Lee's willingness to "sacrifice as many lives as necessary" in an effort to win "spectacular victories that would not only bolster southern spirits but also break—quickly and finally—the northern will to continue the struggle"; see his *Davis and Lee at War* (Lawrence, Kans., 1995), 184 (both quotes), 215, and his *No Band of Brothers: Problems in the Rebel High Command* (Columbia, Mo., 1999). Joseph L. Harsh retorts: "No defensive strategy could prevent eventual defeat." The "surest path to prolong the struggle and afford the South a chance to win the war" would have been "aggressive offensive maneuvering" (*Confederate Tide Rising: Robert E. Lee and the Making of Southern Strategy* [Kent, Ohio, 1998], 144). In other words, the trouble with Lee's strategy was that it was not offensive enough! Gary Gallagher agrees that Lee's victorious offensives were crucial to keeping up Confederate morale (*Lee and His Generals in War and Memory* [Baton Rouge, La., 1998]); he fails to note, however, the cost of heavy casualties in weakening Confederate resolve.

13. Lee, quoted in Freeman, *Lee* 4:120–23; Lee, quoted in Shelby Foote, *The Civil War: A Narrative*, vol. 3, *Red River to Appomattox* (New York, 1974), 939.

14. Tom Hester, in Virginia Writers Project, *The Negro in Virginia* (New York, 1940), 204, quoted in *Weevils*, 138–39. Hester was interviewed in Suffolk, Virginia, by Susie R. C. Byrd, for the Virginia Writers Project's Negro studies project sometime between 1937 and 1939. He turned eighty-nine in 1937, when interviewing began, and would have been sixteen or seventeen at the time of Lee's surrender. As a "free born," who was "paid fo' workin'," he "went over to Richmond an they let me jine up there." He tended horses and drove an ambulance for a Confederate unit until he was captured by Union forces, whereupon "I just stayed roun' de army dere lookin' arter de Yank horses." Thus his reference to "our side" at the end of his description of the surrender. *The Negro in Virginia* included excerpts from only a small number of the project's interviews.

It remains error prone, despite (or perhaps because of) undergoing at least four revisions at the hands of many individuals before publication (*Weevils*, 137–38, xx–xxiii). Hester's account cannot be taken as factual; the rituals described do not square with any other evidence. (See Freeman, *Lee* 4:134–43.) Folklorists consider such stylized and symmetrical structure to indicate that the narrator has told the story many times before, polishing it in presentation and in memory over the years. Such "truth" as it possesses is not the truth of history but that of the human psyche's effort to impose order on chaotic reality.

15. Joshua L. Chamberlain, *The Passing of the Armies* (New York, 1915), quoted in *The Illustrated Confederate Reader*, ed. Rod Gragg (New York, 1989), 134–36. According to historian William Marvel, not only was Chamberlain not in command of the troops accepting the Confederate surrender, but in his moving depiction of the Confederate troops stacking arms for the last time, the "eloquent professor-turned-soldier had employed his own imagination to elevate his place in the proceedings" (*A Place Called Appomattox* [Chapel Hill, N.C., 2000], 260). Chamberlain is a rather contradictory figure, combining exceptional military leadership, perception, and intense religious beliefs with egotism, brutality, and melancholy. See Edward G. Longacre, *Joshua Chamberlain: The Soldier and the Man* (Conshocken, Pa., 1999), esp. 291–93.

16. Thomas L. Connelly coined the term "synthesis of defeat" in his "Robert Penn Warren as Historian," in *A Southern Renascence Man: Views of Robert Penn Warren*, ed. Walter B. Edgar (Baton Rouge, 1984), 17; Caroline S. Jones to Mary Jones, 30 April 1865, in *The Children of Pride: A True Story of Georgia and the Civil War*, ed. Charles Manson Myers (New Haven, 1972), 1268; Mary Chesnut, entry for 23 April 1865, in *Mary Chesnut's Civil War*, ed. C. Vann Woodward (New Haven, 1981), 794.

17. William Faulkner, *Absalom, Absalom!* (New York, 1936), 20.

18. Bertram Wyatt-Brown, *The Shaping of Southern Culture: Honor, Grace, and War, 1760s–1880s* (Chapel Hill, N.C., 2001), 40–41. See also his *Southern Honor: Ethics and Behavior in the Old South* (New York, 1982), 55–59.

19. Thomas, *Lee*, 189; William W. Freehling, "South Carolina's Pivotal Decision for Disunion: Popular Mandate or Manipulated Verdict?" address to the 64th annual meeting of the University South Caroliniana Society, University of South Carolina, 13 May 2000; see also his *The South vs. the South*, 47–65.

20. William Tate, ed., "A Robert E. Lee Letter on Abandoning the South After the War," *Georgia Historical Quarterly* 37 (1953): 255–56.

21. I remember hearing Dabbs tell this story in a symposium I organized at Pfeiffer College, in Misenheimer, North Carolina, in the spring of 1964. Flannery O'Connor, *Mystery and Manners*, ed. Sally and Robert Fitzgerald (New York, 1977), 177; *Piedmont Farmer: The Journals of David Golightly Harris, 1855–1870*, ed. Philip N. Racine (Knoxville, Tenn., 1990), 372.

22. Lee, testimony to subcommittee of the Joint Congressional Committee on Reconstruction, 17 February 1866, quoted in Freeman, *Lee* 1:371, and in Nolan,

Lee Considered, 9. The second Lee quote was published by Rev. Dr. John Leyburn in his "An Interview with Gen. Robert E. Lee," *Century Illustrated Monthly Magazine* 30 (May 1885), quoted in Freeman, *Lee* 4:401, and in Nolan, *Lee Considered*, 24–25. Freeman insists that, while Leyburn published sixteen years after the interview, "as he gave all circumstances of General Lee's visit with absolute accuracy, there is no reason to doubt his direct quotations."

23. "Identity," notes the psychiatrist Erik H. Erikson, "derives from the ways in which history has, as it were, counterpointed certain opposite potentialities: the ways in which it lifts this counterpoint to a unique style of civilization, or lets it disintegrate into mere contradiction" (*Childhood and Society*, 2nd ed. [New York, 1963], 285). The second quotation is from Edmund Leach, "Myth as a Justification for Faction and Social Change," in *Studies in Mythology*, ed. Robert A. Georges (Homewood, Ill., 1968), 186, 198. Leach was writing of the Kachin people of Northeast Burma, but what he says about them is apt for understanding the character of Robert E. Lee.

PART TWO

WAR

Slavery, Nation, and Ideology

————————ᘒᙏᘍ————————

Virginians on the Grand Tour in the 1850s

DANIEL KILBRIDE

Why did Virginia planters, when touring Europe in the 1850s, fail to reflect on slavery or Southern self-consciousness? This question is of interest to historians of the American South, because travelers' failure to do so suggests that historians have overestimated the ideological significance of slavery in white Southern culture. Moreover, what Virginians did reflect on, in particular their intensifying patriotism and pride in American progress and modernity, raises questions about planter-class distinctiveness in the era of sectional conflict. The query is of interest to intellectual historians, because it poses the dilemma of how to interpret silences—and whether silences, or which silences, ought to be interpreted at all. This presents a problem in the intellectual history of the Old South a well as a more theoretical question pertaining broadly to the history of ideas.

For several reasons, this silence—which was relative, not absolute—needs to be explained. To begin with, many Virginia travelers felt compelled by their experiences in the Old World to reflect on their lives in the New. As John Doyle wrote just days after disembarking in Liverpool in 1840, "I cannot help making some remarks on American society."[1]

More to the point, this silence needs to be confronted in view of what most students of Southern culture believe about the centrality of the proslavery argument to it. By and large, the defense of slavery is seen not as a localized, specific response to the rise of antislavery sentiment but as "a key to wider patterns of beliefs and values," a coherent "social philosophy" that "embodied the South's particular perspective on those philosophical, moral, and social dilemmas confronting the nation as a whole." Proslavery thought was thought about society, and European travel was virtually certain to provoke reflection about social and cultural issues. It was also an occasion that inspired a great deal of writing, particularly journal keeping and correspondence. The relative absence of references to proslavery and Southern identity in Virginians' writings during this period of intense sectional conflict is arguably both conspicuous and surprising.[2]

This is so partly because the contrast between the conditions of workers in free societies with the allegedly superior moral and material conditions of Southern slaves was an important part of the proslavery argument. As one critic maintained, the condition of English factory workers "present[s] to the contemplation of the world, scenes of physical suffering, and mental degradation, and moral pollution, to which the annals of African slavery, in its harshest and most unmitigated forms, furnish no parallel." This argument also found its way into some of the period's worst literature. Regaled by a visiting Englishman on the "genius of universal emancipation" to be found in Britain, Mr. Chapman, the Virginia planter from Mary Eastman's *Aunt Phillis's Cabin*, could not contain himself. "I have been to England," he retorted, "and I saw some of your redeemed, regenerated, disenthralled—I saw features on women's faces that haunted me afterward in my dreams. I saw children with shrivelled, attenuated limbs, and countenances that were old in misery and vice." And in the immortal words of William J. Grayson:

> What blessing to the churl has freedom proved,
> What want supplied, what task or toil removed?
> Hard work and scanty wages still their lot,
> In youth o'erlabored, and in age forgot,
> The mocking boon of freedom they deplore,
> In wants and labors never known before.
> Free but in name—the slaves of endless toil,
> In Britain still they turn the stubborn soil.[3]

But proslavery writers did more than merely contrast the living conditions of free and enslaved workers: they literally invited tourists to do the same. In 1851 an antiabolitionist columnist urged antislavery travelers in England "to drop in at the cotton factories of Manchester and Salford, the nail factories of Preston, and, above all, the coal pits in the north of England, where the white images of God, blackened by contact with the foulness of the mines, are harnessed naked to the drags, and perform harder service a thousand feet below the level of the sea than we exact from horses and mules." The sightseer who saw so-called "free white people" toiling in the satanic mills could then write home "and tell us what he thinks of their begrimed ghastliness, as compared with the sleek, oily appearance of the comfortably clothed, well-fed, fat and saucy southern slaves?" Traveling slaveholders were well positioned to be the shock troops of the proslavery argument. Not only were they on the ground, as it were, in free labor societies, and therefore capable of judging between the two systems as informed observers. They also were in foreign lands, particularly Great Britain, whose intellectuals routinely used the South's labor regime to lampoon America's claims to exceptionalism and even respectability.[4]

Travelers were also in a strong position to weigh slave versus free labor systems because of the sights they visited. Virginians abroad did not restrict themselves to museums, castles, palaces, and natural wonders. They took pains to visit factories, farms, and relief institutions— the very places that supplied proslavery theorists with ammunition to use against free labor societies. Travel guides, such as those published by John Murray's London publishing house or the guides to France and Italy published by Galignani's, the English-language bookstore in Paris, supplied travelers with directions, hours of operation, and instructions on securing passage to these places. These books also sought to influence their impressions. John Disturnell's 1853 *American and European Steamship Guide* went well beyond outlining the various routes from Brussels to Paris. It also engaged in political economy. Travelers were advised to view the "splendid mansions" of Antwerp, but only as "memorials of the former opulence of the Burghers" of the city. Many being either boarded up or "only partially inhabited," and "when seen next to the dwellings of poverty or of the hard working laborer, there appears an anomaly irreconcileable with the spirit of the age."[5]

Virginians read a wide variety of materials in preparing for their travels. These works did not determine what they took from their experiences, but they did indelibly shape them. Very little of this material was written from a Southern perspective. No guide to Europe for Southerners appeared in the antebellum period. The overwhelming bulk of the literature that informed Virginians was either cosmopolitan—written for an Anglo-American audience—or American. Much of it was devoted to the determination of national character, of which moral and economic traits were among the most important criteria. John Murray's popular *Handbook for Travellers in Central Italy* observed that it was "impossible to travel over Italy without observing the striking difference between its northern and southern provinces," and urged that travelers "at least regard with respect a people who have done so much in the great cause of human amelioration." Unsaid was the assumption, shared by the great bulk of the *Handbook's* Protestant, upper-class Anglo-American readers, that the Catholicism, underdevelopment, and political fragmentation of central Italy made it worthy of contempt. When Richard B. Gooch toured Italy in the mid-1840s, he read John C. Eustace's *Classical Tour through Italy* (1816), which, he objected, "had a most remarkable prejudice in favor of the Italians and every thing Italian."[6]

Thus, the literature they read in preparing to see Europe invited Virginians to judge societies in national, not local, terms according to their political, moral, and economic qualities. While there were important differences between American and British travel books, both tended to judge Continental societies by how well they conformed to the ideal of progress, which usually has been seen as a distinguishing feature of Northern middle-class identity.[7] Yet some Virginia travelers did use their experiences to address slavery and freedom. The differences between published accounts and writings meant for private consumption are largely superficial. The former sometimes turned overseas travel into an opportunity for proslavery observations, while those writing privately almost never did. Yet even those accounts that hailed the merits of slavery did so tepidly, unsystematically, and with ultimate reference to the superiority of national institutions. Virginians abroad engaged in comparative political economy, always concluding that American institutions were superior because of their commitment to modernity.

The Richmond-based *Southern Literary Messenger* loyally defended slavery in the 1850s, and it featured travel literature prominently. Very seldom, however, did its writers turn the sights and sounds of Europe to the defense of slavery, and those that did so were at best ambivalent. The condition of the poor in Ireland prompted one traveler to reflect on the condition of slaves and free blacks in Virginia in 1852. He attributed Irish poverty to intemperance, "the cruelest slavery on earth." Since this "occurs under the sanction of the British government," he recommended that John Bull ease agitating over a "much less oppressive sort" of slavery in "America, of which she is greatly ignorant." And when he witnessed how women "huddle their tattered calico over their bosoms, as the stranger casts his eye upon them," he "compared them in my mind again with our slaves," certain that "public sentiment . . . would not allow negro women to go about in the garb of these Irish." These observations did not flower into a general critique of free society—to the contrary, in fact. The Irish despised the English, "because they know there is a land of Liberty and Plenty, where they would be welcomed, and yet they cannot reach it." He had "talked with a good many men about America" and had "not met with one—absolutely not with one . . . who has not some stake of Home or Love in our heaven-blessed land."[8]

This account of Ireland integrated some important parts of the proslavery argument, including charges of English hypocrisy, the grinding poverty of free societies, and planter paternalism. In the context of proslavery literature, however, it was a weak indictment. Above all, its praise for the boon of free labor had no place in the ideology of slavery. Other travel articles were not merely unsystematic in defending slavery, but were also ambivalent or even questioning. William Boulwere found "the state of slavery in the Eastern world . . . peculiarly interesting. It differs widely from that in America. It is the slavery of the patriarchal ages." Eastern slavery, being "a misfortune, not a degradation," excited "no feeling of contempt" upon slaves by masters. Few performed menial labor, but filled offices of responsibility and even honor and were "treated with great lenity and kindness." What most "distinguishes this institution from that among us," however, "was the knowledge of the slave, that he is not inevitably doomed to remain in this condition; that his chains are not of iron." Boulwere conceded that his remarks were "confined to the whites," but insisted that "there are instances" where black slaves had "emerge[d] from their condition and reach[ed] high places."⁹

Other writers used their travels to raise disquieting questions about possible contradictions between slavery and progress. While traveling through the Austrian Empire, John R. Thompson, the *Messenger*'s editor, reflected that it was "melancholy to think how the chains of slavery have bound together in one unnatural and overgrown empire people who have no sentiment of union." Yet he was not likening Southerners to oppressed peoples such as "the broken-spirited native of Hungary and the dejected Milanese." In fact, he was analogizing between Southern slavery and the absence of self-determination for ethnic minorities in Eastern Europe. When a Hungarian in his train informed Thompson that the castle he was admiring was in fact "a prison for political offenders" and commented that Americans had "no such thing," Thompson replied, "True . . . but we have slavery."¹⁰

Even more than those writing for publication, Virginians scribbling in private letters and journals used their travels to reflect on the merits and defects of American society. Indeed, their very concept of American nationalism owed a great deal to what they saw in the Old World. Positive references to slavery are conspicuously absent from these writings. Slaveowning travelers believed that Europe was poorer, less developed, more oppressed, and less dynamic than the young republic, but few suggested that the absence of slavery or the shortcomings of modernity had anything to do with these defects. Many of Europe's economic and social problems reflected America's strengths—in particular, social mobility, Protestant faith, and the right to sell one's labor in the marketplace, they believed.

Traveling Virginians did reflect on slavery occasionally, however. Europeans sometimes brought it up when they realized they were in the presence of slaveholders. Cornelia Grinnan complained of the "Wholesale execration of slavery" she encountered in England, "as if it could be swept away easily & speedily, as a parlour table is dusted over." However, it seems that Europeans did not confront Southerners as much as they expected. When the proslavery Philadelphian William Gilpin toured Europe in 1853–54, he told George M. Dallas that he "never—on a single occasion—heard America, or her institutions—

even slavery—alluded to in a sneering or illiberal spirit." At other times the sights and sounds Virginians encountered in the Old World literally compelled them to consider bondage at home. Slavery in the Holy Land prompted Richard Eppes to make a "comparison between the Bedouin Negro slave & as he exists among us" and "Slavery in the East in general." Whether Eppes was comforted or troubled he did not say, but artistic representations of slavery sometimes inspired unsettling feelings. When Eppes's wife, Josephine, saw I Quattro Mori, the statue of Ferdinand I in Livorno, she noticed in particular the "four slaves chained at the corners of the pedestal, writhing with their hands fettered behind them, and faces expressing so much despair and mental suffering as inimitable." And when Anne Gordon visited the British Museum in 1857, she saw plates from the ancient Near East featuring slaves in various poses. She was most impressed by one showing "masters standing over them *with whips raised very threateningly.*"[11]

If their European experiences sometimes called to mind the unsettling aspects of the peculiar institution, other features of European societies illustrated the merits of modernity and progress. When Ambrose Carlton rode around Naples in 1854, he took special notice of the cultivation, which included corn, hemp, flax, almonds, and oranges. Yet what captured his attention was "misery as we would call it, in Va. that I never saw before." He was stunned by the "many poor ragged men, women, and children." As he wrote his wife, "you could not go for 1/4 mile without coming cross some 1/2 dozen in the road . . . with their hat or cap in hand begging for coppers." Virginians sailed or steamed to Europe by way of New York, Philadelphia, or Boston, so many of them had seen destitution. The Old World's seemed far worse. Virginians attributed this to aristocratic privilege and retrograde economic practices, not the absence of slavery or paternal relations. When Carlton visited the winter palace in Naples, he was repelled "to see the millions spent in such a way, for *one man*, when there are *thousands* of *beggars* every where you go." James Gardner observed that "Italy is a poor degraded nation, a nation of beggars" during his 1853 tour. "They have no government," he explained. "This alone is sufficient to cause an American to bless his own country and cast a benevolent sigh of sympathy upon the degraded population of Europe."[12]

In their comments on slavery and free labor, Virginians were broadly representative of Southerners—indeed, of American travelers generally. The juxtaposition of aristocratic grandeur with widespread poverty in Spain prompted Augustin Taveau of South Carolina to declaim against "this Continent, where concentrated wealth can afford to gratify its tastes at the cost of overrunning the land with Beggars . . . thank God I am an American," he wrote his sister. "Ours is the only land of true prosperity & liberty." Taveau's comments suggest that the conflict between free and slave labor may have existed largely in the minds of proslavery theorists. Less ideologically inclined Southerners seem to have believed in the merits of both systems. When Eliza Middleton Fisher got into a friendly argument over abolition with Fanny Kemble Butler in 1845, she pointed out that, based on the "pictures drawn by Dickens & others of the horrible sufferings of the poor in Eng[land] . . . they must be infinitely worse off than the slaves." However, she went on: "blessed God that my lot was cast in a land where all could make an honest living if they wd. only work industriously."[13]

Virginians in Europe were not exactly silent about slavery, obviously, but it is just as clear that, despite plenty of opportunities, they did not engage in the contrasts between free and slave labor that proslavery literature invited them to make. Nor did planters ask about individual slaves or express paternal curiosity about their well-being in their letters home. Other historians have noted this silence, one that speaks to the indifference with which whites viewed their property beyond the services they could render.[14] It is hazardous to interpret such silences, but white Virginians' failure to analogize suggests certain conclusions about upper-class culture in the Old South. It may illuminate differences within the master class itself, between cosmopolitan, sophisticated planters, on the one hand, and parochial sectional ideologues, on the other. This resonates with one historian's conclusion that the absence of "reflections upon the meaning of the American South," as well as the lack of proslavery rumination, "signifies the incompleteness with which antebellum Southerners had alienated themselves from American culture."[15]

White Virginians' comfort with American life can be appreciated by way of contrast with former slaves who traveled to Europe as abolitionist lecturers. They regularly made the comparisons between Old World freedom and New World slavery that their former owners failed to make. In 1851 William Wells Brown visited Oxford, where a man "with the appearance of little or no ability, is here *moulded* into a hero, a scholar, a tyrant, or a friend to humanity." Such sentiments only reinforced his awareness of "the obstacles which the laws of the land, and of society, places between the colored man and education in the United States." And Henry Highland Garnet, born a slave in Maryland, crossed the Atlantic in 1861 on an English steamer, where he "did not receive a look, or hear a word during the whole voyage, that grated upon my very sensitive feelings." The sentiments of Virginia planters could not have been more different. The absence of regional discrimination, not merely proslavery sentiment, in their writings suggests that the sectional conflict remained a political struggle that did not poison other aspects of American society well into the 1850s.[16]

In Michael Frayn's play *Copenhagen*, Werner Heisenberg illustrates his principle of uncertainty by asking what Niels Bohr's wife, Margrethe, knew of his travels from Copenhagen to Leiden in 1925. "A picture postcard from Hamburg, perhaps. Then one from Leiden. There is no track, there are no precise addresses; only a vague list of countries visited." Likewise, there is much that we cannot know of what Virginians experienced, or of what they thought, as they traversed Europe. To allege that they failed to make proslavery observations may suggest more about our own interests than what engrossed Virginians as they toured the Old World. Yet they were not silent. Travelers did not merely send postcards—they wrote letters; they kept journals and diaries. Their silence on slavery and sectional identity amplifies what they did write about, namely how their travels intensified and gave concreteness to their American nationalism. They identified not with a narrow, sectional culture rooted in a proslavery political economy, but a modern, progressive nation based on political and economic freedom. As Conway Robinson wrote in 1853 after crossing Switzerland, "the tendency of a trip to Europe is to make any reflecting American more and more pleased with the republican institutions of his country, and more and more convinced of the manifold advantages resulting from our glorious Union."[17]

Notes

1. John Edward Doyle Diary, 18 December 1840, Doyle Family Papers, VHS.

2. Drew Gilpin Faust, "The Proslavery Argument in History," in her *The Ideology of Slavery: Proslavery Thought in the Antebellum South, 1830–1860* (Baton Rouge, La., 1981), 1.

3. R. T. H., "White and Black Slavery," *Southern Literary Messenger* 6, no. 3 (March 1840): 193; Mary H. Eastman, *Aunt Phillis's Cabin; or, Southern Life as It Is* (Philadelphia, 1852), 95; Grayson, "The Hireling and the Slave," in *The Selected Poems of William H. Grayson*, ed. Mrs. William H. Armstrong (New York, 1907), 23. This contrast was a central part of George Fitzhugh's proslavery argument, though in endorsing the enslavement of working classes, he carried its implications much further than other propagandists were prepared to go. See Fitzhugh, *Cannibals All! or, Slaves without Masters* (1854; rept. Cambridge, Mass., 1960); for analyses of Fitzhugh's influence, see C. Vann Woodward's introduction to *Cannibals All!*, vii–xxxix; Eugene D. Genovese, *The World the Slaveholders Made: Two Essays in Interpretation* (New York, 1969); and Drew Gilpin Faust, *A Sacred Circle: The Dilemma of the Intellectual in the Old South* (Baltimore, 1977), 112–31.

4. "An Abolition Delegate on His Travels," *Sunday Times, and Noah's Weekly Messenger,* 16 February 1851, 2.

5. *Gagliani's New Paris Guide for 1859* (Paris, 1859); *Disturnell's American and European Railway and Steamship Guide, Giving the Arrangement on all the Great Lines of Travel* (New York, 1853), 179.

6. *Handbook for Travellers in Central Italy, Including the Papal States, Rome, and the Cities of Etruria* (London, 1843), xvi; Richard B. Gooch Diary, 25 November 1843, Gooch Family Papers, VHS.

7. On progress as a feature of sectional distinctiveness, see Carol Sheriff, *The Artificial River: The Erie Canal and the Paradox of Progress, 1817–1862* (New York, 1996). For interpretations that rightly contest Sheriff's, see Jonathan Daniel Wells, "The Origins of the Southern Middle Class: Literature, Politics, and Economy, 1820–1880" (Ph.D. diss., Univ. of Michigan, 1998), and Michael O'Brien, "The Lineaments of Antebellum Southern Romanticism," in his *Rethinking the South: Essays in Intellectual History* (Baltimore, 1988), 53.

8. S. L. C., "A Day or Two in Ireland [Copied from My Journal]," *Southern Literary Messenger* 18, no. 5 (May 1852): 273, 275–77.

9. William Boulwere, "Extracts from Notes of a Voyage in the East, in 1843, Part I," *Southern Literary Messenger* 10, no. 6 (March 1844): 172–73.

10. John Reuben Thompson, "Notes of European Travel," *Southern Literary Messenger* 21, no. 9 (August 1855): 547–48.

11. Cornelia Grinnan Diary, n.d. [1855], p. 64, VHS; Henry D. Gilpin to George M. Dallas, 22 June 1853, vol. 41, Gilpin Family Papers #238, Historical Society of Pennsylvania, Philadelphia; Richard Eppes Journal, 25 April 1849, Eliza

(Pleasants) Gordon Diary, section two; Josephine Dulles (Horner) Eppes Diary, 11 January 1851, section eight, Eppes Family Muniments, VHS; Anne Eliza (Pleasants) Gordon Diary, 15 July 1857, VHS.

12. Ambrose Carlton to Mary Ann Dow (Gardner) Carlton, 22, 26 May 1854, Ambrose Carlton Papers, 1854–78, section two, VHS; James H. Gardner to Phebe P. Gardner, 12 November 1853, folder 3, section eight, Gardner Family Papers, VHS.

13. Augustin L. Taveau to Catherine Waring, March 1853, Augustin Louis Taveau Papers, DU; Eliza M. Fisher to Mary H. Middleton, 10 February 1845, in *Best Companions: Letters of Eliza Middleton Fisher and Her Mother, Mary Hering Middleton, from Charleston, Philadelphia, and Newport, 1839–1846*, ed. Eliza Cope Harrison (Columbia, S.C., 2001), 428.

14. Steven M. Stowe, *Intimacy and Power in the Old South: Ritual in the Lives of the Planters* (Baltimore, 1987), xvii; Jane Turner Censer, *North Carolina Planters and Their Children, 1800–1860* (Baton Rouge, La., 1984), 149; and Jan Lewis, *The Pursuit of Happiness: Family and Values in Jefferson's Virginia* (Cambridge, UK, 1983), 141. Charles Manigault's concern for his slaves is documented in the letters he wrote from Europe, reprinted in *Life and Labor on Argyle Island: Letters and Documents of a Savannah River Rice Plantation, 1833–1867*, ed. James M. Clifton (Savannah, Ga., 1978).

15. William Wells Brown to Frederick Douglass, 10 September 1851, in *The Black Abolitionist Papers*, 5 vols., ed. C. Peter Ripley (Chapel Hill, N.C., 1985-), vol. 1, *The British Isles, 1830–1865*, 303; Henry Highland Garnet to Julia Garnet, 13 September 1861, ibid., 497. Regarding the experiences of black abolitionists in Great Britain and on the Continent, see R. J. M. Blackett, *Building an Antislavery Wall: Black Americans in the Atlantic Abolitionist Movement, 1830–1860* (Baton Rouge, La., 1983), and *Liberating Sojourn: Frederick Douglass and Transatlantic Reform*, eds. Alan J. Rice and Martin Crawford (Athens, Ga., 1999).

16. Michael O'Brien, "Italy and the Southern Romantics," in his *Rethinking the South*, 109, 99.

17. Michael Frayn, *Copenhagen* (London, 1998), 67; Conway Robinson to James Alfred Jones, 11 September 1853, Conway Robinson Letterbook, Robinson Family Papers, 1836–99, VHS.

Reluctant Protestant Confederates

The Religious Roots of Conditional Unionism

CHARLES F. IRONS

Evangelicals throughout the Confederacy—including those in Virginia—gave vigorous support to their region's war for independence. Scholars have documented how Southern churchmen ennobled the Confederate struggle by portraying it as a holy one, and how Protestant clerics were among the last to let go the dream of an independent Southland. Indeed, as late as March 1865, pastors from each of the Virginia's major denominations publicly offered "their services to the Government to address the people, encourage hearty support of the Government, moral firmness, and that faith which Christians may illustrate in such a cause."[1]

Evangelical solidarity during the Civil War, however, masks the reluctance of Upper South Protestants to embark on the Confederate experiment. Though before the war they stood shoulder-to-shoulder with their coreligionists in the Cotton South on the justice of slavery and the need for ecclesiastical separation from Northern abolitionists, white Protestants in Virginia emphatically rejected secession, on moral grounds, until the eleventh hour.

The principled resistance to secession of Virginia's lay and ordained evangelicals reveals several truths about the sectional crisis. First, white Virginians considered slavery and secession distinct and divergent moral issues. Second, evangelical Virginians' particular ecclesiastical history prepared them to accept civil debates over the future of slavery with more grace than could their coreligionists farther south. Third, and most important, it was white Protestants' long defense of the Union that persuaded them that they held the moral high ground when they finally did secede in April 1861. By waiting to secede until Lincoln requisitioned troops, white evangelicals could more easily interpret their rebellion as just resistance to a tyrant.

Even scholars who recognize the prominent role that men and women of faith played in the sectional crisis have failed to distinguish between the sensibilities of Upper and Lower South believers, or to acknowledge the circuitous route that white Virginians took toward secession. In the works of Eugene Genovese, Mitchell Snay, James Farmer, C. C. Goen, and others, the same Southern nationalist and Deep South clerics tend to stand in for the entire antebellum Southern church, with Louisiana's Benjamin Palmer, Georgia's Stephen Elliot, and—above all—South Carolina's ubiquitous James H. Thornwell representing Southern Christendom. Virginia's Robert Lewis Dabney is now included as an occasional member of this pantheon, but his presence only highlights another bias: the tendency to allow the Presbyterian Church, a distant third in terms of membership to the Baptists and Methodists, to speak for all denominations.[2]

This homogenization of Southern religion across states and denominations is especially ironic in light of the sensitivity that the academy has displayed toward the Upper South's—and Virginia's in particular—distinctive political caution and economic diversification. In virtually all accounts of Southern churchmen during the antebellum years, Virginia churchgoers appear to be marching in step with their Deep South brethren, becoming more enamored with both slavery and Southern independence annually. Though thoroughly committed to enslaved African labor, the Old Dominion's churchmen were in actuality—like most of their fellow statesmen—what Daniel Crofts and William Freehling have termed "Reluctant" Confederates.[3]

The Unionism of Virginia's white Protestants, based on their religious convictions, appears paradoxical in comparison with the leading role that residents of that state played in the pursuit of ecclesiastical separation in the 1830s and 1840s. Virginia Presbyterians George A. Baxter and William S. Plumer had helped James Thornwell orchestrate the Old School/New School split in their denomination in 1837. After the initial schism, Plumer began publication in Richmond of a new denominational journal, the *Watchman of the South*, and, along with Baxter, successfully prevented New School sympathizers from being seated at the 1838 General Assembly. Six years later, Virginia Baptists James Taylor and Jeremiah Bell Jeter exercised leadership in their own denominational schism. The two called for an independent Southern Baptist Convention in 1844, and Jeter invited his coreligionists to meet in Augusta, Georgia, "to confer on the best means of promoting the Foreign Mission cause, and other interests of the Baptist denomination in the South." Yet another Virginian, Methodist William A. Smith, played a corresponding role in the national councils of his denomination. Also in 1844 he put forth a motion to split the Methodist Episcopal Church into Northern and Southern jurisdictions. From the time he became the editor of the *Virginia Conference Sentinel* in 1836, Smith had editorialized that Southern Methodists needed to be vigilant against the machinations of Northern abolitionists and speculated that ecclesiastical division might be desirable.[4]

In each denomination, Virginia clergymen cited their resentment of the intrusion of antislavery ideas into national forums as their key motivation for schism. Having led the charge to separate from their Northern brethren ecclesiastically, Virginia pastors and their flocks nonetheless then labored with equal vigor to preserve the political union. Only when Lincoln demonstrated his willingness to use force to coerce the Deep South did Virginia's religious leaders endorse secession.

White Virginia Protestants pursued this course because they considered slavery and secession distinct moral issues, though historians continually conflate the two.[5] Most scholars use the intensity of a cleric's pronouncements in defense of slavery to gauge the depth of his secessionist sentiment, even though developments in the political sphere show that proslavery could be compatible with a variety of orientations toward the Union. Bertram Wyatt-Brown, for example, in his recent book *The Shaping of Southern Culture*, cites ministerial ambivalence over slavery as proof positive of clerical reservations about secession. "We are concerned here with the holdouts, as it were, the leaders of the more conservative denominations who saw clearly the perils of disunion," he states in his chapter on "Church, Honor, and

Disunionism." As evidence, he continues, "Far from endorsing slavery's positive goodness, Presbyterian and Episcopal ministers in particular sounded various themes on the subject. None was hostile, but few called it holy."[6] Wyatt-Brown's assertion of a complete correspondence between proslavery and pro-secession does not describe the behavior of Virginians of faith in the secession crisis.

Disentangling white Virginia evangelicals' feelings for slavery and secession is important. While they did not endorse secession until war was virtually upon them, they affirmed the legitimacy of slavery time and again, especially after Nat Turner's 1831 rebellion. At that time, Virginians in both the legislature and the churches determined that, rather than give up slavery, they would make the institution safer and stronger. For their part, lawmakers bolstered the slave regime through tougher laws governing slave assembly and literacy.

White evangelicals, meanwhile, sought to make slavery more secure by bringing slaves into their churches, where the whites could supervise black evangelicals and teach them a Gospel of submission. The mission to the slaves co-opted would-be dissenters against the South's peculiar institution by allowing churchmen uneasy about slavery to sublimate their concerns for blacks by working to Christianize them. Robert Ryland, pastor of Richmond's First African Baptist Church from 1841 to 1865, was one of thousands who worked out his own reservations about the slave system through ministry: "Since the passage of a law by the Virginia Legislature, forbidding all colored preachers to minister to their people in divine things, [I] felt that all the ministers of Christ, and especially those of [my] own denomination, were called on to put forth new efforts to evangelize the people of color."[7]

Committed to slavery, many Virginia whites nonetheless preferred the Union to an experiment with Southern independence. These Unionists insisted that Northerners would keep the promises that their forefathers had made in the Constitution, including the protection of white Southerners' property in persons. Sounding this theme, Episcopalian William C. Rives began reminding his fellow Virginians in the late 1850s that the Constitution and Supreme Court protected slavery absolutely. In May 1859 he chided secessionists: "the supreme judicial tribunal of the United States has, by its solemn and irreversible judgments, surrounded the rights and institutions of the

South, in the only points in which they have ever been supposed to be open to invasion, with an impassable wall of defence." Rives maintained this line months after the election of 1860; in early March 1861, in a speech on the proceedings of the Peace Conference, he assured his listeners that, "By the proposed plan, every possible approach by which the rights and interests of the South could be threatened or assailed—every conceivable avenue through which the agitation of the slavery question could be renewed—is forever cut off and hermetically closed." He closed his speech by quoting Matthew 19:6, sure to resonate with Virginia's majority evangelical population: "What God has joined together, let no man put asunder."[8] Most Virginia voters agreed with Rives and rejected secession in an election held on February 4, 1861, to choose representatives to a statewide constitutional convention; out of 152 delegates, only about 30 were outright disunionists.[9]

Prominent Upper South clerics preached that God endorsed slavery and at the same time demanded fidelity to duly constituted authorities; loyalty to the Union was a religious duty. Southern Methodists, in the same 1858 resolution in which they struck Francis Asbury's rule identifying slavery as an evil from their *Discipline*, clearly articulated the Christian theory of civil obedience: "We recognize the Constitution and Government of the United States," they affirmed, "and obedience to them as a religious duty, and pledge ourselves, in our very profession of faith, to fidelity to the country and her authority." Virginia divines continued to preach this message after Lincoln's election. In an attempt to soothe the sectional tensions, Presbyterian pastor Robert Lewis Dabney penned "A Pacific Appeal to Christians" that circulated in the *Central Presbyterian* in January 1861, with the signatures of several dozen leading Presbyterian ministers, sundry representatives of other denominations, and faculty members of Virginia Military Institute, the University of Virginia, and Washington College appended: "All Southern Christians would deplore an unnecessary rupture of the Federal Union bequeathed to us by our heroic sires, as marring their glorious work, and showing ourselves unworthy of their inheritance," and "as covering the claims of American Christianity and republicanism with failure and disgrace before the world."[10]

Many proslavery Virginians and their peers in the Upper South thus voted Unionist because they perceived religious scruples to stick with the federal bargain. Calling attention to the difference between proslavery and pro-secession should not undermine the identification of slavery as the chief cause of the Civil War, but merely show that there was a powerful religious component to Virginians' debate over when to break the federal bonds. John Minor Botts and other Virginia Unionists, when they chanted the refrain "If there is no violation of the Constitution, you have no right to withdraw as a member of the body," appealed directly and intentionally to the duty Protestant Virginians perceived to honor duly constituted authorities.[11]

Virginia churchmen's tradition of channeling debates over slavery out of their sanctuaries and into the civil sphere also contributed to the particular nature of their Unionism. The fire-eating slave states of the Deep South had no analog to the turbulent period of antislavery agitation in Virginia in the early national period, when white members of each of the state's major denominations banished discussion of slavery from the churches. By 1820 assemblies of Virginia Baptists, Methodists, and Presbyterians had each ruled that the civil government had the exclusive right to legislate on the contentious issue of slavery. Episcopalians, who did not become a significant factor in the state's religious life until the late 1820s, never felt the necessity of making such a resolution, for antislavery did not threaten to disrupt the ranks of the denomination with the highest proportion of slaveowners.[12] Denominational leaders were generally careful not to rule that slavery was a "positive good"; rather they chose to leave politics to politicians and willfully to forget that slavery was a moral as well as a political question.

Virginia's Baptists, Methodists, and Presbyterians in the early national period shuffled conversation about slavery from their churches to the statehouse. The Baptist General Committee, after their condemnation of the principle of chattel slavery in 1790 drew angry protests from constituent associations, decided in 1793 "that the subject be dismissed from this committee, as believing it belongs to the legislative body."[13] Virginia Methodists had to some extent extinguished antislavery conversation within the state in 1785, when they bullied the General Conference into rescinding its prohibition on slaveowning, but they sealed the matter in 1816 by forcing the General Conference "to admit that to bring about such a change in the civil code as would favor the cause of liberty is not in the power of the General Conference."[14] In 1800 Presbyterians in the Virginia Synod took a similar step. They acknowledged that some of their members disagreed with slavery but warned that "to refuse to hold Christian communion with any who may differ from us in sentiment & practice in this instance would . . . be a very unwarrantable procedure." Virginia evangelicals in the three largest denominations agreed that their churches were not appropriate venues for discussion of the South's most distinctive institution.[15]

The historical memory of these battles against the discussion of slavery in religious organizations set white men and women in the older, Upper South states (and above all in Virginia) apart from their coreligionists at both higher and lower latitudes. Virginians perceived national debate over slavery—instigated by antislavery or abolitionist Northerners accustomed to discussing social causes in church—as a violation of their pledge not to discuss it publicly. By contrast, Protestant leaders from the Deep South perceived the debates of the 1830s as fresh threats to their interests. Virginians displayed indignation over a broken faith during the denominational schisms and lamented that abolitionists were poisoning God's kingdom with contentious political issues. Delegates from the Gulf States, in contrast, displayed indignation that anyone would question their God-given right to own slaves and denied the right of even secular authorities to interfere with slavery. Influenced by these Deep South representatives, delegates at the first meetings of the Southern Baptist Convention and the Methodist Episcopal Church, South, each passed resolutions far stronger than had any Virginia church on slavery. Methodists, for example, went further than their 1816 moratorium on antislavery agitation and boldly declared the laws of slavery immutable by any authority: "We wholly disclaim any right, wish or intention to interfere with the civil and political relation between master and slave; we consider the subject as having been put beyond the legislation, by the General Government."[16]

Virginia's Protestants, in contrast, did believe that conversation about slavery had a place in the civic sphere. Virginia Unionists believed that discussion alone could not hurt them; conversation itself terrified many farther south. Botts, for one, urged Virginians not to worry about Northern hostility to the peculiar institution until the Republicans put concrete actions behind their threats of interference. "When they come here to take control of my domestic concerns, or attempt a practical interference with them, it will be quite time enough for me to find a remedy—it is always at hand, and it is not necessary to arm the State against Mr. [Hinton Rowan] Helper, Mr. Helper's book [*The Impending Crisis of the South*] or any sixty-eight endorsers of that or any other book in print." In contrast, New Orleans's Benjamin Palmer preached that the representatives of the federal government blasphemed Almighty God by daring to discuss slavery: "These great questions of Providence and history must have free scope for their solution; and the race whose fortunes are distinctly implicated in the same is alone authorized, as it is alone competent, to determine them."[17]

Augusta County Methodists provided proof in the summer of 1860 that Virginia evangelicals were still willing to tolerate discussion of slavery in the civil sphere while rejecting it ecclesiastically. Until that month, they and thousands of other Methodists in western Virginia and along the Maryland border had remained members of the Baltimore Conference. This conference straddled the Mason and Dixon line and included—as did no other—roughly equal parts slaveholding and nonslaveholding regions. From its earliest days, Methodists in this unusual body balanced antislavery and proslavery sentiments. They did not allow slaveowners to be preachers, nor did they expel them from fellowship or label slaveholding a sin. Members of the Baltimore Conference agreed to disagree on the justice of slavery and avoided discussion on the topic. Following the denominational schism of 1844, the conference continued its affiliation with the Methodist Episcopal Church, North, and became the largest slaveholding jurisdiction within that body.[18]

In May 1860 delegates to General Conference of the Methodist Episcopal Church, North, passed a resolution that condemned slavery as a sin and—had it been confirmed—would have required white Methodists in the anomalous Baltimore Conference to give up their slaves or forfeit membership. In local meetings throughout the conference's jurisdiction, Virginia Methodists met to protest the report. Many whites, including those in Staunton, emphasized their willingness to remain in fellowship with antislavery members of the Baltimore Conference who had not tried to force their hand on slavery. The Staunton group expressed their "continued and unabated confidence in the Baltimore Conference," in fact. But they could not stand the larger church's interference with their domestic institutions and resolved "that the time has fully come for a separation of the Baltimore Conference from the jurisdiction of the General Conference." As had most of Virginia's slaveholding Methodists in 1844, Methodists in the Shenandoah Valley embraced ecclesiastical division when their codenominationalists proposed further limits on their rights as masters. And again like most Virginia Methodists, they overwhelmingly voted against secession at the polls only six months later.[19]

The reluctance of white Virginia churchmen to unite with their brethren further south in support of the secessionist cause raises questions of the relationship between ideology (or belief) and material interest so prominent in the historiography of Southern religion. Scholars such as Christine Heyrman and Donald Mathews have argued that Southerners compromised their ethical standards early in the national period to attract more and more wealthy white members. According to Mathews, material interest guided white Protestants in the South from their acquiescence to slavery in the 1790s until after the Civil War, when a few prophetic whites broke free from the shackles of mammon. "Because of their place in society," he critiqued, "white Evangelicals were too conscious of their own respectability and too crippled by their ethnocentrism or racism to sense the agony and alienation of the cross and therefore to understand the Gospel as a truly liberating force."[20] The differing beliefs about secession among Protestants in the Upper and Lower South raises this issue of material interest in the context of the 1860s: Did the Deep South's greater material interest in slavery compel the churchgoers of this region to read the Bible differently and to reach different conclusions about the justice of secession?

Material interest did indeed influence convictions about secession, but in a way that left room both for human greed and for spiritual and intellectual integrity. Protestants in all regions of the country believed that disunion and disobedience to civil authorities was sinful, *unless* some other party abrogated the federal compact and thereby released them from the obligation of submission. Southerners professed this belief with almost complete unanimity, and it made Thornwell and other future Confederate champions, too, Unionists well into the sectional crisis.[21] Thus, material interest did not distort the apprehension of the moral issues relevant to the act of secession—virtually all churchgoing Southerners believed they owed fealty to the national compact—but it did affect the threshold at which a Southern Protestant considered the Constitution violated by Northerners and therefore nullified. Those more invested in slavery possessed a more delicate trigger and required less evidence of Northern bad faith before embracing secession than did Virginians.

For most citizens of Virginia, the election of Lincoln did not, by itself, as it did for many farther south, signal a violation of the compact. Georgia congressman Howell Cobb, using religious language, founded his lament for the Union immediately following Lincoln's victory: "The broken Constitution and violated compact formed the only Union we ever recognized; and if you would still have us to love and preserve it, restore to it that vital spirit of which it has been robbed by your sacrilegious hands, and make it again what our fathers made it—a Union of good faith in the maintenance of constitutional obligations." With Republican ascendancy, South Carolina's Thornwell also determined that the compact had been violated and cast aside his own lingering doubts about secession: "We know the people of the South," he said, and they would have remained loyal "as long as the Constitution of the United States continued to be sincerely observed." By December 1, 1860, an editorial writer for the Augusta (Georgia) *Daily Constitutionalist* also saw the Constitution as a dead letter: "The argument is exhausted, or has at least grown tiresome. Let us stand by our rights without fear or bravado." He went on, "Having failed to secure them in a Union where a controlling majority is against us, we must, as prudent men, seek new guards for future security."[22]

But a majority of white Protestants in the Commonwealth waited until Lincoln called for troops and coercion became a reality before conceding that the Constitution had been broken. The Charlottesville

Review of January 4, 1861, summarized their political creed: "We are among those who believe that the United States is a government, and not a league. We regard the Constitution as a fundamental law, and not as a treaty. We consider that we are citizens of the United States, and owe an allegiance to the Federal Government. Any resistance to the Federal authority we regard as rebellion." Presbyterian pastor and professor Robert L. Dabney, in a letter to his mother on December 28, 1860, accused South Carolinians of committing such rebellion: "As for South Carolina, the little impudent vixen has gone beyond all patience. She is as great a pest as the Abolitionists."[23]

After April 15, though, most conditional, religious Unionists castigated Lincoln and endorsed a new political order. J. M. Broadus, a Virginia Baptist, declared on April 27, "if Virginia cannot belong to the Union without servile degradation from Northern aggression and domination, then I am for Virginia and nothing else at present."[24] William Meade, the Unionist bishop of Virginia's Episcopal Church— and soon the senior bishop of the Confederacy—in his annual address before the denomination's General Convention explained his own conversion to secessionist: "I have clung with tenacity to the hope of preserving the Union to the last moment," he insisted. "But the developments of public feeling and the course of our rulers have brought me slowly, reluctantly, sorrowfully, yet most decidedly, to the painful conviction, that notwithstanding attendant dangers and evils, we shall consult the welfare and happiness of the whole land by separation."[25]

Amelia County Presbyterian minister Richard McIlwaine demonstrated how decisive a shift occurred after Virginia Protestants determined that Lincoln had invalidated the Constitution and declared war on the Southern people. News of the president's call for troops did not reach McIlwaine on the day of its issue, and he had stayed up until midnight trying to convince a fellow churchman of the justice of the Unionist position. When he saw printed news of the proclamation the next morning, he later recounted that he "and the people of Virginia generally flopped over to the other side, became rabid Secessionists and were ready for a fight." McIlwaine eventually helped to raise a volunteer infantry regiment and was elected its third lieutenant. Believing with Bishop Meade that "if war should actually come upon [Virginians,] it will be on our part one of self defence, and therefore, justifiable before God," he and other Protestant Virginians joined the mad rush in April 1861 to fend off the invaders from the North. The disappointed Unionists at Charlottesville's *Review* phrased it best: "And now while President Lincoln holds in suspense the uplifted gauge of battle, we warn him in the name of the former Union party in Virginia, that there are no divisions here now."[26]

The conditional Unionists in the Virginia secession convention also abruptly changed their minds when the president committed the federal government to a policy of coercion. Before South Carolina forces fired on Fort Sumter, on April 4, delegates registered a 90–45 vote against secession. As soon as they heard of Lincoln's call for troops on April 17, however, eighty-seven men voted to accept an ordinance of secession and only fifty-five to reject it. At least thirty-five delegates had changed their vote on the basis of Lincoln's request for men. William Sutherlin, a Danville moderate, was one of them. He exclaimed, "I have been a Union man, but, my God, I have never been a submissionist. . . . I have a Union constituency who elected me by a majority of one thousand, and I believe now that there are not ten Union men in that county today." Samuel Staples of Patrick County also switched his vote. "Ten days ago, I was known as a Union man," he announced at the convention, but coercion meant that the "Convention having exhausted all peaceable measures to save the Union and avoid a resort to arms, has no alternative left but to adopt an ordinance of secession."[27]

Any attempt to understand the discontinuous journey of white Virginians toward secession must take into consideration their religious beliefs. Virginia pastors and laymen's understanding that God approved slavery did not necessarily translate into support for Southern independence, and many evangelicals labored in defense of the Union. The more they identified scrupulous adherence to the letter of the Constitution as a religious duty, however, the more prepared these Virginians were to condemn Abraham Lincoln once he settled upon a policy of coercion. As Nelson County Episcopalian William D. Cabell fumed in his diary of April 17, 1861: "Lincoln having ordered up 5000 troops to coerce the seceding states I this day change my position and am for opposing him to the bitter end. Having been cool & con-

servative up to this date I now feel thrice armed for the combat—Ma~
the god of battles be with us!"[28] With other Virginia Protestants, Ca~
bell had come to believe Southerners fully justified in prosecuting a~
violent a defensive war as necessary to protect Southern liberty an~
true religion.

Notes

1. Willard E. Wight, "The Churches and the Confederate Cause," *CWH* 6 (De-
   cember 1960): 373. Recent works that stress religious support for the Confed-
   eracy include Beth Schweiger, *The Gospel Working Up: Progress and the Pulpit in*
   Nineteenth-Century Virginia (New York, 2000); Drew Faust, *The Creation of*
   Confederate Nationalism: Ideology and Identity in the Civil War South (Baton
   Rouge, La., 1998); and Stephanie McCurry, *Masters of Small Worlds: Yeoman*
   Households, Gender Relations, and the Political Culture of the Antebellum South
   Carolina Low Country (New York, 1995). The seminal work remains James W.
   Silver, *Confederate Morale and Church Propaganda* (1957; rept. New York, 1967).
2. Eugene D. Genovese, *A Consuming Fire: The Fall of the Confederacy in the Mind*
   of the White Christian South (Athens, Ga., 1998), and other works; Mitchell
   Snay, *Gospel of Disunion: Religion and Separatism in the Antebellum South* (Cam-
   bridge, UK, 1993); James Farmer, *The Metaphysical Confederacy: James Henry*
   Thornwell and the Synthesis of Southern Values (Macon, Ga., 1986); and C. C.
   Goen, *Broken Churches, Broken Nation: Denominational Schisms and the Coming of*
   the American Civil War (Macon, Ga., 1985).
3. Daniel W. Crofts, *Reluctant Confederates: Upper South Unionists in the Secession*
   Crisis (Chapel Hill, N.C., 1989); William W. Freehling, "Virginia's (Reluctant)
   Decision to Secede: Slave or States Rights or ?," paper presented at the Douglas Southall Freeman and Southern Intellectual History Conferences, 21 February 2002.
4. Jeter quotation from Robert A. Baker, *Relations between Northern and Southern*
   Baptists (1948; rept. New York, 1980), 76. Though there is debate over how
   much slavery factored into the 1837 Old/New School split, I have followed
   those who believe that slavery lay at the heart of the conflict, among them H.
   Shelton Smith, *In His Image, But . . . : Racism in Southern Religion, 1780–1910*
   (Durham, N.C., 1972), 79–86. William A. Smith is the chief villain in Donald
   Mathews, *Slavery and Methodism: A Chapter in American Morality, 1780–1845*
   (Princeton, N.J., 1965).
5. An exception is Schweiger, *Gospel Working Up*, 93–94.
6. Bertram Wyatt-Brown, *The Shaping of Southern Culture: Honor, Grace, and War,*
   1760s–1880s (Chapel Hill, N.C., 2001), 155.
7. Robert Ryland, "Origin and History of the First African Church," in *The First*
   Century of the First Baptist Church of Richmond, Virginia, 1780–1880 (Richmond,
   1880), 245–72, quotation at 252. For more on this process, see also Janet Duits-

man Cornelius, *Slave Missions and the Black Church in the Antebellum South* (Columbia, S.C., 1999); Milton C. Sernett, *Black Religion and American Evangelicalism: White Protestants, Plantation Missions, and the Flowering of Negro Christianity, 1787–1865* (Metuchen, N.J., 1975); and Charles F. Irons, "'The Chief Cornerstone': The Spiritual Foundations of Virginia's Slave Society, 1776–1861" (Ph.D. diss., Univ. of Virginia, 2003).

8. "Speech of Hon. Wm. C. Rives, in the City of Richmond, May 3, 1859," *Richmond Whig and Advertiser,* 6 May 1859; *Southern Pamphlets on Secession, November 1860–April 1861,* ed. Jon L. Wakelyn (Chapel Hill, N.C., 1996), quotations at 363, 368.

9. Shanks, *Secession Movement,* 153; Crofts, *Reluctant Secessionists,* 140.

10. Alexander Gross, *A History of the Methodist Episcopal Church, South* (New York, 1904), 66; Thomas Cary Johnson, *The Life and Letters of Robert Lewis Dabney* (Richmond, 1903), 215–18.

11. John Minor Botts, *The Past, the Present, and the Future of Our Country: Interesting and Important Correspondence between Opposition Members of the Legislature of Virginia and Hon. John Minor Botts, January 17, 1860* (Washington, D.C., 1860), 12.

12. This is a fact generated by Episcopalians themselves, from the *Journal of the Sixty-Fifth Annual Convention of the Protestant Episcopal Church in Virginia* (Richmond, 1860), 65: "If this is a correct estimate, then, of the colored population in Virginia, not more than eight or nine thousand are brought under the influence of the ministry of our Church, though far the largest part of them are under the control of those who profess and call themselves Episcopalians."

13. *Minutes of the Baptist General Committee, at Their Yearly Meeting, Held in the City of Richmond, May 8th, 1790* (Richmond, 1790); *Minutes of the Baptist General Committee, Holden at Muddy-Creek Meeting-House: Powhatan County, Virginia, May, 1793* (Richmond, 1793), VBHS.

14. Quotation from Gross, *A History of the Methodist Episcopal Church, South,* 8; see also William Warren Sweet, *Virginia Methodism: A History* (Richmond, 1955), 199–200. The best book on early Southern Methodism is Cynthia Lynn Lyerly, *Methodism and the Southern Mind, 1770–1810* (New York, 1998).

15. Quoted in Ernest Trice Thompson, *Presbyterians in the South, Volume One: 1607–1861* (Richmond, 1963), 326–27.

16. Quoted in Anne C. Loveland, *Southern Evangelicals and the Social Order, 1800–1860* (Baton Rouge, La., 1980), 202.

17. Botts, *Correspondence,* 7; Rev. Benjamin Palmer, *The South: Her Peril and Her Duty* (New Orleans, La., 1860), in Wakelyn, *Southern Pamphlets,* 67; Hinton Helper, *The Impending Crisis of the South: How to Meet It* (New York, 1857). Sixty-eight Northern members of the Senate and the House of Representatives endorsed the antislavery arguments of Helper, a North Carolinian.

18. Mathews, *Slavery and Methodism,* has the best pre-1844 information on the Baltimore Conference.

19. Quotations taken from an article in Staunton's Whig organ, the *Republican*

Vindicator, 29 June 1860, 3. These and other articles on religion in Augusta County may be accessed through Edward L. Ayers and William G. Thomas, "The Valley of the Shadow," http://jefferson.village.virginia.edu:8090/xslt/servlet/ramanujan.XSLTServlet?xml=/vcdh/xml_docs/valley_news/eveTopics.xml&xsl=/vcdh/xml&xsl=/vcdh/xml_docs/valley_news/topics.xsl&list=civic&area=a.

20. Donald Mathews, *Religion in the Old South* (Chicago, 1977), 184 and Christine Heyrman, *Southern Cross: The Beginnings of the Bible Belt* (New York, 1997).

21. One example is Farmer, *Metaphysical Confederacy.*

22. Cobb, *Letter . . . to the People of Georgia* (Washington, D.C., 1860), in Wakelyn, *Southern Pamphlets,* 90–91; James H. Thornwell, *The State of the Country* (New Orleans, La., 1861), ibid., 160; "The Argument Is Exhausted—Stand by Your Arms!" *Daily Constitutionalist,* 1 December 1860, in *Southern Editorials on Secession,* ed. Dwight Lowell Dumond (1931; rept. Gloucester, Mass., 1964), 280–84, quotation 284.

23. "Coercion," *Review,* 4 January 1861, in Dumond, *Southern Editorials,* 387–90; Johnson, *Letters of Robert Lewis Dabney,* 215.

24. Quoted in Archibald Thomas Robertson, *Life and Letters of John Albert Broadus* (Philadelphia, 1901), 183.

25. *Journal of the Sixty-Sixth Annual Convention of the Protestant Episcopal Church in Virginia, Held in St. Paul's Church, Richmond, . . . May, 1861* (Richmond, 1861), 28.

26. Ibid., 27; Richard McIlwaine, *Memories of Three Score Years and Ten* (New York, 1908), 184–85; "[The War of Revenge]," *Review,* 19 April 1861, in Dumond, *Southern Editorials,* 504.

27. Both quotations from David Bert Jeffus, "Invitation to a Carnival of Death: The Virginia State Convention of 1861, February 13–April 17" (M.A. thesis, Univ. of Virginia, 1994), 51–52; table 1 for vote results.

28. William D. Cabell Journal, 1861 (January–November), Cabell Family Papers, UVA.

Christian Love and Martial Violence

Baptists and War — Danger and Opportunity

WAYNE WEI-SIANG HSIEH

Evangelical Christianity shaped life in Confederate Virginia from se-cession to defeat. The Baptist denomination, in particular, claimed 42 percent of Virginia's full-fledged church members. During the seces-sion winter of 1860–61 and the first years of war, Baptists paid special attention to the problem of despair and a growing hatred for invading Yankees. Ordained ministers, the acknowledged leaders and represen-tatives of Baptists (and other evangelical denominations), articulated an idiom that helped sustain their own and their congregations' mo-rale throughout the war—and their understanding of the sacrifices that came with war. An examination of the Richmond-based *Religious Herald*, the premier print-organ of Virginia Baptist clergymen, as well as some of the papers left by Baptist ministers permits an exploration of the ways in which evangelical Virginians faced the Civil War.[1]

Too often scholars take an unwisely skeptical approach to those matters of the spirit that animated so many people in earlier times. Pious Virginia Baptists were by no means limited to the ministry, es-pecially in light of women's simultaneous dominance of church mem-bership and exclusion from the pulpit. Nonetheless, an examination of the abundant records left by Baptist ministers regarding their activi-ties not only indicates a high degree of loyalty to both their principles and the Rebel cause but also suggests what was happening among the rank and file in the Baptist faith. Virginia Baptists—lay and clerical to-gether—did not represent white popular opinion in its entirety in the state, but they did represent a substantial segment of it. The members of the Baptist clergy had to struggle to reconcile Christian love with martial violence, but they eventually came to see in the Army of Northern Virginia's religious revivals more wartime hope than danger for the cause of Christ.

Even after Abraham Lincoln's election to the presidency in November 1860, many of Virginia's Baptist clergy wanted nothing to do with the secession movement. Robert Ryland, the distinguished white minister of the First African Baptist Church in Richmond and president of Richmond College, wrote that month to his son, "I am opposed to secession though I don't see how it is to be avoided." The next month, shortly before South Carolina seceded, Jeremiah Jeter, pastor of Richmond's influential First Baptist Church, wrote to a colleague in Greenville, South Carolina, that despite his distaste for Northern agitation on slavery, "I cling with great tenacity to the Union. With all our perplexities, we have been the freest, happiest, and most prosperous nation that the sun has ever shined on." Reflecting many ministers' reluctance to engage in openly political activity, T. W. Robert, a Baptist minister who worked in central Virginia, recorded in his diary on election day 1860 that "for the first time I cast a vote, in any political context," although he did not record who he voted for.[2]

Faced with a potentially explosive political situation, Unionist Baptist clergymen invoked the jeremiad and Fast Day traditions to explain and cope with the secession winter of 1860–61. The jeremiad tradition—which originated in the books of the Hebrew prophets, especially Jeremiah—provided a religious frame of reference used in America since the days of the Puritans and the first Virginia colonists. In this worldview, God linked a special destiny to special religious obligations; if those obligations were not fulfilled, God's punishments would be swift and sure. God would only stop chastising his wayward people when they humbled themselves before Him and petitioned for His pardon through a day of fasting or some other act of penitent worship.[3]

Shortly after Lincoln's election, the *Religious Herald*, in a piece titled "National Chastisements," cited Jeremiah 16:5 in a representative rendition of the jeremiad: "I have taken away my peace from the people, even loving kindness and mercies." Americans had previously enjoyed a worldly peace, "the temporal prosperity of the nations," the

Herald noted, but the peace had disappeared, because "an incensed holiness prompts it. . . . An exhausted patience permits it. . . . An immutable purpose demands it. . . . An irresistible arm accomplishes it." God's chastisements were dreadful, because "when loving kindness no longer stays the rod, but wields it, how severe must the stroke be!" The *Herald* closed with a grim exhortation: "Is it not well in these times of national commotion to lay such truths to heart—and to seek unto the Lord with earnest supplication, that His peace may not be taken away from us because of our iniquities as a nation."[4]

For the *Herald*, which was still holding to the Union, the term "nation" referred to North and South together, and both sections stood guilty of iniquity. Jeremiah Jeter, in his letter of December 1860, had also talked about the guilt of both sections, asking: "Will it not be sad, if between Northern fanaticism and Southern rashness the best government that the world has ever seen, the work of our revolutionary fathers, the admiration of the friends of freedom in all nations, and the last refuge of republican liberty, should perish?" Reflecting Christian providentialism, Jeter declared: "My only hope is in God."[5]

In Virginia in late 1860 and early 1861, the clergy invoked the idiom of the jeremiad to support the cause of Unionism. On December 3, the Baptist ministers of Richmond called for a fast day in early January, with the comment that "section is arrayed against section, party against party, and fanaticism and passion seem likely to usurp the place of reason and patriotism. Our government, the work of our revolutionary fathers, long the safeguard of our liberties, and the admiration of the world, seems to be on the very verge of disruption—an event fraught with consequences which no mortal can foresee." The ministers prayed that, with proper penitence by Virginians, "God may avert the judgments which our national iniquities have provoked" and "inspire our public men with wisdom and moderation" to preserve the Union.[6]

These ministers feared the prospect of secession and civil war. In March, the month before Fort Sumter, the *Herald* highlighted Edmund Burke's ominous calculation that war had taken 35 billion lives throughout human history. And yet Unionist Baptist ministers in Virginia believed that a disastrous civil war might well serve a purpose ordained by Providence. The editors at the *Herald* printed a letter from a correspondent in Louisiana complaining that in the Gulf States, "almost all our most intelligent and able ministers are engaged in secular pursuits, and preach only once in a while." The writer mused that "perhaps God is about to send civil war upon us, and so desolate our land and impoverish us, as to bring us to that humility which ought to be the habilament of ever[y] minister of Jesus."[7]

Whatever might happen, the ministry believed that it would be part of God's plan. A week before the bombardment of Fort Sumter, the *Herald* printed a poem titled "Wait," the last lines of which read:

> Be assured the future story
> Of the days now dark to you,
> Will record His work of glory—
> Wait, and see what God will do.[8]

The poem must have seemed to readers especially hopeful in so ominous a time. After Fort Sumter on April 12 came Lincoln's call for volunteers on April 15, followed soon by Virginia's secession.

For all their piety and sincerity as well as their reluctance to countenance secession, these men of the cloth soon became enthusiasts for the Rebel cause. Evangelicalism and Confederate nationalism were intertwined in a complex braid of meaning and causality, and in view of the prevailing interpretation of their relationship, that braid must be reexamined.

On the instrumental front, Charles Royster has argued in *The Destructive War* that Americans, in the North and the South alike, attempted to settle the vexatious question of nationhood with violent and destructive measures. He observes that in this bloody struggle, "drastic measures" became rationalized by powerful "claims to righteousness." Royster has also contended that an appetite for destructive war was present in both sections and waiting for fulfillment from the war's beginning, that "Americans did not invent new methods of drastic war during the Civil War so much as they made real a version of conflict many of them had talked about from the start." Royster's treatment of religion reflects this rendition of events. He describes how Americans likened destructive war to the Atonement and compares it to a "sacramental mystery, the central act of which was bloodshed."[9] It may indeed be true that large numbers of Americans saw the war's bloodletting as a sacred cleansing, but it is surely significant that many religiously committed Virginians had at least some qualms about such a use of religious imagery.

Virginia Baptist sources, at least, contain little evidence giving positive support to Royster's picture of a bloodthirsty civilian population. In fact, from the very start, the clergy fretted publicly about the evil results of military violence. To be sure, later on they resigned themselves to the inevitability of ruin and death—but they retained hope that such tragedies would release new energy for the evangelical cause. Never did they exult in the military slaughter as some sort of self-justifying sacrament.

In fact, Jeter declared in a sermon in 1861 to his congregation that *'the claims of piety are paramount to the claims of loyalty.'* But since almost all of Virginia's Baptist ministers saw the Confederate cause as just, they saw no real conflict between piety and citizenship. In Jeter's view, *'The duties of citizenship and of piety are perfectly compatible.* The same wise and gracious authority that enjoined duty to Caesar, enjoined duty to God. . . . Indeed a man cannot be a good Christian who is not a good citizen.'[10]

Confederate loyalties notwithstanding, ministers jealously protected the independent prerogatives of religion against the needs of a wartime state. Baptist clergymen from west of the Blue Ridge worried that Christians would be overcome with wartime excitement. As early as October 1861, they declared: "In the midst of national confusion and moral insensibility, we should ever be found at our posts, as good soldiers of the cross, with arms and armor bright, fighting the good fight of faith. Let us not yield too much to the pressure of the prevailing excitement; but 'be steadfast, unmovable, always abounding in the work of the Lord.'" The *Herald* reprinted a warning that "patriotism is not religion, and no substitute for it, for it embraces the discharge of but a single duty or class of duties." From the pulpit, Jeremiah Jeter warned his Richmond congregation that "it is folly to suppose that services rendered to Caesar can absolve [anyone] from [an] obligation to serve God."[11]

These clergymen were calling not for destructive and patriotic warfare but for a cautious recognition that the ends of God and man

might not be congruent. In the words of "Athanasius" in the *Herald*
"If, in my judgment, there ever was a just cause for war, Virginia ha:
such a cause at present. . . . But all this does not relieve *us* from our *full
share of responsibility* for the awful civil conflict in which we are about
to engage. For, no matter how triumphant we may be on every battlefield, yet the scourgings to which we will be subjected are terrible to
contemplate."[12]

In contrast to Royster's argument that Americans saw the war as a
means by which, with battlefield carnage, they could atone for their
sins, these Baptist ministers saw the war as a tremendous stimulant for
sin and what they called "demoralization." When ministers spoke of
"demoralization," they did not merely mean a reduction in what we
now call morale or esprit, a concept of motivation disconnected from
morality. Instead, they meant de-*moral*-ization in terms of an increase
of vice in the army.

These temptations seemed especially dangerous to many evangelicals early in the war. The month after the shelling of Fort Sumter, the
Religious Herald moaned that "the flower of our churches are enlisted
for this struggle, and it is sad to think of how many temptations will
beset them, and of the probability that many will be led into the paths
of vice, and have their Christian character shipwrecked." The *Herald*'s
readers could not have been pleased by a soldier's letter that complained: "It is very hard to live a Christian life here." Many of these
early fears about demoralization were grounded in fact. The Confederate armies suffered from a range of camp vices throughout the entire war, including gambling, swearing, drinking, prostitution, and
other common soldiers' vices. To mark a fast day in 1862, Jeter told his
congregation, "I am more afraid of our own sins than of the arms of
our enemies. I fear *drunkenness*. It is prevailing among officers and soldiers—increasing—demoralizing our armies—preparing us for defeat and ruin."[13]

An article in the *Religious Herald* titled "The Demoralization of
War" gave one of the most explicit and articulate formulations of war's
moral dangers. The authors feared bad company, lack of a regular Sabbath, martial courage turned into indifferent recklessness, and separation from the religious influences of home. Other evangelicals echoed

the *Herald*'s concerns about male separation from the domestic feminine sphere. Two months after the firing on Fort Sumter, a tract agent
found soldiers eager for religious tracts because "being separated from
wives, mothers, sisters and other loved ones, they long for, and heartily
respond to expressions of sympathy, affection and Christian influences." The authors of "The Demoralization of War" further warned
that "while we believe that there is a gospel for the bullet and the bay-
onet, and that the 'devout soldier' may preserve a consistent, nay, an
eminent piety, when lending his energies to the vigorous prosecution
of just, defensive war;—we cannot blind ourselves to the peculiar
moral and spiritual hazards of military life. This is the shore most
thickly strewn with the wreck of souls!" In contrast to a postwar conception of uniformly pious Confederate armies, the *Herald* worried
that demoralization operated like an "infection" that "spreads beyond
the camps and a whole people breathes it."[14]

In striking contrast to Royster's portrayal of an America preoccupied
with drastic and violent measures, the authors feared above all else that
the Southern people would fail, in the *Herald*'s words, to "fulfill the
Christian law of love to its enemies in arms!" Clergymen consistently
linked wartime brutalization with an inability to love one's enemies. In
June 1861 another commentator in the *Herald* told soldiers that they
should pity their opponents, because if they lost that Christian trait,
"it will be an end far worse than the desolation of your homes and
the destruction of your property." Robert Ryland, in a published letter, demanded that his son "should not, even in the hour of deadly conflict, cherish personal rage against the enemy" but, rather, "pity them
even in the act of destroying them." Ryland also pointed, as the polar
opposite of proper Christian conduct, to the supposed iniquities of
Northern Christians who advocated aggressive warfare. The *Herald*
reprinted from the Nashville *Christian Advocate* an article that ex-
horted Christians to remember, "Love is the royal law, and its dues are
not intermitted even in war." Printing a story of a Confederate soldier
praying for a dying Federal, The *Herald* noted that such action "somewhat softens the aspect of the present unnatural war." The Federal was
a Christian, and his Confederate coreligionist allowed him a dignified
Christian death in a scene that "was solemn and impressive."[15]

Christ's atonement had been a personal shedding of blood that did not directly harm even his persecutors; there were limits to how far an analogy of war and atonement could be sustained to support "destructive war." Virginia Baptist clergymen could not simply ignore Christian doctrines about peace and love; they had to find some way of reconciling Christian love and martial violence. Although these men of the cloth could call on the long tradition of Christian "just war" doctrine, their evangelical beliefs nonetheless forced Virginia's Baptist ministers to make the taxing demand that soldiers love the same men they killed. The explanation seems to lie in the stern evangelical emphasis on sanctified conduct among the saved.[16]

Such concerns were expressed well into the war. In April 1863 Jeter warned his congregation, "The times are trying. War, of almost unexampled dimensions and ferocity, is raging," and the times are "fraught with danger to piety." He went on: "We are in danger of being led by the excitement of the times to forget or neglect our Christian duties. . . . We are in danger of becoming discouraged by the troubles of the times in our efforts to promote the cause of Christ. . . . We are in danger from the aggressions of our enemies of cherishing an unchristian spirit toward them." In May 1863 the *Herald* continued to insist that Christians "are required to love their enemies, to bless those that curse them, to do good to those that hate them, to pray for those who despitefully use them and persecute them." Furthermore, "if Christians are not careful while striking for their country, to maintain the spirit of their Master, how shall they hope for that Master's help?"[17]

This is not to claim that all ministers refrained from expressions of bloodlust. F. McCarthy, a minister who had graduated from Richmond College, joined the Confederate army and went as far as to write in the *Herald* that "if any Southern man lacks the anger (I know he does not lack the courage) to march to the battlefield and butcher the monsters that have invaded our soil with intentions worse than murderous, I call upon such a one to sit down and reflect on the putrid qualities of the Northern heart and their base designs upon us and ours, until no chain will be strong enough to keep him from their throats." But more representative of the *Herald*'s tone is a reprinted piece arguing that ministers "should not run five hundred or a thousand miles to imbrue their hands in the blood of their enemies, when there are thousands and tens of thousands who are eager for the fray and whose special calling it is not to preach peace." Ministers of this less-pugnacious persuasion frequently saw a regimental chaplaincy as the best way to reconcile patriotism with the demands of their divine office.[18]

The more optimistic ministers sought salvation not in destructive bloodletting, but in the age-old evangelical practice of conversion. Shortly after Virginia's secession, the *Herald* expressed a hope that "we may find the time of the country's war, the time as well of the Church's progress." A correspondent for the *Herald* reported with satisfaction in May 1861 that the Georgia units arriving in Richmond were commanded by and filled with pious Baptists. Whatever the ambivalence of some of his colleagues, the scene of these devout troops allowed him to declare, "I have never understood the compatibleness of Christianity with war as I see in it in the present struggle for Southern independence. Never have I seen or read of greater promptness on the part of Christians of all denominations, to shoulder the musket in defense of their homes, their families, and all that makes life desirable." In a letter reprinted in the *Religious Herald*, one chaplain reported: "the morality of the camp is excellent. It is far beyond my most sanguine expectation. Mothers, you need not tremble!" Another chaplain exclaimed in late 1861, "I think I have never occupied a field that afforded an equal opportunity for usefulness."[19]

As the war dragged on into 1862, Virginia's Baptist clergy began to search for signs of Christian virtue in the Confederate armies. A. E. Dickinson, who directed Baptist colportage to soldiers in Virginia, believed that "the fields are white unto the harvest." Another minister hoped that the physical dangers of war would make men more receptive to the evangelical message. The army correspondent of the *Charleston Courier* observed, in a letter reprinted in the *Herald*, "There is something irresistible in the appeal which the Almighty makes when he strikes from your side, in the twinkling of an eye, your friend and comrade." Given soldiers' close proximity to death, he explained, "the recent battles have done more to make converts than all the homilies and exhortations ever uttered from the pulpit. A man who has stood upon the threshold of eternity while in the din and carnage of the fight, has listened to eloquence more fiery and impressive than ever came from mortal lips."[20]

For these ministers, the "destructive war" was not so much a "vicarious" experience (to use a chapter title of Royster's *Destructive War*), associated with both rational political ends and a mystical bloodlust. Rather, it was a stimulant for individual evangelical conversion to the cause of the Prince of Peace. Indeed, Virginia's Baptist clergy had too many evangelical scruples to exult in the war's carnage. In March 1862 the *Herald* reprinted an article urging its readers to "pray, then for our enemies, since Christ had commanded us so to do—pray in sincerity and with fervor."[21]

Virginia's Baptist ministers found a way of explaining and living with war, but their solution centered on the large evangelical revivals that broke out intermittently in the Army of Northern Virginia starting in the fall of 1862. Another major revival, the so-called "Great Revival" along the Rapidan, caught fire in the winter of 1863–64, and yet another set of revivals took hold in the siege lines of Richmond and Petersburg in the winter of 1864–65. Confederate evangelicals as a whole, including Baptists from Virginia, had helped bring about these revivals through a massive program of army evangelization.[22]

The evangelical clergy hoped that the war's trying circumstances might help them convert large numbers of young and impressionable men ripe for conversion—the same groups that before the war had been so much more difficult to convert than the women who dominated church membership rolls. A. E. Dickinson exulted in a letter from Staunton in October 1862 that "never have I known such eagerness to hear and to read the Gospel as is manifested by the convalescent soldiers here." J. William Jones, a Baptist minister who would later form a key role in the articulation of post–Civil War Lost Cause religion, marveled in the spring of 1863 that "it was a touching scene to see the stern veteran of many a hard-fought field, who would not hesitate to enter the deadly breach or charge the heaviest battery, trembling under the power of Divine truth, and weeping tears of bitter penitence over a misspent life." Baptist clergymen in Virginia focused their efforts on personal conversion, with the war's terrors providing a means to focus a young soldier's mind on the hereafter, not on Royster's mystical and violent form of atonement that saw violence as a self-justifying end.[23]

According to the historian Richard Beringer and his coauthors, when Confederates began to lose battles, they also forfeited, many believed, divine favor as well. The result was a diminishing of morale, which in turn engendered more defeats. The Beringer thesis underplays the potential restorative effects of religion for morale. The scholar Drew Gilpin Faust has observed that the "the most dramatic outbursts of religious enthusiasm followed fierce and bloody battles—especially losses," and such, as we have seen, was certainly the case in Virginia. Recent work by Harry Stout and Charles Grasso has also shown that evangelicalism buttressed Confederate nationalism on the home front, where Confederate clergymen portrayed the South as a "chosen people" who would triumph against any odds if they would only do proper penance for their many sins. The Confederacy's collapse had more to do with martial defeat on the battlefield than with a collapse of morale partly grounded in Confederate premillennialism.[24]

Whatever the political situation, whether it be the secession winter or full-blown war, Baptist clergymen never stopped being Baptist clergymen. Although convinced that the Southern cause was more agreeable to the Heavenly Father than Northern efforts to subdue the Confederacy, they delivered stern jeremiads replete with sin and doom. Many Confederates in the first months of war may have perceived the conflict as some grand outing, but an evangelical faith provoked ministers to worry about the effect of war on the morals of their parishioners. Faced with Christianity's injunction to turn the other cheek, the clergy urged their followers in the armies to love those whom they regrettably had to kill. As the war dragged on, they reconciled themselves to its consequences, not by giving up prior convictions in the face of overwhelming events, but by overcoming the demoralizing tendencies of war itself through revivals among the troops. In a sense, Baptist ministers believed that they had subdued even war—in evangelical doctrine, an inherently evil event—for the cause of righteousness.

Baptist ministers did what they could to reconcile the Confederate cause with their evangelical faith. That reconciliation survived the war itself, even when defeat and devastation stunned them with the unexpected news of their Virginia hero's surrender at Appomattox. Lee, although less venerated than the Presbyterians' Stonewall Jackson, Virginians commonly portrayed as another Christian paladin. Early in the war, an officer reportedly commented that "in addition to all I have said about Gen Lee, the best thing, after all, is, that he commits his plan to the Almighty. When he has made a plan, he, as a Christian, looks to God to help him carry it out."[25]

Few clergymen, even at the close of the war, would have dared to challenge that appraisal. The leaders of Virginia Baptists never wavered in their wartime support of the Confederate cause and deeply mourned its demise. Nonetheless they probably never regretted their initial reluctance to wage war, though few would have dared to repeat those early jeremiads about the corruptibility of military bloodshed and the moral dangers that warfare aroused. Some had predicted the grievous outcome. But none was bold enough in the postwar years to proclaim that God's judgment, with the strength of Yankee arms, had punished their fellow Virginians, destroyed their old ways of living, and freed their slaves.

Notes

1. For the importance of the ministry, see Mitchell Snay, *Gospel of Disunion: Religion and Separatism in the Antebellum South* (Cambridge, UK, 1993), 1–2, 7; Beth Barton Schweiger, *The Gospel Working Up: Progress and the Pulpit in Nineteenth-Century Virginia* (New York, 2000), 8; Harry S. Stout and Christopher Grasso, "Civil War, Religion, and Communications: The Case of Richmond," in *Religion in the American Civil War*, eds. Randall M. Miller, Harry S. Stout, and Charles Reagan Wilson (New York, 1998), 318–19; Drew Gilpin Faust, "Christian Soldiers: The Meaning of Revivalism in the Confederate Army," *JSH* 53 (February 1987): 64–65. For church figures, see Schweiger, *Gospel Working Up*, 198 (these relate to Virginia's prewar boundaries and date from 1850—and, whatever their accuracy, suffice to demonstrate that Baptists were an important denomination in Virginia). For the importance of the *Religious Herald* (cited hereafter as *RH*), see ibid., 69.

2. Schweiger, *Gospel Working Up*, 51, 93 (Ryland quotation); Jeter's letter reprinted in Archibald Thomas Robertson, *Life and Letters of John Albert Broadus* (Philadelphia, 1901), 179 (for background on Jeter, see Schweiger, *Gospel*, 3); T. W. Robert diary, 6 November 1860, VBHS.

3. See Perry Miller, *The New England Mind: From Colony to Province* (Cambridge, Mass., 1953), 27–39. For the use of the jeremiad during the secession winter, see Snay, *Gospel of Disunion*, 200–204, and Schweiger, *Gospel Working Up*, 93–94.

4. "National Chastisements," *RH*, 29 November 1861.

5. Roberts, *Life and Letters of John Albert Broadus*, 180.

6. Snay, *Gospel of Disunion*, 200–204; "A Day of Fasting and Prayer," signed J. B. Jeter, *RH*, 6 December 1860.

7. "The Terrible Havoc of War," *RH*, 14 March 1861; "Louisiana Correspondence," *RH*, 4 April 1861.
8. "Wait," *RH*, 4 April 1861; Schweiger, *Gospel Working Up*, 94–95.
9. Charles Royster, *The Destructive War: William Tecumseh Sherman, Stonewall Jackson, and the Americans* (New York, 1991), xi, 39, 266.
10. Jeremiah Jeter, sermon on Matthew 22:21, Sermon Book (1861), VHBS.
11. Eighteenth Annual Report of the Western Association of Baptist Churches in Virginia, printed in *RH*, 10 October 1861; "Patriotism and Religion," signed Southern Presbyterian, ibid.; Jeter quoted in Schweiger, *Gospel Working Up*, 95.
12. "Volunteers for the War," signed Athanasius, *RH*, 23 May 1861; see John Wesley Brinsfield, W. C. Davis, Benedict Maryniak, and James I. Robertson Jr., *Faith in the Fight: Civil War Chaplains* (Mechanicsburg, Pa., 2003).
13. "Book Distribution among Soldiers," signed A. E. D, *RH*, 16 May 1861; "A Christian Soldier's Letter," signed C. M., *RH*, 27 June 1861; Jeremiah Jeter, sermon on Jonah 3:5–10, Sermon Book (1862), VHBS; see also Bell Irvin Wiley, *The Life of Johnny Reb: The Common Soldier of the Confederacy* (1943; rept. Garden City, N.Y., 1971), chapter 3.
14. "The Demoralization of War," *RH*, 23 May 1861; "Tracts for Soldiers," signed W. J. Crowder, *RH*, 20 June 1861. For similar examples of worries about demoralization, see Christopher H. Owen, *The Sacred Flame of Love: Methodism and Society in Nineteenth-Century Georgia* (Athens, Ga., 1998), 105–6.
15. "The Demoralization of War"; "To the Soldiers of the South," *RH*, 27 June 1861; Ryland letter, dated 17 July 1861, reprinted in *RH*, 15 August 1861; "Love Your Enemies," signed *Nashville Chris. Adv.*, *RH*, 20 June 1861; "Prayer for a Dying Enemy," *RH*, 22 August 1861.
16. For the ministry's use of "just war" doctrine, see Stout and Grasso, "Civil War," 324.
17. Jeremiah Jeter, Sermon Book (1860–61), sermon titled "The Danger of the Times" (although these sermon notes are in a sermon book marked 1860–61, Jeter dated them April 1863); "Hatred of our Enemies," *RH*, 7 May 1863.
18. "The Ethics of War," signed F. McCarthy Jr., *RH*, 6 June 1861; *Due West Telescope* quoted in "Ministers as Soldiers," *RH*, 3 October 1861. For ministers becoming chaplains, see Schweiger, *Gospel Working Up*, 97.
19. "The Crisis," *RH*, 25 April 1861; "Christian Patriotism," signed Jos. Walker, *RH*, 9 May 1861; *Laurensville Herald* quoted in "Ministers as Soldiers," *RH*, 3 October 1861; Dr. Cross quoted in "Army Chaplain," *RH*, 10 October 1861.
20. "Religious Condition of Our Soldiers," signed A. E. Dickinson, *RH*, 15 May 1862 (for background on Dickinson, see Schweiger, *Gospel Working Up*, 144); *Charleston Courier*, 10 August 1862, quoted in "Religion in the Army," *RH*, 21 August 1862.
21. Royster, *Destructive War*, 241; *Southern Presbyterian* quoted in "Praying for our Enemies," *RH*, 6 March 1862. For examples of continued sentiment that war was an evil, see "War," *RH*, 13 February 1862, and "How long, O! Lord, how long?" *RH*, 8 May 1862.

22. For the scale of missionary efforts by evangelicals (including Baptists), see Schweiger, *Gospel Working Up*, 101; see also Faust, "Christian Soldiers," 66, 69, and Wayne Hsieh, "'Stern Soldiers Weeping': Confederate Clergymen and the Civil War" (M.A. thesis, Univ. of Virginia, 2002).

23. Dickinson quoted in J. William Jones, *Christ in the Camp or Religion in the Confederate Army* (1887; rept. Harrisonburg, Va., 1986), 294; Jones letter quoted ibid., 297. For Jones's later importance, see Charles Reagan Wilson, *Baptized in Blood: The Religion of the Lost Cause* (Athens, Ga., 1980), chapter 6.

24. Richard E. Beringer, Herman Hattaway, Archer Jones, and William N. Still Jr., *Why the South Lost the Civil War* (Athens, Ga., 1986), 94, 98, 102, 362–63; Faust, "Christian Soldiers," 72; Stout and Grasso, "Civil War," 341, 346–47. See also Gardiner H. Shattuck Jr., *A Shield and a Hiding Place: The Religious Life of Civil War Armies* (Macon, Ga., 1987), 10–12.

25. "Religious Condition of Our Soldiers." For Jackson, see "War Notes," signed Ecclesiastes, *RH*, 5 June 1862; "War Notes," *RH*, 10 July 1862; *Richmond Christian Advocate* quoted in *RH*, 7 May 1863, under "Items"; see also James I. Robertson Jr., *Stonewall Jackson: The Man, the Soldier, the Legend* (New York, 1997). On Lee's religious background, see Emory M. Thomas, *Robert E. Lee: A Biography* (New York, 1995), 45–46.

Religious Belief and Troop Motivation

"For the Smiles of My Blessed Saviour"

JASON PHILLIPS

The horrors of war and the constant reality of death caused many soldiers to think seriously about what ministers might call the state of their souls. This mode of thought became almost a preoccupation with some Confederate soldiers. In October 1864, with the following entry, Capt. Joseph Manson of the Twelfth Virginia Infantry began a diary that could more appropriately be called a prayer book: "I begin today to note down in this little book, the dealings of God with my soul. . . . The world has lost much of its power over me & I feel that I can cheerfully exchange the greatest attractions [of earth] for the smiles of my blessed Saviour. . . . His kind hand has been thrown around me & my life has been prolonged. . . . Oh God show me the path of duty & incline my heart to walk therein." Instead of detailing the daily traffic of men and arms or his contact with comrades and family, Manson scribbled down the movements of his soul. That seemed more important—the search for God and salvation beyond the terrors of war. With an enormous enemy force only yards away and pangs of hunger in his gut, the captain admitted, "It is a constant struggle with me to keep my mind in exercise upon eternal things." Certain that death would come to him soon, he prayed, "Oh God may I be found with my face towards the Celestial City & my Armor on."[1]

Manson began his diary in the trenches of Petersburg, where thousands of soldiers found religion because it offered them two invaluable gifts: an explanatory system to make sense of the war and a code of behavior to guide them past the temptations of camp and the perils of combat. Within the ranks, Christianity countered fears of death, promoted discipline and morality, relieved the stresses of combat and fatigue, and alleviated boredom. Yet for believers, spirituality promised more than an entrance into the next world; it accounted for the good, evil, fortune, and hardships of this one. Religious explications of their life and times shaped how thousands of Rebels viewed the war and expected it to end. Drawing support from a host of influences—the tenor of antebellum Southern evangelicalism, reassurances from Confederate clergy, government propaganda, the encompassing presence of spirituality in the armies—many Confederates believed that God favored their cause and would deliver them victory. Even in the final months of the struggle, many soldiers displayed remarkable confidence that the Almighty would save them from ruin if they fulfilled their obligations to Him, if they upheld their covenant. This belief that they were on the winning side of Providence delayed realization of the war's outcome from the Rebellion's final defenders and, thus, helped to prolong the bloodshed and suffering.[2]

The popular idea that Southern religion, particularly its Christian fatalism, lowered Confederate morale and eroded the war effort is grossly inaccurate. Some historians contend that Southern evangelism's focus on individual salvation and the afterlife undermined the political activity and secular labors required to win the war. Civil War historian Steven Woodworth has well documented the religious fidelity of soldiers in both the Confederate and the Union ranks. Nonetheless, other scholars aver that Southern guilt over slavery, when combined with the fear of God's wrath, created a subconscious expectation of defeat. Or, as the authors of *Why the South Lost the Civil War* contend, "God's will became a psychological bridge to the acceptance of defeat." According to historian Larry Logue, as casualty lists swelled and military setbacks multiplied, the religious and psychological inclinations of the South toward defeat "served as a self-fulfilling prophecy."[3]

Notwithstanding such opinions, countless Confederate letters and diaries reveal continued faith in God's favor and Providence. On Christmas Day 1864, Edward Crenshaw sat in his winter quarters hoping for holiday joy or "good news from our armies to cheer me." None came. "But the blessed thought that God, in his infinite mercy, gave his only begotten son as an atonement for our sins, cheers me and gives me new life." "I will not despair when we have such a God to aid us," Crenshaw reasoned, "for he has said that he will protect the weak and aid those who are deserving and he will hear the prayers of those who call him in an humble and contrite spirit.—He will do what is best for us; his will will be done and not that of our enemies." Crenshaw did not fathom that God's will could correspond to Northern war aims. In a letter to his father in January 1864, Reuben Pierson expressed unquestioning confidence in God's favor: "While we . . . fight in a holy and just cause we need have no fears of being enslaved by so brutal and cruel enemies as those against whom we are fighting." According to Pierson, "God who rules the destiny of all things and is a God of wisdom and of justice will never suffer a determined and Christian people to be overcome by a cruel Tyrant but will be their deliver[er] as in the days of old." Pierson thought that a God who led "the children of Israel dry-shod through the Red Sea" could and would find a way to give the Confederacy independence.[4]

From today's perspective, it is difficult to imagine how Rebels like Crenshaw and Pierson found hope and signs of God's favor in the closing months of the conflict. Historical hindsight and current paradigms of psychology and religion encourage us to view late Confederate optimism as delusional. In part, though, thousands continued to believe that Providence smiled on them, because God provided assurances that no other source could promise. In the maelstrom of combat, no other factor, not comrades, fortifications, weapons, tactics, or heroism, could shield soldiers from death; only God could. Likewise from a Christian perspective, nobody else, not the president, a general, a trusted friend, or even an entire army could guard soldiers' families from destitution or invasion like Jehovah could. No doubt thousands of Rebels hoped and prayed for that protection as Federal armies wrecked the home front. Finally, when Confederates suffered one setback after another in 1864 and 1865, no other element, not foreign powers, Copperheads, Gen. Robert E. Lee, or even devotion to the cause, could guarantee victory like the promise of God's favor could. Because of these comforts, Christianity was a powerful sustaining force for Confederate morale throughout the war and particularly toward the end.

The conviction that God would providentially deliver them independence continued to embolden many Rebels late in the war, in part because the roots of these thoughts were deeply embedded in Southern religion. Throughout the antebellum period, Southern identity gravitated not only away from the North but toward God. The growth and separation of evangelical Protestant denominations in the South, clerics' support of slavery and disunion, and the millennialism of American civil religion fostered a heavenly focus that raised Confederates' perceptions of their country and its cause to a sacred level. Civil War soldiers were children of the Second Great Awakening. For those who participated in the evangelical movement, personal salvation gave meaning and joy to their lives. While this emphasis drew some people, like Joseph Manson, to inward reflection and a private relationship with their Maker, other Christians focused on how the outer world was infused with a divine presence. Nineteenth-century Christians considered God an active agent in all their affairs. Just as no soul could avoid God's judgment, nothing God created was beyond His control. On a daily basis, God directed the course of nature, individual humans, and entire civilizations. Though His motives were unknowable, many Americans in general and Southerners in particular believed in Providence, or the idea that God governs the universe toward a moral finale. Trusting that the world would end as described in the Book of Revelation, evangelicals considered all history a part of God's progression toward Judgment Day and the final triumph of good over evil.[5]

When the war came, Southerners comprehended events through the interpretive prism of scripture, like 2 Chronicles 7:13–14: "The calamaties and scourges which befall nations, are ordered by and are under the control of an Allwise though mysterious Providence." Likewise, a pamphlet that circulated through Confederate camps asserted that "the only proper view of this Revolution, is that which regards it as the child of Providence." Seeing the war through this spiritual framework comforted Rebels, because it used traditional beliefs drawn from antebellum religion when people needed constancy most. The worldview assured Confederates that their Maker ordained the war. Moreover, belief in Providence did not permit accidents or fortune. Every effect had a cause, every death served a purpose, and every victory or defeat meant something. Seeing the Almighty directing the carnage helped Southerners fathom the magnitude of the struggle, while it averted the blame for deaths numbering in the hundreds of thousands.[6]

Besides concerns over personal salvation, concepts of Providence are the most prevalent religious ideas found in soldiers' wartime writing. For many Rebels, viewing themselves as pawns produced a fatalistic conviction that surviving the struggle was beyond their control and in the hands of the One who oversaw the paths of bullets and the fates of men. Confederates used the mystery of Providence to explain how they had passed through the surrounding death of battles unscathed. After fighting at Burgess Mill in February 1865, Joseph Manson confided in his diary, "I am not able to express my gratitude to God for having covered our heads in the day of battle. His good providence has spared us a little longer whilst so many have been called away! . . . I commit all into the hands of Him who gave me my life & who will take it at the most appropriate time." After Spottsylvania Court House, a hand-to-hand struggle of men in mud that affected the hardest veterans, Robert Stiles wrote home that "Nothing but God's Providence over us has shielded us from greater losses. . . . God has been very near to both of your boys I hope and believe darling Mother."[7]

Rebels were perhaps fatalists for accepting their status as pawns, but they also believed that God protected the lowliest trooper who prayed with true reverence. In fact, some men were so convinced of a connection between personal piety and God's protection that they encouraged family members back home to lead moral lives on their behalf. When Charles Fenton James learned that his sister Emma attended dancing parties, he feared that her conduct would jeopardize God's protection over him in battle. He wrote her a strong rebuke: "Suppose that while you were upon the dancing floors, you were to hear that one or both of your brothers had fallen in some battle, what would be your feelings then? . . . And do you have any guarantee that such will not be the case when you go to the ball room?" James chastised Emma for neglecting her duty not only to God and her country but also to her brothers in uniform. In a world where God's hand touched everything, a person's conduct could have far-reaching consequences.[8]

Because Providence explained the divine hand in history, the idea also influenced how soldiers perceived the war's progress and expected it to end. When bravado alone failed to convince Rebels that they would overcome the odds their country faced, the men found comfort and courage in St. Paul's assurance to the Romans, "that all things work together for good to them that love God, to them who are called according to His promise." A Confederate clergyman echoed this faith when he stated, "If we, as a State, and confederation of States, officially and privately, nationally and individually, trust obediently in God, He will be our deliverer."[9]

Soldiers who listened to sermons, read religious pamphlets, or meditated over scripture found many instances of God saving His children from mighty foes. Shortly after Gettysburg, a chaplain spoke on this subject to a brigade of Lee's army in Orange County, Virginia. He reminded the men: "Large armies and great powers do not always conquer the smaller and weaker. The Bible and history show that the reverse comes nearer being true." After recounting at length how Macedonians, Athenians, Romans, Englishmen, and Russians had beaten their enemies despite enormous odds, the chaplain addressed the history of Lee's troops. According to him, from Manassas to Gettysburg the Confederate army had always vanquished larger forces. As the chaplain put it, "Often they have more than doubled you, and yet they have never beaten you. Under God you have always mastered the field." According to this interpretation, the history of Lee's army paralleled biblical accounts of the Israelites' miraculous triumphs. Just as outnumbered forces led by Moses, Joshua, and Gideon slew thousands with the aid of divine power, Lee's men scattered the Northern multitudes by God's blessing.[10]

Church leaders repeated this message for the rest of the war. In 1864, while Lee's troops fought a continuous campaign against Grant's army from the Wilderness to the trenches of Petersburg, Confederates read religious pronouncements like this one: "The progressive proofs of God's good providence, in our behalf, strengthen the conviction that the period of our deliverance is not remote. Step by step, have we been led through the bloody scenes of our national drama, by the most manifest interposition of his hand. . . . Have we been brought so far, only to be abandoned in the last stage of the journey, and to perish in the passage, as a monument of Divine delusion?"[11] Most Confederate soldiers did not think so. Within their worldview, defeat would signify that God had tricked and forsaken them, and that was unthinkable.

What started as a belief in Providence and an assumption that they were holier than the Yankees, grew into a certainty of invincibility—they could not lose, because God favored their cause. Instead of hoping that their country was on God's side, many Confederates came to believe that God was on their country's side. How did these convictions differ? The first one, more consistent with evangelicalism, envisioned the Creator as an unknowable arbiter over battlefields, whose design was Providence's progress. Hoping the Confederacy was on God's side emphasized citizens' obligations to Him as well as to their country. Some strands of this thought persisted in fast day sermons until the end of the war. Clergy continued to implore Rebels to repent of their sins in order to deserve divine aid. But over time even fast day sermons highlighted the Confederacy's special place in God's heart and stressed how He was directing them to victory. This emphasis signaled the second, more fanatical vision of God as an omnipotent and ever-present ally, whose plan was Confederate independence.

A common sentiment voiced by Rebel soldiers illustrates the fine line between these two perspectives and reveals the core assumptions of Confederate religion and the unconquerable mentality. As William Casey put it, "If God is for us, who can be against us." Casey's "if" could represent the conditional and mysterious nature of providential aid. Perhaps Casey and others meant that no one can be certain of God's allegiance in war, but *if* He is for us, no one can defeat us. William Nugent voiced this perspective: "We have nothing to fear if we have the approving smiles of Heaven and are true to ourselves." The meaning changes dramatically, however, when we interpret "if" as a synonym for "because." Perhaps Casey and others meant, "Because God is for us, who can be against us?" Such an expression assumed divine sanction and thus ultimate victory for the Confederacy. Thomas Hampton supported this latter interpretation when he stated without equivocation, "I feel assured that God is for us & who can be against us."[12]

A cavalryman explained, in a letter to his sister-in-law, how this mentality affected his perspective. In January 1865 James Keith believed that "the end may not be far off & the sun of peace with happiness in every ray may yet shine out to gild the evening of our days. . . . the eye of faith see[s] only the silver lining of the cloud & look[s] to him who has promised never to desert those who put their trust in him." By seeing only silver linings, Keith and many of his comrades viewed military reverses from a peculiar angle. If God favored the Confederacy, no number of Union victories could lead the enemy to ultimate triumph. Confederate soldiers believed the Creator planned for their independence, but only after the Rebels repented and followed His lead with greater reverence. Therefore, Confederate setbacks resulted from God chastening His people for their sins and not from Union prowess. After enduring a month of Grant's overland campaign, Sgt. Rawleigh Downman wrote to his wife, "Look to Him & call upon Him for strength. Whom He loveth He chasteneth—and we must bear his rod with resignation though to our mortal eyes it seemeth grevious. In all things let us bless God though at times his hand He laid heavily upon us." As late as March 1865, Edward Crenshaw echoed James Keith's meteorological metaphor and sought brightness amid the gloom. He confided in his diary: "The South is being sorely tried, and if she is not found wanting in the balance, the dark clouds of adversity will soon clear away from her horizon and the bright sun of victory will shine out resplendently."[13]

Men who possessed this perspective found hope in the darkest circumstances. Because they connected their country's military success to its piety, public manifestations of faith were "bloodless victories" toward their final triumph. In particular, national days of thanksgiving, prayer, and fasting brought the Confederacy closer to God and, thus, closer to independence. As Stephen Elliott affirmed in a fast day sermon in April 1864, "we have so often seen the gathering fury of our enemies dispersed by God in answer to our humble prayers—scattered and rolled back in blood and confusion—that we come to day boldly to the throne of Grace, firmly believing that our prayers, and supplications, if offered with pure hearts and clean lips, will return to us laden with blessings from the Lord of Hosts, the God of the armies of Israel." Charles Fenton James agreed with Elliott and offered an opinion popular among soldiers when he told his sister, "It is a notable fact that we have never yet met with disaster immediately after a fast day. Our arms have always been blessed with success; and not until the people, in the exultation that follows success, have forgotten the giver of all victory and rejoiced in their own strength and given themselves up to pleasure, have our armies met with reverses."[14]

Revivals within the ranks were compelling symbols of Confederate piety and God's presence. In October 1864 an artilleryman noted: "The revival is spreading & pouring in our Battn, & among our infantry support. Four out of five officers, in one of our batteries have been hopefully converted & many of the men. I mention the officers first, only because religious awakening is less common among them, & they are likely to exert more influence for good. . . . God be with us, our prospects are yet bright." Revivals were also significant for the spectacle of piety they produced. Just as grand reviews and sham battles impressed soldiers with their army's material power, great revivals awed the men with their collective moral strength. The sight of thousands of comrades seeking God's forgiveness and protection convinced many Rebels that their army was as holy as Joshua's Israelites. According to their perspective, each baptism or conversion of a soldier increased God's favor and brought the Confederacy one step closer to peace and independence.[15]

Soldiers' religious perspectives, and the assurance of ultimate victory they encouraged, contribute to our understanding of troop motivation, because they suggest new ways for scholars to study the subject. James McPherson and others have asked "what they fought for"; this essay asks instead why they fought on. Most historians agree that Confederates fought for their people and principles. Protecting loved ones at home and comrades in the ranks steeled Rebel resolve. Believing that the cause was just and that duty bound them to persist also motivated them. But why Rebels continued to fight for people and principles despite the long odds of 1864 and 1865 requires further examination. This issue addresses another element of motivation—hope.[16]

Reid Mitchell understood the difference between inquiring what they fought for and why they fought on when he asked, "Why did the Confederate soldiers continue to give their loyalty to the army and government at Richmond long after victory could be expected?"

Countless Rebel diaries and letters, even those written in the waning months of the war, point to an unlikely but compelling answer: many Confederates persisted because they still thought they could win. Despite internal turmoil and external pressures, regardless of major setbacks at Gettysburg and Vicksburg, and then the fall of Atlanta and Abraham Lincoln's reelection, many Confederate soldiers still hoped for, and even expected, ultimate victory and independence.[17]

But how could this be? And why did some men continue to fight for cause and comrades after others deserted? By relying on religion, some Rebels continued to find God's presence and assurances in the trenches around Petersburg. Their Christianity offered hope, not despair. In his classic work on Confederate religion, James Silver concluded that "morale was a thing of the spirit." Having people and ideals to fight for is an important part of soldiers' motivation, but sustaining hope in success and survival is an equally crucial component of their temperament. After serving in World War I, Lord Moran noted that his men had varying capacities for courage, and every soldier had a limit to the amount of horror and stress he could withstand. Perhaps the capacity for hope among troops is a similar phenomenon. War tests all its participants, and some expend hope for victory before others. In the Army of Northern Virginia, those who lost all hope most likely deserted—and thousands did so in the last months of the war. Those who remained to the end of the struggle often exhibited an unconquerable mentality that would have led some of them to their death on April 9, 1865, had General Lee not raised the white flag. As sociologist Peter Berger explained, "the power of religion depends, in the last resort upon the credibility of the banners it puts in the hands of men as they stand before death." Confederate religion was very powerful for many soldiers, and they lofted their banners of faith for contemporaries—and scholars—to see.[18]

Finally, was this unconquerable mentality a product of wartime self-delusion or a perspective grounded in nineteenth-century Southern beliefs and experiences? The complete answer is both. Nevertheless, most historians who identify the mentality stress its psychological deception. Reid Mitchell called it "insane Confederate optimism." Richard Beringer and his collaborators described it as "unrealistic bravado." They correctly assert that fanaticism and fears of the leveling consequences of Northern victory promoted the unconquerable mentality. In many respects, Confederate religion *did* encourage self-delusion and escapism. Less than a month before Appomattox, Robert Stiles admitted that "God has been good & merciful in taking away the once *abiding* consciousness of desolation." But as historians, we must pause and ask ourselves, is the undefeated mentality "insane" and "unrealistic" from the Rebels' point of view—or from ours? Our knowledge of psychology and the war's outcome must not supplant the fact that Confederates saw a different war from a bygone perspective. In other words, there is little doubt that the soldiers' worldview ill prepared them for defeat, but their vantage point was not irrational or contradictory within their own time and place.[19]

Because Rebels' providential theory of deliverance minimized humanity's role in the war's outcome, it underestimated the very factors that caused Confederate defeat: deficient supplies and manpower, international isolation, a strangling blockade, the disintegration of slavery, Northern power and determination, and disaffection within the ranks and at home. Believers convinced themselves that God could and would overcome these challenges. In the end, the unconquerable mentality *was* encouraged by some of the central religious beliefs of the nineteenth-century South. In particular, faith that God would intercede on Rebels' behalf was not a reactionary hope spawned by the war's conditions but a sincere expectation consistent with their evangelical inheritance. Seeing a God of Battles scattering the enemy and delivering victory may be unusual from today's perspective, but it was not so from the Confederates' point of view. When the promise of Providence vanished at Appomattox Court House, men like Charles Fenton James and Robert Stiles faced a direct challenge not only to their patriotism but to their Christianity as well. A closer examination of Rebel religion will better illuminate how white Southerners saw the war, handled defeat, envisioned the future, and memorialized the past.[20]

Notes

1. Joseph Richard Manson Diary, 27 October, 8 November, 17 December 1864, VHS.

2. Randall M. Miller, Harry S. Stout, and Charles Reagan Wilson, eds., *Religion and the American Civil War* (New York, 1998); Bell I. Wiley, *The Life of Johnny Reb: The Common Soldier of the Confederacy* (Indianapolis, Ind., 1943); Drew Gilpin Faust, "Christian Soldiers: The Meaning of Revivalism in the Confed-

erate Army," *JSH* 53 (February 1987): 63–90; Larry J. Daniel, *Soldiering in the Army of Tennessee: A Portrait of Life in a Confederate Army* (Chapel Hill, N.C., 1991), 115–25; Samuel J. Watson, "Religion and Combat Motivation in the Confederate Armies," *Journal of Military History* 58 (January 1994): 29–55. "Religion" and "Christianity" were not synonymous terms for every Confederate, but because correspondence from Jewish soldiers and men of other faiths was not found for this essay, only the Christian dimensions of Southern religion are considered here. Moreover, "Southerner" and "Confederate" or "Rebel" were not synonyms either, but herein *Southerner* refers to white Southerners who supported the Confederacy.

3. Steven E. Woodworth, *While God Is Marching On: The Religious World of Civil War Soldiers* (Lawrence, Kans., 2001); Gardiner H. Shattuck Jr., *A Shield and Hiding Place: The Religious Life of the Civil War Armies* (Macon, Ga., 1987), 10–12; Richard Beringer, Herman Hattaway, Archer Jones, and William N. Still Jr., *Why the South Lost the Civil War* (Athens, Ga., 1986), 353 (first quotation), 360 (second quotation); Larry M. Logue, *To Appomattox and Beyond: The Civil War Soldier in War and Peace* (Chicago, 1996), 78.

4. Edward Crenshaw, "Diary of Captain Edward Crenshaw, of the Confederate States Army," *Alabama Historical Review* 2 (Fall 1940): 367; Thomas W. Cutrer and T. Michael Parrish, eds., *Brothers in Gray: The Civil War Letters of the Pierson Family* (Baton Rouge, La., 1997), 224.

5. For the origins and pervasiveness of providential beliefs in the South, see John B. Boles, *The Great Revival: Beginnings of the Bible Belt* (Lexington, Ky., 1996), 25–35 (originally published in 1972 as *The Great Revival, 1787–1805: The Origins of the Southern Evangelical Mind*).

6. An example of how this Scripture was used can be found in Thomas S. Dunaway, *A Sermon Delivered by Elder Thomas S. Dunaway, of Lancaster County, Virginia, before Coan Baptist Church* [4138–2] (Richmond, 1864), 3; Joseph M. Atkinson, *The Giver of Victory and Peace: A Thanksgiving Sermon, Delivered in the Presbyterian Church, September 18, 1862, Raleigh, N.C.* [4123] (Raleigh, [1862?]), 11 (second quotation). These and all subsequent sermons are contained in the Confederate Imprints Microfilm Series; the number in brackets after the title is that sermon's identification number in the CIMS. For religion's contributions to Confederate nationalism, see Drew Gilpin Faust, *The Creation of Confederate Nationalism: Ideology and Identity in the Civil War South* (Baton Rouge, La., 1988), and Mitchell Snay, *Gospel of Disunion: Religion and Separatism in the Antebellum South* (Cambridge, UK, 1993).

7. Joseph Richard Manson Diary, 8 February 1865, VHS; Robert Augustus Stiles to Caroline Clifford Stiles, Spottsylvania Court House, Sunday [5 May 1864?] Robert Augustus Stiles Papers, VHS; James M. McPherson, *For Cause and Comrades: Why Men Fought in the Civil War* (New York, 1997), 63; Woodworth, *While God Is Marching On*, 27–39.

8. Charles Fenton James to Emma James, 13 February 1865, Charles Fenton

James Letters, VHS; McPherson, *For Cause and Comrades*, 64–67; Kurt O. Berends, "'Wholesome Reading Purifies and Elevates the Man': The Religious Military Press in the Confederacy," in Miller, Stout, and Wilson, *Religion and the American Civil War*, 139.

9. King James Bible, Romans 8:28; William Rees, *A Sermon on Divine Providence* [4185–1] (Austin, Tex., 1863), 11.

o. J. J. D. Renfroe, "The Battle is God's": A Sermon Preached before Wilcox's Brigade [4186] (Richmond, 1863), 7.

1. D. D. Doggett, *The War and Its Close* [4137] (Richmond, 1864), 19; Berends, "Wholesome Reading," 152–53.

2. William Casey to his mother, 28 June 1864, William Thomas Casey Papers, VHS; William Nugent to Eleanor Nugent, 25 June 1864, in *My Dear Nellie: The Civil War Letters of William L. Nugent to Eleanor Smith Nugent*, eds. William M. Cash and Lucy Somerville Howorth (Jackson, Miss., 1977), 185; Thomas Hampton to Jestin Hampton, 29 April 1864, Thomas B. Hampton Letters, Univ. of Texas Center of American History; James W. Silver, *Confederate Morale and Church Propaganda* (Tuscaloosa, Ala., 1957), 38; Berends, "Wholesome Reading," 147.

3. James Keith to Sarah Agnes (Blackwell) Keith, 15 January 1865, Keith Family Papers, 1831–1916, VHS; Rawleigh William Downman to Mary Alice (Macgruder) Downman, 20 June 1864, Downman Family Papers, VHS; "Diary of Captain Edward Crenshaw," 364.

4. Stephen Elliott, *Gideon's Water-Lappers: A Sermon Preached in Christ Church, Savannah* [4143] (Macon, Ga., 1864), 5; Charles Fenton James to Emma A. James, 13 February 1865, James Letters; W. Harrison Daniel, *Southern Protestantism in the Confederacy* (Bedford, Va., 1989), 29.

5. Robert Augustus Stiles to Mother, 2 October 1864; Stiles Papers; Berends, "Wholesome Reading," 135, 140–41, 146; James I. Robertson Jr., *Soldiers Blue and Gray* (Columbia, S.C., 1988), 186–88.

6. McPherson, *For Cause and Comrades*; Gerald Linderman, *Embattled Courage: The Experience of Combat in the American Civil War* (New York, 1987); Earl Hess, *Liberty, Virtue, and Progress: Northerners and Their War for the Union* (New York, 1988).

7. Reid Mitchell, *Civil War Soldiers* (New York, 1988), 168.

8. Silver, *Confederate Morale*, 42; Charles McMoran Wilson Moran, *The Anatomy of Courage* (1945; rept. Boston, 1967); Peter Berger, *The Sacred Canopy: Elements of a Sociological Theory of Religion* (New York, 1990), 51.

9. Mitchell, *Civil War Soldiers*, 191; Beringer, et al., *Why the South Lost*, 87; Robert Augustus Stiles, 21 March 1865, Stiles Papers.

o. For discussions of how defeat challenged the faith of some Confederates, see John B. Boles, *The Irony of Southern Religion* (New York, 1994), 96–98, and Eugene D. Genovese, *A Consuming Fire: The Fall of the Confederacy in the Mind of the White Christian South* (Athens, Ga., 1998).

Promoting the Confederate Nation

―――――――――― ⟨⟩ ――――――――――

The Southern Illustrated News *and the Civil War*

IAN BINNINGTON

On September 6, 1862, the Richmond publishing house of Ayres and Wade issued the first copy of the *Southern Illustrated News*. Just a week earlier, Gen. Robert E. Lee's forces had bested John Pope's Federals at the second battle of Bull Run (or Manassas). And on September 4, the Army of Northern Virginia had started to cross the Potomac River in its invasion of Maryland. The editors of the *News*, in their inaugural comment on "The Times," noted that hopes were running high for the Confederate nation, with spirits buoyed by repeated victories against inferior Union generals:

> From the dark gloom of despondency, our people have been elevated into the clear sunlight of hope. Light has literally come out of darkness, confidence has succeeded to a state very nearly resembling despair, universal cheerfulness has assumed the place of general depression. In such a condition of the public mind our journal makes its appearance, like an emanation from an atmosphere brilliant with anticipations of prosperity yet to come.[1]

Historical hindsight reveals that the *News* was chasing rainbows when it forecast such a bright future for the Confederacy's national project. Early September 1862 proved just a brief interlude before the meat grinder of Antietam (or Sharpsburg) and the issuance of the Preliminary Emancipation Proclamation.

Regardless, in this fleeting historical moment in September 1862 can be seen the centrality of the Confederate military to its national endeavor. It was not lost on the editors of the *News* that the future prosperity to which they looked would come at the hands of the Confederacy's "great leader, and the gallant army which he commands"—Gen. Robert E. Lee and the Army of Northern Virginia.[2] To cement the role of the military in its conception of the Confederate nationalist project, the first issue of the *News* featured Gen. Thomas "Stonewall" Jackson on its first page. Virtually every subsequent issue of the journal featured another military portrait. For the *News*, the generals and the nation ran together.

A nation needs symbols and heroes upon which to focus its attention. A nation in the act of self-creation needs them even more. A nation seeking to constitute itself through war, as the Confederacy did, might well tend to concentrate on the virtues and achievements of its military men. This certainly was not the only symbolic foundation of the Confederate nation, or the first. But as the American Civil War progressed, Confederate iconography became inextricably tied to the fortunes of the military, and the generals came to represent the Confederate nation to itself. Lee and Jackson appear at the center of this wartime nationalist production, the general for the ages and his doughty and tenacious lieutenant.

The first issue of the *News* made clear the dualistic problem of employing military men as nationalist heroes. On the one hand, they promised great victories, and a consequent growth of patriotism and loyalty as well as the ultimate promise of independence. But on the other hand, they carried the potential for defeat, disillusion, subjugation, and even death. A nation at war lives or dies on the qualities of its military—a blindingly obvious statement to be sure, but one that had important implications for the burgeoning nationalist project of the Confederacy. The *News* cast itself as a literary journal, one devoted to the fight for "our intellectual, as well as political independence," as one of their correspondents put it, so the editors tended to see the stories of the war through a literary and intellectual lens.[3]

In their "Salutatory" welcome to new readers, the editors of the *News* pointed to the power of battlefield stories to inspire, a power that "mere literary or artistic novelties" could not match. As they put it, "there is a deeper pathos, a loftier poetry in the incidents of yesterday's battle-field than belong to the most tuneful measures, while Jack Morgan and Jeb Stuart surpass all the knighthood of romance."[4] So Confederate military prowess loomed large as a unifying factor, something Southerners could gaze upon with pride. We know this was built on the sandy foundation of a few victories over poorly led foes, but a few victories proved an ample fabric from which to spin a nationalist mythology, with only a toehold in strategic realities.

From the outset, this mythology of victory was tenuous and undermined by the continuing possibility of defeat at the hands of those same Federals. This points to the danger of creating a mythology at the same time as its story was playing out. Another article on the same page made this clear. Under the heading, "Resting on Their Laurels," the *News* sternly admonished unnamed generals from letting fame and success go to their heads:

> It is curious to observe that so soon as opinion crowns some of our generals with a little airy fame, they deem their fortune made and their duty ended. They forget that their scrap of good deeds past are being put in a huge wallet at Father Time's back, along with the other "alms for oblivion," and that, whilst they feast their ears on the few lingering echoes of popular applause, even then they are in danger of going quite out of fashion, and like a rusty mail, hanging "in monumental mockery."

Yet public disapproval was not the most important thing here, for the nation or the Cause. The key is that the people—whom the *News* presumed it could speak for—had serious and weighty expectations of their generals that they would disappoint at their peril. From the Confederacy's leaders, "who are endowed with every quality of nature with which the hero should be gifted," said the *News*, "every thing is demanded"—military victory, conduct appropriate for a Southern gentleman, and ultimately independence and enduring nationhood.[5]

The centerpiece of the *Southern Illustrated News*, the thing that cemented its commitment to the Confederate nation and to the position of its putative military heroes, was its ongoing series of front-page portraits of leading military figures. Many of these were, as the name of the journal might suggest, illustrated with engravings of the men under discussion. The first engravings were small head shots, but starting with Turner Ashby in the sixth issue, they presented the occasional cavalier-like pose on horseback. Starting with Robert E. Lee in the nineteenth issue, in January 1863, the *News* offered full-page portraits of the generals, complete with accompanying artillery pieces and Confederate flags.[6]

After Lee, such luminaries as Albert Sidney Johnston, Lloyd Tilgham, James Longstreet, and Pierre Beauregard were feted with full-page spreads. Exceptions to this domination of the front page by generals (and the occasional naval officer) included "Vicksburg, Mississippi" (in the ninth issue) and "The Society of Women" (in the fifteenth).[7] Moreover, even when the front page was taken, portraits of generals continued in the interior pages, with Braxton Bragg and Jeff Thompson featured respectively in these instances. In sum, military leaders figured centrally in the image of the Confederacy presented by the *Southern Illustrated News*. And in a pre–mass media society, images like this no doubt had great power to make their points and stir a sense of patriotism and nationalism.

The first issue of the *News* contained, just under its masthead, a profile of Stonewall Jackson, and Jackson's career illustrates the dangers of relying on military leaders as exemplars of national virtue. According to the *News*, Stonewall was immune to the "prejudice and bigotry of rank," and he was a soldier's soldier, a leader "daunted by no danger, exhausted by no toil, caught by no stratagem." Perhaps more than all of this, he was marked by a "rigid remembrance of Divine power."[8]

In terms of temperament and character, Jackson was perhaps the perfect expression of the Confederate general. He also inspired literary flourishes from the correspondents and contributors to the *Southern Illustrated News*, including Hard Cracker's "Foot-Cavalry Chronicle" and "Jackson's Foot-Cavalry"; "Stonewall Jackson's Way," supposedly found on the body of a sergeant in Stonewall's brigade; and Virginia Norfolk's "Over the River," allegedly based on Jackson's last words. As one of the tributes noted: "The foe had better ne'er been born / Than get in Stonewall's way."[9] In fact, Stonewall appeared to inculcate more devotion from the partisans of the *News* than any other person.

And yet Stonewall was human, and his mythic status was ultimately disfigured by his death in May 1863, after the battle of Chancellorsville, at the hands of what we would call today "friendly fire." In its edition of August 29, 1863, the *News*, partly in an effort to publicize a book on Jackson published by Ayres and Wade, devoted its front page to "Recollections of Stonewall Jackson." Their opening comments drive home the point that dead military heroes, who die in the service of the current nation, rather than in the mythic past, present a particular problem to the development of a sense of nationalism.

JACKSON IS DEAD.
Seldom have words penetrated more deeply to the heart of a great nation. The people of the Confederate States had begun to regard this immortal leader as above the reach of fate. He had passed unhurt through such desperate contests; his calm eyes had surveyed so many hard fought battlefields, from the commencement of the combats to their termination, that a general conviction of the hero's invulnerability had impressed every heart—no one could feel that the light in those eyes of the great soldier would ever be quenched.[10]

And yet it got worse, for the *News* then discussed the vital link between Jackson and Robert E. Lee, one that was now broken by Jackson's demise: "Lee is the exponent of Southern power of command; Jackson, the expression of its faith in God and in itself, its terrible energy, its enthusiasm and daring, its unconquerable will, its contempt of danger and fatigue, its capacity to smite, as with bolts of thunder, the cowardly and cruel foe that would trample under foot its liberty and religion." And then it got worse even still, for in the view of this author, Stonewall "was no accidental manifestation of the powers of faith and courage. He came not by chance in this day and to this generation. He was born for a purpose."[11] And yet this man was dead—at the hands of his own soldiers, although the *News* never appeared to report this fact. Certainly, there was the hope that "his fiery and unqualifying spirit would survive in his men," but that was little more than wishful thinking. The Confederacy had lost a man apparently born to deliver them victory, who was the arm of God and General Lee on the battlefield, and the expression of the South's martial characteristics.

How could the Cause survive Jackson's demise? And in the case of the *Southern Illustrated News*, with so much of the nationalist spirit and vigor invested in this one figure, how could its vision of Confederate nationalism survive? The *News* appeared to offer no answer. Some historians have noted that Stonewall's tragic death dissociated him from the reality of the Confederacy's ultimate defeat, and thus made his canonization by the advocates of the Lost Cause easier than his sometimes-checkered record as a general might warrant. While that may be true, it should not lead one to underestimate the very real impact his death had on the Cause—on the Confederacy—before its surrender necessitated the creation of a Lost Cause myth.[12]

Yet what of Lee, "the exponent of Southern power of command," who remained alive, in good health, and at the head of his army? Part of the problem seems to be that, although they mouthed platitudes about the relationship of Jackson and Lee, the editors of the *News* appear to have seen the fate of the Confederacy bound up more in Jackson than in Lee. So the position of Robert E. Lee in the military pantheon of the *Southern Illustrated News* is something that needs attention.

In the inaugural issue, Lee was "our great leader," "our gallant leader," and his befuddlement of McClellan before Richmond in the Peninsular campaign was held to contain "some of the most splendid combinations known to the art of war, the conception of which has placed the author in the first rank of generals." Later issues continued this hyperbolic praise. Introducing their portrait of Lee in the nineteenth issue, in January 1863, the *News* noted that "the achievements of General Lee form the most remarkable chapter, not only in the history of the present gigantic war, but in some respects, in the entire annals of war itself." The editors pointed to the Peninsular campaign as a brilliant episode in the career of the Confederacy's "distinguished chieftain." When the *News* again featured Lee on the front page, in October 1863, it quoted Union general Winfield Scott describing Lee as "the greatest military genius in America, myself not excepted."[13] They also ranked him among the greatest generals in the history of the world, alongside Epaminondas of Thebes, Julius Caesar, Gustavus Adolphus, Frederick the Great, and Napoleon Bonaparte.[14]

Yet the *News* misreported Lee's name throughout its entire publication run—he was always Robert Edmund Lee rather than Robert Edward Lee. And perhaps more significant, not only was Stonewall Jackson the first general portrayed, in the first issue of the *News*, but also Lee was the nineteenth. Before the *News* turned its attention to their "great leader," they profiled John H. Morgan, Sterling Price, Turner Ashby, Ben McCulloch, Joe Johnston, Braxton Bragg, Leonidas Polk, A. P. Hill, William Cabell, Bankhead Magruder, Nathan Davis, Jeff Thompson, Frank Cheathem, and two naval officers, Cdr. M. F. Maury and Adm. Franklin Buchanan.[15] It may be that the answer to this conundrum is as simple as the lack of a suitable engraving of Lee—the one used in the January 17, 1863, issue was taken from a decade-old photograph, described as the only one "extant" of the general.

It also may be that Lee's reputation in late 1862 and early 1863 was not as stellar as the *News* seemed to imply. On the one hand, he was their greatest chieftain, but on the other, he was only a few months removed from being Granny Lee, the timid and frustrated military adviser to the Confederate president.[16] If Lee was so central to the Confederacy's national project—and what the *News* said never wavered from this analysis—why was his profile printed after so many others, including at least three of his subordinates in the Army of Northern Virginia?

Lee inspired none of the literary output from the contributors to the *News* that Jackson did. Jeb Stuart had a poem or two, and even—improbably—Joe Johnston had one ode penned in his honor. Paul Hayne's poem about Jeb Stuart urged Confederates to

> drink to a spirit as leal and true
> As ever drew blade in a fight,
> And dashed on the Tyrant's lines of steel
> For God, and a Nation's Right!

John R. Thompson's poem, commemorating Joe Johnston's "exile" to the Department of the West, concluded:

> One flash of his sword when the foe is hard prest,
> And the Land of the West shall be free!

But never Lee—no poem for him.[17] Did this fact represent the editorial inclinations of the journal—or the colorlessness of Lee's popular image?

One clue can be found in the language used to describe the two men. Jackson was the heart of the Confederacy's military, representing its "faith," "energy," "enthusiasm," "daring," "contempt of danger," "capacity to smite," and "unconquerable will." Lee was a military technician of the highest order, but he never inspired the same linguistic flights—he remained a mechanic of the military arts rather than a poet. Jackson was a romantic hero to inspire the generations, Lee rather more mundane. While always given his due, Lee was seemingly never embraced to the same extent. Even at the height of Lee's wartime achievements, his mythic status never seemed to rival that of Jackson, his subordinate colleague.

In a culture that tended toward self-romanticization (and still does now), the exploits of dashing heroes were essentialized and elevated to mythic status. Southern wartime literature, too, manifested a fascination with military heroes. For example, in Sally Rochester Ford's *Raids and Romances; or, Morgan and his Men*, General Morgan's first appearance in the text is accompanied by a description bordering on the adulatory—his horsemanship was elegant, his features "bespoke daring and determination," his mustache was "trimmed with exquisite precision," he was handsome and immaculately clothed, and he manifested both "manly dignity" and "graceful ease."[18] And, as Ford also made clear, Morgan was a chivalrous gentleman—in contrast to the barbarous and depraved Yankees, a theme also reflected in the pages of the *News*.

In an October 1862 article entitled "The Yankee Spirit of Rapine," the *Southern Illustrated News* accused the Federals of desiring "extermination, and all the horrors of indiscriminate emancipation," reenacting the "worst days of the Terror in France," and threatening to 'deluge the whole land with blood!" The *News* castigated Northern generalship, whether Pope the poltroon, "Hunter the Hound," or "Butler the Beast."[19] Southern generalship, by contrast, was seen as urbane, civilized, sanctified by the Lord, and expressive of the best features of Southern society and culture. Yet mounting failures bloodied the troops in gray and the prospects of independence. The South's generals proved increasingly unable to deliver on the hopes that had been invested in them to secure a Confederate nation.

Notes

I wish to acknowledge the critical readings of this essay provided by O. Vernon Burton and David F. Herr.

1. "The Times," *The Southern Illustrated News* 1, no. 1 (6 September 1862): 5 (hereafter cited as *News*).

2. Ibid.

3. M. Louise Rogers, "Glad Greetings We Send Thee," *News* 1, no. 6 (18 October 1862): 3.

4. "Salutatory," *News* 1, no. 1 (6 September 1862): 4.

5. "Resting on their Laurels," *News* 1, no. 1 (6 September 1962).

6. "General Turner Ashby," *News* 1, no. 6 (18 October 1862): 1; "General Robert Edmund Lee," *News* 1, no. 19 (17 January 1863): 1. W. B. Campbell completed most of the engravings presented in the *News* after its first few issues.

7. "Vicksburg, MS," *News* 1, no. 9 (8 November 1862): 1; and "The Society of Women," *News* 1, no. 15 (20 December 1862): 1.

8. "General Thomas J. Jackson," *News* 1, no. 1 (6 September 1862): 1.

9. Hard Cracker, "Foot-Cavalry Chronicle," *News* 1, no. 6 (18 October 1862): 3; Hard Cracker, "Jackson's Foot-Cavalry," ibid., 8; "Stonewall Jackson's Way," *News* 1, no. 14 (13 December 1862): 7; Virginia Norfolk, "Over the River," *News* 2, no. 3 (25 July 1863): 18. The *News* reported Stonewall's last words as "Let us cross over the river, and rest under the shade of the trees."

10. "Recollections of Stonewall Jackson," *News* 2, no. 8 (29 August 1863): 57.

11. Ibid.

12. On this, see Gary W. Gallagher, "The Making of a Hero and the Persistence of a Legend: Stonewall Jackson during the Civil War and in Popular History," in his *Lee and His Generals in War and Memory* (Baton Rouge, La., 1998), 101–17, esp. 111–14.

13. "The Times," *News* 1, no. 1 (6 September 1862): 5; "General Robert Edmund Lee," *News* 1, no. 19 (17 January 1863): 2; "General Robert Edmund Lee," *News* 2, no. 15 (17 October 1863): 1.

14. A series portraying the lives of these military exemplars was run in the *News* between 26 September (2, no. 2) and 24 October 1863 (2, no. 16).

15. I have not yet been unable to track down the third and fourth issues of the *News*, but internal evidence suggests that Lee was not featured in either of them.

16. On Lee's transformation in the popular imagination during 1862, see Gallagher, "The Idol of His Soldiers and the Hope of His Country: Lee and the Confederate People," in his *Lee and His Generals in War and Memory*, 3–20, esp. 8–11.

17. Paul H. Hayne, "Stuart," *News* 2, no. 13 (6 December 1862): 7; John R. Thompson, "A Word with the West," *News* 1, no. 14 (13 December 1862): 4.

18. Sally Rochester Ford, *Raids and Romances; or, Morgan and his Men* (1863; rept. New York, 1866), 28.

19. "The Yankee Spirit of Rapine," *News* 1, no. 5 (11 October 1862): 5; "A Farewell to Pope," *News* 1, no. 2 (11 September 1862): 3.

War Comes Home

⟨ccc⟩

Confederate Women and Union Soldiers

LISA TENDRICH FRANK

On a warm and humid Sunday, June 19, 1864, Lucy Breckenridge's world fell apart. She and the other elite white women of her Virginia household had spent three exhausting years adjusting to wartime shortages, fears, and sacrifices. At this point, though, a greater threat appeared—the arrival of Union troops at the plantation gate. No longer could women like Breckenridge enjoy the traditional protections usually afforded civilians. Without regard for the rules of polite society, the Federals ransacked the house. Breckenridge described her "fright" at the behavior of "one impudent scamp" who continually demanded that the women pull out the brandy. She told him repeatedly that she and the women in her house had none to offer. Assuming that she was lying, the Yankee soldier cursed her while violently opening drawers and cupboards and making a great mess of things. Her contact with this "fearfully insolent man" and his comrades ultimately led Breckenridge to judge "what horrible things men are."[1]

Breckenridge's experience with Union soldiers during Philip Sheridan's 1864 Shenandoah Valley campaign was scarcely an isolated incident. Across Virginia and throughout the Confederacy, hundreds of elite white Southern women had similar encounters with invading enemy soldiers and came to share her gloomy assessment. Verbal and physical assaults on Confederate women and their domestic property revealed that they had become part of the Union's determination to bring the South to the point of surrender.

As Breckenridge's experience in Virginia's Shenandoah Valley demonstrates, the Civil War drew white Southern women into the orbit of a hostile male population. No longer shielded by the men of their family or by nineteenth-century deference toward women, slave-holding females could not escape confrontations with Union soldiers who treated them as enemies. In these interactions, femininity became both a weapon for women to draw upon and a weakness for soldiers to prey upon. In some cases, soldiers used notions about femininity to their advantage. They attacked such material indicators of femininity as fancy dresses. The purpose of bringing the war to the home front was to demoralize wealthy Confederate women and thus bring the war to a quickened conclusion.

Reshaping their roles in both their domestic and civic lives, slave-holding women became energetic participants in the battle for Southern nationhood and, as such, targets for enemy armies. Union soldiers, recognizing elite Southern women's roles in the development and preservation of Confederate nationalism, were determined to crush such support.[2] Consequently, in 1864 Union military policy concentrated on destroying the Southern will to fight. This revised policy focused on all civilians, especially white women on plantations. Union troops recognized that female enemies could not be treated as combatants, but they would still be regarded as enemies.

Slaveholding women became acceptable targets for Union policies as a result of their outspoken hostility and participation in the Southern war effort. They were not necessarily the demure belles and shy matrons that Union troops expected to meet. As recent work has shown, before the war many of them had drawn attention to themselves in public situations as outright secessionists. Far from politically ignorant, educated women of the South paid close attention to the events around them and kept journals in the 1850s and 1860s to record the tumultuous events. They even took a significant part in campaigns and elections, earning them the gratitude of politicians for their efforts behind the scenes.[3] In addition to recording their impressions in personal diaries, elite women read the news and discussed it in depth with friends and family of both sexes.

When the secession crisis came to a climax in the presidential election of 1860, these plantation women had much to say on the issue. As self-proclaimed patriotic Southerners, many appealed to their husbands' sense of familial duty to encourage secession and thereby protect hearth and household from "black Republicans" and abolitionists.[4] Others, more prudent, were "Conditional Unionists," but they, too, once Virginia rallied to the new Confederacy after the firing on Fort Sumter, made themselves indispensable to the war effort. White women encouraged their brothers, husbands, and male kinfolk to enlist in the armed services, and they supplied the newly formed regiments with food, clothes, and medical supplies. They appealed to their men to act manly, valorous, and honorable in fulfilling the obligations of the soldier. Those who refused the call to arms would soon find themselves social pariahs in the eyes of the ladies.

Emma Edmonds, a Union spy, marveled that Confederate women were "the best recruiting officers," as they refused "to tolerate, or admit to their society any young man who refuses to enlist."[5] They taunted, cajoled, and shamed white men into the army. For example, one dedicated "fire-eater" broke off her engagement to a man who did not enlist. She sent him a petticoat, a skirt, and a note reading, "wear these, or volunteer."[6] In a published poem, "If You Love Me," another woman encouraged her sweetheart to enlist:

> If you love me, do not ponder, . . .
> Join your country in the fray. . . .
> Be her own and my defender—
> Strike for freedom to the last.[7]

Privileged white women determined to fill the army because, as Virginian Judith McGuire confided to her journal, "We could not bear that one of [the men of our family] should hesitate to give his life's blood to his country."[8] Furthermore, they felt confident that the fight for an independent Southern nation would prevail. As Caroline Davis asserted, "The cause of the South is just & I pray for its success. Aye! & it will succeed there is no such thought as 'fail' in a Southern heart."[9]

Elite women's confidence in their new nation and their soldiers marched arm in arm with a virulent antipathy toward the enemy. The Union's shift from a focus on the battlefield to direct assaults on Southern civilians provoked many female Confederates to view Northern soldiers as "demons." The enemy presence in militarily occupied areas could be, and was, tolerated as a consequence of war, but Southern women frequently concluded that Union soldiers took things too far. When, in 1861, the Union imprisoned a group of vocal Southern women and their young daughters in Washington, D.C., men and women across the Confederate states voiced their outrage. In November 1861 Rose O'Neal Greenhow, a Southern spy and one of the arrested women, proclaimed in the *Richmond Whig* that Union actions illuminated "the cruel and dastardly tyranny which the Yankee government has established at Washington." Greenhow hoped that "the incarceration and torture of helpless women, and the outrages heaped upon them . . . will shock manly natures and stamp the Lincoln dynasty everywhere with undying infamy." Enraged by their arrest, but confident of their place in history, the women in custody saw themselves as martyrs to the Confederacy. Greenhow asserted that she wrote her "Letter from a Southern Lady in Prison," because "my sufferings will afford a significant lesson to the women of the South, that sex or condition is no bulwark against the surging billows of the 'irrepressible conflict.'"[10]

Eugenia Yates Levy Phillips, as she prepared for her own internment, objected to what she called "a new era in the History of the Country, one which marks the arrest and imprisonment of women, for political opinions!" The women's bravery, sacrifice, and dedication to their nation became clearer, she continued, as they "immediately prepared with courageous hearts, inspired with the thought that we were suffering in a noble cause, and determined so to bear ourselves, as not to shame our southern countrywomen."[11] Through their objections to their treatment, both Greenhow and Phillips demonstrated a belief held by many elite women that their sex placed them beyond the scope of punishment. In addition, they played upon their confinement to enhance Southern patriotism, to demonstrate the necessity of the Confederate war and total separation from the North.

The imprisonment of elite female Confederates in 1861 foreshadowed the troubles white women across the South would face in the future. In May 1862 reports of Maj. Gen. Benjamin Butler's actions in occupied New Orleans further excited Confederate tempers. After women in the city shunned and even attacked the Union soldiers there, Butler issued his infamous General Order 28, which stated that any woman who showed disrespect for the occupying Union troops would be treated as a prostitute; that is, Confederate women could be stripped of the protections normally afforded them as white women. News of Butler's attempt to subdue and control the Confederate women in New Orleans through the "Woman Order" spread quickly across the South. White women and men denounced it. They agreed with Gertrude Thomas, who denounced Butler as someone whose name "th[r]ough all coming ages will be branded with the reputation of being the most vile loathsome of all God's creation."[12] Confederates viewed "Beast" Butler's improper treatment of white women as unforgivable. Even though it was wartime, white Southern women expected that men, including the enemy, would treat them with respect. Even after perceived outrages by Butler and others, Southern white women, assuming that even in wartime their gender and race afforded them protection, continued to appeal to the enemy for personal guards for their homes.[13]

In 1864 Union policy shifted to one directly aimed at the Confederate home front and at its civilian population as enemies of war. Hoping to hasten the end of the war, U.S. general Ulysses S. Grant directed two of his commanders, Philip H. Sheridan and William Tecumseh Sherman, to bring the war to the Virginia and Georgia home fronts. In September, Grant ordered Sheridan to "do all the damage . . . you can" to turn the Shenandoah Valley into "a barren waste."[14] Grant expressed the hope that the soldiers on this campaign would "eat out Virginia clear and clean as far as they go, so that crows flying over it for the balance of this season will have to carry their provender with them."[15] Sheridan and his men took these orders to heart, seizing or destroying all flour, grains, and livestock as well as burning civilians out of their homes.

Not only did Sheridan and his troops destroy things that directly assisted the Confederate war effort, they also struck at the heart of the feminine sphere by invading homes and destroying domestic treasures. As they carried out their home front objectives, few Union soldiers sympathized with the plight of their wealthy female victims. Many supported Sheridan, who "[did] not believe war to be simply that lines should engage each other in battle." This, the commander continued, was the case especially because Confederate "women did not care how many were killed, or maimed, so long as war did not come to their doors, but as soon as it did come in the shape of loss of property, they earnestly prayed for its termination. . . . As war is a punishment, if we can, by reducing its advocates to poverty, end it quicker, we are on the side of humanity."[16] Sheridan believed in the utility of bringing war to the Confederate home front and the slaveholding women who occupied it. Consequently, Sheridan denied elite Southern women their protected status, and instead engaged them as enemies. The Union's method of "hard war," which included the invasion of the domestic sphere, guided Union actions throughout the South beginning in 1864.[17]

Despite their varied attempts to prepare for invasion, white Southern women could not anticipate the havoc that Union soldiers would ultimately wreak in their homes. During the 1864 campaign, Union troops in the Shenandoah Valley vandalized and sacked houses from top to bottom, particularly those belonging to the wealthier families. The destructiveness was not confined to parlors and dining rooms, where silver and valuable glass might be found. Soldiers also tore up, scattered, or looted the furnishings and jewelry in the bedrooms, a sphere that more intimately belonged to the women of the household. Indeed, the soldiers singled out the trappings of domesticity— women's wardrobes, fine china, silver candlesticks, glass vases, private journals, sewing supplies, and fancy linens. From her home near the University of Virginia, one woman described how "the stragglers intruded themselves and ran all over the house, ransacking bureau drawers, trunks and wardrobes. Taking out the ladies' underclothes and dresses and finally dressing themselves up in them and wildly dancing about the yard, much to the terror of the ladies."[18]

This humiliating scene was repeated in other invaded homes. In some instances, Union soldiers jumped up on piano tops to dance, scar, and finally kick apart the instrument. Slaveholding women often rushed in horror to pen and paper to record their distress for themselves and their loved ones. They filled diaries and letters with vivid accounts of Union soldiers whom they disdainfully called "fiends" and other epithets. These missives, they hoped, would help fuel the anti-Northern sentiments of others.[19]

Elite women took special pains to hide their most valuable domestic treasures. At the same time, they often naively convinced themselves that even Union foot soldiers would feel bound by nineteenth-century rules of propriety. Consequently, "she-Rebels" shielded their personal property in "feminine" places they assumed were inviolable. One Virginian assumed she had found a safe place for her valuables when she "put all her silver and things in her baby's crib. The baby was asleep and the old nurse was sitting by rocking it." Much to her surprise, the Union soldiers "turned the baby out on the floor, found and took the hidden treasure."[20]

Many a Virginia woman also hid personal and monetary valuables on her person, presuming that her body remained untouchable even if her domestic sphere was not. One woman congratulated herself for hiding her gold twenty-dollar pieces in what turned out to be a secure place. "After gravely debating the matter as to whether they should be put into the chimney, sewed into the mattress or worn in a belt we determined the safest mode of carrying them would be to rip up some flannel strips, which decorated her homespun . . . skirt . . . and sew the coins at intervals under it all around. This we did and she wore her fortune thus encircling her as long as there was a yankee in sight." Others hid bulkier items in their skirts. Susan Blackford wrote her husband, "I took my silver sugar-dish, cream pot, bowl, forks and spoons and put them into the legs of a pair of your drawers . . . tying up each leg at the ankle and buckling the band around my waist. They hung under, and were concealed by my hoops." This hefty bundle "did well while I sat still, but as I walked and when I sat down the clanking destroyed all hope of concealment."[21] Still, she hoped it would protect her valuables. Others secreted items of sentimental value. Lucy Breckenridge "basted all of Tommy's letters in my flannel skirt. . . . I was so burdened with letters, journal, silver, etc., that I don't think I could have walked far."[22] Her immobility seemed a small price to pay to preserve things she held dear.

As they anxiously awaited the arrival of invading Union troops, many Confederate women feared sexual assault more than any potential material loss. They knew that Union soldiers would arrive at their homes, so they "were then in a state of dreadful expectancy, not knowing at what moment the vile things might return," as Caroline Davis wrote, and "afraid to undress at all that night."[23] Despite their assumptions that their bodies would remain untouched, elite women still feared the possibility of rape by enemy soldiers, who had already disregarded so many presumed gender boundaries. Women in the path of the invasion did not know how far Northern men—especially African American soldiers, who were often seen as hypersexual— would go beyond the dictates of civilized warfare. Rumors circulated about sexual assaults across the region. As one woman reported, although some "had been spared personal outrage . . . where the negro troops had been let loose, the accounts were awful."[24]

Word spread quickly of such atrocities. White women across the South could hardly believe the "the treatment our people in Va" at "the hands of these bands of scoundrels under Sheridan." North Carolinian Catherine Edmondston was especially infuriated by the "details of the outrage of *twenty five* ladies by that band [of Negroes under a white officer] alone [that] have been filed in Richmond!" The consequences of invasion were so horrible that she refused to record all of the details. "One [woman] was!—but my pen shrinks from the recital." Furthermore, "Many are *dead* & some with a far less happy fate live shrieking maniacs or sunk in hopeless misery." Edmondston, like others, was shocked by reports of the soldiers' outright disregard for gender boundaries. "Whilst one reads the catalogue of horrors it seems more like a recital of the conduct of the Sepoys in India than that of a nation nominally at least Christian!"[25]

Despite the women's realization that the war had reached their doorsteps, the behavior of Union troops during the Shenandoah campaign still came as a terrifying shock. After the soldiers had departed, one woman mourned that "hardly a house . . . has not been up turned & robbed."[26] Others described their personal encounters with the marauders. E. W. Harrison described her confrontation with one soldier who "said he had strict orders to search every part of the house for arms and rebels." The soldier "came up stairs," where they "searched every trunk and chest in the hall, read some of Mary Harrison's letters, and took her thimble, went into my room, opened every wardrobe and bureau drawer. . . . Finally when he opened my top drawer and took out a small pin box, I could not resist the temptation of saying, Which do you expect to find in that, arms or rebels?"[27] Caroline Davis described how her "dear old home-stead has been ransacked from 'head to foot' seven times." The tenor of the searches made the pillaging unbearable. "It is hard *hard* to bear having these despicable men searching into every place, & stealing whatever valuables they can find ordering one about as if they were dogs prying into ladies wardrobes . . . their taunts & insults are hard enough to endure."[28] Stunned by the behavior of the troops, Davis and others bristled at the violation of their gender ideals and domestic space.

By making civilian life as difficult as possible, the Union's "hard war" not only aggrieved those in Sheridan's path but also other civilians, especially elite women, across the Confederacy. In South Carolina, Emma Holmes recorded a Virginia woman's description of "Hunter's late raid, in which her house had been sacked, & *every thing* carried off—every particle of grain meat, or food in every possible shape inanimate or living . . . in fact all she owned in the world, save her wedding ring, & an indifferent change of clothing." This had been no ordinary raid: "The house was not only completely stripped but the walls ripped open, & even the ashes barrels & *privies* searched for hidden articles." She found this especially appalling, because the house was filled with "an aged man, his sister & her four little children, his wife & one little child." When the woman appealed to General Hunter for help, "He told her, he was glad of it, for that the *women* & *children were* the *very* fiends of *this war,* sending their husbands, fathers & brothers into the army. He meant to humble the pride of the haughty Virginians to the very dust, & that if he did not do it that time he would sweep the earth so clean that it would be incapable of affording nourishment." Holmes recorded with pride the response of this Confederate woman: "The spirit of the Virginian mother & matron only rose the higher, & she declared she would be willing to lose 10,000 times as much for the great cause."[29]

As the response of the "Virginian mother and matron" reveals, elite Confederate women often challenged the invasion of their domestic sphere. Unable to prevent Hunter's "underling Captain Martindale," who "executed [Hunter's] infamous order and burned [her] house," Henrietta Lee sent an angry letter to the commander. She appealed to him as a man, repeatedly asserting herself as "a helpless woman whom you have cruelly wronged," and whom he should have protected. However, Lee did not confine herself to a polite inquiry into the matter, but instead verbally attacked Hunter, with a tone and approach that perhaps no Southern lady would have used during peacetime: "Hyena-like, you have torn my heart to pieces! for all hallowed memories clustered around that homestead; and demonlike, you have done it without even the pretext of revenge, for I never saw or harmed you." Lee asserted that Hunter's "name will stand on history's pages as the Hunter of weak women, and innocent children; the Hunter to destroy defenceless villages and beautiful homes—to torture afresh the agonized hearts of widows . . . the Hunter with the relentless heart of a wild beast, the face of a fiend, and the form of man." His ordered attack on the Southern household, she assured him, would guarantee that "the curse of thousands, the scorn of the manly and upright, and the hatred of the true and honorable, will follow you and yours through all time, and brand your name infamy! infamy!"[30]

The assault on civilian properties did not demoralize slaveholding women. Determined to resist the Union invasion, plantation women began to think how best to defend themselves. Twenty-eight ladies of Harrisonburg, Virginia, wrote to Secretary of War James A. Seddon in December 1864 to offer a novel plan. "With the permission of the War Department we will raise a full regiment of ladies—between the ages of 16 and 40—armed and equipped to perform regular service." These women were further willing "to endure any sacrifice—any privation for the ultimate success of our Holy Cause."[31] If the enemy engaged women as combatants, they wanted to be able to fight back. Other women appealed to their soldier husbands, brothers, and fathers to redouble their military exertions. One outraged woman sent a directive to her husband. "Shoot them, dear husband, every chance you get. Hold no conference with them. They are devil furies who thirst for your blood and who will revenge themselves upon your helpless wife and children. It is God's will and wish for you to destroy them. . . . it is your Christian duty."[32]

Many of the elite white Virginia women who faced Sheridan's troops vowed never to surrender. Fanny Taylor Dickinson even despised the Union soldiers who served as her protectors. As she listened to her guard talking, "my heart rebelled so against them and my blood boiled as I heard him talk about all shaking hands and living under the stars and stripes once more."[33] Such a reunion, she thought, was impossible after the treatment to which these men had subjected Confederate women. Hers was not an uncommon reaction. Others used the invasion of the home front as a way to inspire the troops in the field. After Sheridan's men had scoured her home and humiliated her, E. W. Harrison felt renewed dedication to the cause. When confronted with an enemy soldier who had gathered up her clothes to take with him and told the women of the household, "we are going to make good Union people of you this *trip*," Harrison's sister announced: "That is the way to make [Confederate] patriots of us, not Union people." Harrison agreed, "of course we feel more intensely patriotic than ever, and never for an instant doubt that we will eventually be successful."[34]

Scholars of the Civil War have often assumed a distinction between home front and warfront that the experiences of many elite Virginia women belie. The Union assault on Southern domesticity brought white Virginia women to center stage of the Civil War. No longer safeguarded by their gender, class, or men, they found themselves unprotected subordinates, a position once reserved for slaves. Union soldiers assumed that placing elite women into this demeaning position would change their outlook on the war. However, it seldom led Confederate women to abandon their cause or country. Instead, it fueled their hatred of the Yankee invaders and rekindled their passionate loyalty to the cause of white supremacy and Southern independence. While the conquest by the Union armies freed the slaves, that triumph did not emancipate Virginia women, much less their men, from the cultural and racial traditions of the Old South. General Sheridan's destructiveness ignited the fires of bitter resentment throughout the Shenandoah Valley. That hatred of Yankee success and grief for a world lost forever would linger for many years to come in white Virginia women's minds and hearts.

Notes

1. Mary D. Robertson, ed., *Lucy Breckenridge of Grove Hill: The Journal of a Virginia Girl, 1862–1864* (Columbia, S.C., 1994), 193 (19 June 1864).
2. Many scholars assume that elite Confederate women's patriotism had limits and therefore diminished as the war lengthened and casualties mounted. However, the experiences and reactions of plantation women in the path of Sheridan's campaign in the Shenandoah—like those of elite women who faced Sherman's

troops in Georgia and the Carolinas late in the war—belie this conclusion; see Lisa Tendrich Frank, *Home Fires Burning: The Gendered Implications of Sherman's March* (Athens, Ga., forthcoming). For discussions of women's roles in undermining Confederate nationalism, see Drew Gilpin Faust, *Mothers of Invention: Women of the Slaveholding South in the American Civil War* (Chapel Hill, N.C., 1996); Faust, *The Creation of Confederate Nationalism: Ideology and Identity in the Civil War South* (Baton Rouge, La., 1988); George C. Rable, *Civil Wars: Women and the Crisis of Southern Nationalism* (Urbana, Ill., 1989); Victoria E. Bynum, *Unruly Women: The Politics of Social and Sexual Control in the Old South* (Chapel Hill, N.C., 1992); Laura F. Edwards, *Scarlett Doesn't Live Here Anymore: Southern Women in the Civil War Era* (Urbana, Ill., 2000); Catherine Clinton, *Tara Revisited: Women, War, and the Plantation Legend* (New York, 1995); Paul D. Escott, *After Secession: Jefferson Davis and the Failure of Confederate Nationalism* (Baton Rouge, La., 1978); Richard E. Beringer, Herman Hattaway, Archer Jones, and William N. Still Jr., *Why the South Lost the Civil War* (Athens, Ga., 1986), 64–81 ("Southern Nationalism"), 424–42 ("Why the South Lost").

3. Elizabeth R. Varon, *We Mean To Be Counted: White Women and Politics in Antebellum Virginia* (Chapel Hill, N.C., 1998).

4. On this point, see Stephen A. Channing, *Crisis of Fear: Secession in South Carolina* (New York, 1974), 178, 287.

5. Emma E. Edmonds, *Nurse and Spy in the Union Army: Comprising the Adventures and Experiences of a Woman in Hospitals, Camps, and Battle-Fields* (Hartford, Conn., 1865), 332.

6. William Stevenson, *Thirteen Months in the Rebel Army* (New York, 1862), 195.

7. J. Augustine Signaigo, "If You Love Me," reprinted in William Gilmore Simms, *War Poetry of the South* (1866; rept. New York, 1972), 312.

8. Judith White McGuire, *Diary of a Southern Refugee, during the War* (Richmond, 1889), 33 (18 June 1861).

9. Caroline Kean (Hill) Davis Diary, 24 April 1861, VHS.

10. Rose O'Neal Greenhow, "Letter from a Southern Lady in Prison to Seward—The Cowardly Atrocities of the Washington Government," *Richmond Whig*, November 1861, Leila [Elliott] Habersham Papers 1861–62, Georgia Historical Society.

11. "Journal of Mrs. Eugenia Phillips Wife of Philip Phillips of the City of Washington, Counselor at Law," 23 August 1861–26 September 1861 (28 August 1861 entry), LC.

12. *OR*, ser. 1, vol. 15, p. 426; Virginia Ingraham Burr, ed., *The Secret Eye: The Journal of Ella Gertrude Clanton Thomas, 1848–1889* (Chapel Hill, N.C., 1990), 206–7 (2 June 1862). See also C. Vann Woodward, ed., *Mary Chesnut's Civil War* (New Haven, 1981), 343 (21 May 1862).

13. Faust, *Mothers of Invention*, 198; Jane E. Schultz, "Mute Fury: Southern Women's Diaries of Sherman's March to the Sea, 1864–1865," in *Arms and the Woman: War, Gender, and Literary Representation*, eds. Helen M. Cooper,

Adrienne Auslander Munich, and Susan Merrill Squier (Chapel Hill, N.C., 1989), 59.

14. Ulysses S. Grant to Philip Sheridan, 26 August 1864, *OR*, ser. 1, vol. 43, pt. 2, p. 202.

15. Ulysses S. Grant to Henry Halleck, *OR*, ser. 1, vol. 40, pt. 3, p. 223. On the escalation of Union tactics, and the hardening of attitudes on both sides, see Charles Royster, *The Destructive War: William Tecumseh Sherman, Stonewall Jackson, and the Americans* (New York, 1991).

16. Philip Sheridan, as quoted in Roy Morris Jr., *Sheridan: The Life and Wars of General Phil Sheridan* (New York, 1992), 179.

17. Mark Grimsley distinguishes "hard war" from "total war" by pointing to the restraint of Union Soldiers; see *The Hard Hand of War: Union Military Policy toward Southern Civilians, 1861–1865* (New York, 1995), 4–5. See also Reid Mitchell, *The Vacant Chair: The Northern Soldier Leaves Home* (New York, 1993), 100.

18. Susan Leigh Blackford to Charles Minor Blackford, 6 March 1865, *Letters from Lee's Army*, ed. Charles Minor Blackford III (New York, 1947), 283.

19. Similar acts occurred throughout Sherman's March as well. See Frank, *Home Fires Burning*.

20. Susan Leigh Blackford to Charles Minor Blackford, 6 March 1865, *Letters from Lee's Army*, 283.

21. Ibid., 281.

22. *Lucy Breckenridge of Grove Hill*, 192 (16 June 1864). Sometimes slave women also concealed things on their bodies to protect them from invading Union troops; see E. W. Harrison to Mrs. James L. Henderson, 14 March 1865, "Sheridan's Raiders," *William and Mary College Quarterly Historical Magazine* 17 (April 1909): 293.

23. [Julia Porter Read] to [?], [18] April 1865, Read Family Papers, VHS.

24. Emma E. Holmes Diary, 2 August 1864, USC.

25. Beth G. Crabtree and James W. Patton, eds., *"Journal of a Secesh Lady": The Diary of Catherine Ann Devereux Edmondston, 1860–1866* (Raleigh, N.C., 1979), 589–90 (14 July 1864).

26. Davis Diary, 12 June 1864.

27. E. W. Harrison to Mrs. James L. Henderson, 11 March 1865, "Sheridan's Raiders," 289–90. See also Elizabeth R. Baer, ed., *Shadows on My Heart: The Civil War Diary of Lucy Rebecca Buck of Virginia* (Athens, Ga., 1997), 298–301 (19 August 1864); Mary Virginia Deans Mayer to Anna D. Smith, 18 August 1864, Smith Family Papers, VHS.

28. Davis Diary, 12 June 1864. See also Nancy Emerson, 9 July 1864, Memoranda of Events, Thoughts &c 1862 [sic], UVA.

29. Emma E. Holmes Diary, 2 Aug. 1864. Women who appealed for protection from the invading troops often used their femininity to justify their claims; see *Lucy Breckenridge of Grove Hill*, 193–94 (19 June 1864).

30. Henrietta B. Lee to Gen. [David] Hunter, 20 July 1864, Civil War Collection—Confederate Items, Manuscripts and Rare Books, CWM.

31. Irene Bell, Annie Samuels, and others to Secretary of War James A. Seddon, 2 December 1864, as cited in Gary W. Gallagher, *The Confederate War: How Popular Will, Nationalism, and Military Strategy Could Not Stave off Defeat* (Cambridge, Mass., 1997), 77.

32. Quoted in William Blair, *Virginia's Private War: Feeding Body and Soul in the Confederacy, 1861–1865* (New York, 1998), 144.

33. Fanny Taylor Dickinson Diary, 4 April 1865, VHS.

34. E. W. Harrison to Mrs. James L. Henderson, "Sheridan's Raiders," 288 (11 March 1865), 292 (12 March 1865). Blair, *Virginia's Private War,* 143–44, observes: "Violations of women, whether symbolically or physically, sparked the strongest reactions over treatment of civilians." See also Davis Diary, 12 June 1864.

Race and Retaliation

The Capture of African Americans during the Gettysburg Campaign

DAVID G. SMITH

As the Army of Northern Virginia marched north from Virginia in June 1863, it engaged in mass captures of civilians. From Pennsylvania, scores, perhaps hundreds, of African Americans—fugitive slaves and free blacks—were seized and sent south. The capture of these black civilians took place from the time Gen. Robert E. Lee's troops entered the state until at least the battle of Gettysburg.[1] Newspaper accounts, soldiers' letters, and local diaries all reported the capture, flight, or concealment of African Americans, from the upper Shenandoah Valley in Virginia to the Pennsylvania capital, Harrisburg. One Confederate soldier described his unit's activities near Chambersburg, Pennsylvania, as "Boys capturing negroes and horses." Another wrote to his family that his brother had "captured several Negroes and is sending them back."[2] According to witnesses near Greencastle, a Confederate captain seized two fugitives who he claimed belonged to his family, and he issued a chilling threat: "When they had destroyed Penn[sylvania] they would return that way and take off every neager."[3]

Much of this mayhem occurred at the hands of the leading elements of the army, but the evidence implicates units from every one of Lee's infantry and cavalry corps. Many of these soldiers came from Virginia, and ascertaining why these troops, at this point in the Civil War, engaged in the mass capture of black civilians is important to understanding the war's meaning for Confederate Virginians. The captures demonstrated continuity with Confederate policies and practice aimed at maintaining the subjugation of African Americans. They also illuminate change—a dramatic, midconflict response to an increasingly bitter and retaliatory war that, through the Union's Emancipation Proclamation and the arming of black soldiers, threatened the social, cultural, and economic system of Virginia and the Confederacy.[4]

While exploring the motivations behind the Confederate actions, this essay in no way intends to minimize their gravity. The human costs were very real. Rachel Cormany of Chambersburg reported that Confederate troops were "hunting up contrabands and driving them off in droves. O! how it grated on our hearts to have to sit quietly and look at such brutal deeds." (*Contrabands* was a Civil War term used by both sides to refer to black refugees from the South.) What Cormany witnessed was repeated in many places. Dozens of African Americans were seized near Chambersburg and Greencastle, and captures were also reported near Mercersburg, Gettysburg, York, and elsewhere in Pennsylvania and Maryland.[5]

Many of the captured African Americans had fled from servitude in Virginia, and their forcible reenslavement underscored their tenuous position, caught between a vengeful South and a largely uncaring North. Most of the captives appear to have been sent to local jails in the Shenandoah Valley to be reclaimed; others were sold almost immediately to slave traders; and a number (mainly those who claimed to be free) were held in military prisons in Richmond and elsewhere. Since many of the prisoners were sold, reclaimed as fugitives, or forced to labor in Confederate prisons or on military projects, I call the actions aimed at their seizure "slave raids."

The precise number of individuals swept up by the Confederate army may never be known, but it appears that in Pennsylvania alone at least several hundred were captured. When this number is added to the black civilians captured earlier in the Gettysburg campaign (mainly around Martinsburg and Winchester, Virginia, and Rockville, Maryland), the total taken may have exceeded one thousand. Many other long-standing residents fled the region permanently, so the raids ravaged the area's African American communities.[6]

The flight and capture of African Americans was reported in the Northern press at the time, but these events were largely forgotten in the selective amnesia that has affected the nation's memory of the Civil War since Reconstruction. Even when these incidents appear in historical scholarship, their significance has often been missed. Any discussion is usually brief, and some historians have portrayed the raids as aberrational, performed by guerrillas or renegade soldiers.[7] To the contrary, the capture of African Americans during the campaign was more typical than previously believed. Soldiers participated from many units—indeed, from every part of Lee's army—often with the direct approval of their immediate commanders, and almost certainly with the acquiescence or approval of higher command.

The raids must be placed in the context of the Civil War's eastern theater. When the war broke out, many Northern military commanders ordered their soldiers to suppress slave revolts and return escaped slaves. After initial defeats, and as African Americans began to flee to Union lines in increasing numbers, resistance to returning fugitives grew, because slave labor helped feed and protect Confederate armies, and it released Confederate men for military service. From 1862 on, black men—some of them fugitives—began volunteering for the Union army. To white Virginians, this raised the specter of insurrections, race war, and the collapse of slavery.[8]

The response was swift. While Confederate forces probably captured and returned fugitive slaves from the beginning of the war on, it is certain that a number of incidents occurred in Virginia during 1862. Large numbers of African Americans were seized near Winchester, at the fall of Harpers Ferry, and during Maj. Gen. J. E. B. Stuart's raid into Pennsylvania in October.[9] In March 1863 policy was developed in Richmond and reinforced in a circular from Lee's headquarters. Lists were to be compiled of fugitives "arrested" by the army, and the slaves sent to special depots near Richmond.[10] When Lee's forces marched into Pennsylvania in June, the Confederate army had an opportunity to extend its established practice of recapturing fugitive slaves to the rich agricultural areas just north of the Mason-Dixon line. A Southern war correspondent reported that even private citizens were following Lee's army as it moved north, hoping to reclaim "stolen negroes and horses."[11]

Many soldiers and slaveholding Virginians felt justified in the captures. Dr. Philip Schaff of Mercersburg reported that Confederates told him that in seizing the African Americans, "they were only reclaiming their property which we had stolen and harbored."[12] A number of Virginia units were based on militia organizations formed in the aftermath of John Brown's raid at Harpers Ferry, or manned by soldiers who had served on slave patrols.[13] Some of these soldiers, whether from slaveholding families or not, had few qualms recovering slaves "stolen" by "abolitionists." In addition, recapturing fugitives who had escaped from the Shenandoah Valley could help ease labor shortages in that critically important Confederate breadbasket.

By midwar, the slave raids involved more than simply restoring fugitive slaves to their masters, as important as that was in bolstering Confederate Virginia's social and economic system. The raids also represented retaliation and reprisal. Retaliation meant levying a punishment on an enemy for offenses against the laws of war as an appropriate means of deterring future violations.[14] Retaliation, or the threat of it, flourished during the American Civil War, in part because civil wars had an uncertain status in the law of nations. After all, international law was supposed to govern conduct between two sovereign powers, not, at least as the Union would define the conflict, two warring sections of the same country.[15] Even when Union authorities drafted new army regulations applying international law to the Civil War (the "Lieber Code"), these instructions still permitted retaliatory conduct.[16]

Early threats of retaliation in the Civil War involved military and maritime prisoners. Later, as the Union army slowly advanced, the opportunity for injuries to Southern citizens multiplied. By summer 1862 the early Union policy of protecting Southern civilians and property was weakening. In December Maj. Gen. Robert H. Milroy threatened to force the citizens of Virginia's Shenandoah Valley to take loyalty oaths, betray guerrillas, and supply his army with food.[17]

Lee characterized these actions as a "system of oppression" and warned, at the request of Confederate president Jefferson Davis, of "stern retaliatory measures." He dropped this threat when the Union general-in-chief Henry Halleck assured him that Milroy's worst abuses were not authorized by Federal command. At this stage in the war, Lee did not favor tit-for-tat reprisals. He believed that retaliation was a losing game for the Confederates, justified only "in very extreme cases," as it would subject Southern civilians caught between the two armies to increasing levels of mistreatment.[18]

While Lee backed away from a policy of retaliation, many of his soldiers did not. Already angered by reports of Union abuses, they had witnessed Federal conduct firsthand in December 1862, when Union artillery shelled Fredericksburg and its civilian population. This stoked desires for revenge, particularly among Virginians in Lee's army. As most of Lee's forces remained in the Fredericksburg area for months afterwards, their anger festered. Some army units raised money for the victims, and one Confederate artillery officer made it a special point to revisit the town (and fix the destruction in his memory) before his unit redeployed north to Pennsylvania. During the invasion, a local witness reported that Confederate troops repeatedly proclaimed that they were avenging Union depredations in Virginia, "especially for Fredericksburg."[19]

Desires for revenge were not limited to rank-and-file soldiers and junior officers. One of the most impassioned complaints against restrained warfare came from Maj. Gen. Lafayette McLaws, an accomplished division commander from Georgia. Writing to his wife as his troops moved north, McLaws explained his rationale for a retaliatory policy that could include the capture of civilians:

> It is reported that our army will not be allowed to plunder and rob in Pennsylvania, which is all very well, but it would be better not to publish it as we have received provocation enough to burn and take and destroy, property of all kinds and even the men, women & children along our whole border.
>
> In every instance where we have even threatened retaliation, the enemy have given [way]—and I am strongly in favor of trying it the very first chance we get.[20]

This excerpt makes it clear that Lee's rejection of a retaliatory policy worked at cross purposes to the anger of much of his army. During the campaign, Lee issued two orders (General Orders No. 72 and 73) to protect the property of Pennsylvanians from unauthorized or uncompensated seizure. Some historians, including noted Lee biographer Douglas Southall Freeman, have used the directives to emphasize Lee's aspirations to run a Christian campaign, but they have overestimated the orders' scope and effectiveness. Lee's purpose, as historian Edwin Coddington has pointed out, was to restrain indiscriminate rampage—not to prevent the army from gathering supplies in Pennsylvania. Property and persons were seized under the authority of the army. In addition, the orders were not fully obeyed and some theft and plunder did occur.[21] Ironically, attempting to turn the soldiers' anger away from the property of white Pennsylvanians may have increased the danger to the unprotected African American population living on the border.

Even with the widespread desire for revenge, not every Confederate who entered Pennsylvania engaged in the slave raiding. Many arrived too late. By June 22 Chambersburg businessman William Heyser was reporting that all of that town's African Americans had disappeared. Later, a South Carolina soldier writing from there remarked, "It is strange to see no negros." Chambersburg was the seat of Franklin County, home to eighteen hundred African Americans in 1860, and the destination of many black refugees during the war. By late June 1863, nearly all of this population had fled, hidden, or been captured.[22]

Where opportunities did arise, however, slave raiding appears widespread. Reports indicate the involvement of a significant number of units. Although Lee's Army of Northern Virginia included soldiers from throughout the Confederacy, much of the evidence implicates units from Virginia, where many Union depredations had taken place.[23]

Brig. Gen. Albert Jenkins's cavalry brigade was the first Confederate unit to invade Pennsylvania in June 1863. For months, warfare had ravaged this unit's home areas in southwestern Virginia, and almost as soon as they entered Pennsylvania, plundering and slave raiding began. Various accounts connect Jenkins's brigade to the capture of a substantial number of African Americans. Capt. John Mosby's partisan rangers, Capt. John McNeill's partisan rangers, and Brig. Gen. John Imboden's cavalry brigade also were involved. All of these units were mounted, and all searched widely in Pennsylvania for horses, cattle, and, it seems, African Americans.[24]

Maj. Gen. J. E. B. Stuart's cavalry corps also seized black civilians during the campaign, despite operating detached from Lee's army for much of the time. The *New York Times* reported that as many as one hundred African Americans were captured in the seizure of a wagon train near Rockville. In a letter home, Lt. George Beale of the 9th Virginia Cavalry said that he recognized some of the fugitives as being from his locality in Northern Virginia. It is not surprising, then, that another correspondent reported "contrabands" traveling with Stuart's column in York, Pennsylvania.[25] The fact that Stuart was out of communication with Lee for nearly a week and yet engaged in the same capture of black civilians as the rest of the army underscores the likelihood that some policy, formal or informal, sanctioned these actions during the Gettysburg campaign.

Even though Stuart's, Imboden's, and Jenkins's commands were all involved, cavalry forces were not the only ones participating in the raids. So were units from every infantry corps from Lee's army. Lieut. Gen. Richard Ewell's Second Corps seems particularly involved. Consisting of Early's, Rodes's, and Johnson's divisions, it was the first Confederate infantry corps to enter Pennsylvania. "The rebels under Gen. Ewell are in Pennsylvania and are accomplishing their object in capturing horses, Negroes, and cattle," wrote a Winchester Unionist on June 23. One of Early's sergeants wrote, "I do not think our Generals intend[ed] to invade except to get some of our Negros back which the Yankees have stolen and to let them [Pennsylvanians] know something about the [hardships of] war." A soldier in Rodes's division wrote to his family on July 7 from Staunton, asking his brother if he wanted a "little Yankee," saying nearly a thousand prisoners (including small children) had come from Winchester "in all colors, ages, sizes, sexes, and from all nations." In Pennsylvania, Maj. Gen. Robert Rodes became personally involved in efforts to recover captured African Americans who had been liberated by local citizens.[26]

The raiding continued after Ewell's corps passed through the Cumberland Valley and moved toward Harrisburg. A letter reportedly found on the Gettysburg battlefield, written by a Confederate colonel, William S. Christian, implicates his command, the 55th Virginia Infantry regiment. In the letter Christian stated, "We took a lot of negroes yesterday [June 27]. I was offered my choice, but as I could not get them back home," and "my humanity revolted at taking the poor devils, . . . I turned them all loose." The 55th Virginia was part of Henry Heth's division of A. P. Hill's Third Corps, which entered Pennsylvania after most African Americans in Franklin County had fled. Christian's regiment, though, was one of the first units to travel from Chambersburg to Cashtown over the South Mountain, and this maneuver may well have uncovered unlucky African American families hiding in the mountains.[27]

Even the last Confederate troops to enter Pennsylvania were involved. Maj. Gen. George Pickett's division was the rear guard of the army for much of the campaign, but even some of his soldiers captured African Americans (such as the captain, mentioned at the beginning of this essay, who seized two of his family's slaves near Greencastle). On July 1, 1863, the commander of the Army of Northern Virginia's First Corps, Lt. Gen. James Longstreet, issued the fateful order to Pickett to move his infantry division from Chambersburg toward Gettysburg. The order ended with the statement, "The captured contrabands had better be brought along with you for further disposition." This innocuous-sounding sentence is actually quite significant. Regardless of who had authorized the capture of African Americans, Longstreet's order shows that Lee's army wanted to maintain control of the prisoners. (Longstreet was Lee's senior corps commander and de facto second in command; one historian believes that Longstreet even ordered the captures directly.)[28]

In summation, the evidence indicates the involvement in the slave raids of units from every single infantry and cavalry corps of Robert E. Lee's army. This includes the first and last elements of the army to enter Pennsylvania, as well as the infantry unit that opened the battle of Gettysburg (Heth's division) and the one that gave its name to the battle's deadly climax (Pickett's division). Even noted Confederate generals such as Longstreet, Pickett, and Rodes were involved to some degree. These facts alone suggest that the slave raids were more widespread and more typical than scholars have previously believed.

Some Confederate soldiers probably were just following orders in capturing African Americans; others may have delighted in defying Lincoln's Emancipation Proclamation. The preliminary proclamation was issued on September 22, 1862, but it did not become official until January 1, 1863, only six months before Lee's army entered Pennsylvania. The proclamation raised Southern fears of slave rebellion and provoked calls for violent retaliation. The editor of the *Richmond Daily Whig* urged that groups of desperados be formed to raid into enemy territory, destroying cities, houses, barns, and bridges. "We can no onger be held to the practice of civilized war," he warned.[29] Many Southerners soon realized, however, that outside of the specter of slave revolt, the proclamation would be ineffectual unless Union forces advanced further south.

The prolonged Confederate debate over the proper response to the Emancipation Proclamation must be understood, rather, in the context of a more immediate, associated concern: black Union troops. By mid-1862, the first regiments had been formed and had seen combat, and African American soldiers had been captured. What was to be done with this new class of prisoner, whose very existence touched the deepest Southern fears? One initial response was to suggest killing them all. In fact, Gen. Pierre Beauregard vehemently endorsed a proposal in the Confederate Congress to execute every single Union soldier, white or black, captured after January 1, 1863.[30] On December 23, 1862, Jefferson Davis proclaimed that captured African American soldiers who were fugitive slaves were to "be treated according to the laws of [the] States" "to which they belong." This was disingenuous, however, since Secretary of War James Seddon and Davis had already determined that armed, rebellious African Americans were subject to the death penalty in every Southern state. Seddon himself advised summary executions rather than trials in most cases.[31]

The Confederate leadership soon realized, though, that since many of the black soldiers were fugitive slaves, the disposition of their cases could involve issues of property rights as well as the laws of war. Mass executions could also complicate foreign relations, and bring about Union retaliation and fearsome resistance on the part of black soldiers. Soon Confederate authorities were urging only a few of the captives be executed as examples. Various proposals surfaced in the Confederate Congress to return captured fugitives, even if they were Union soldiers, to their owners. If their masters could not be found, the fugitives could be sold and the proceeds could be pooled and distributed to slaveowners who had lost slaves during the war. One congressman proposed instead that the money from the capture of unclaimed fugitives be divided among the soldiers who had captured them.[32] Many Confederate soldiers read the Richmond papers (in which the proceedings of the Congress were published) and may have learned of this proposal. This, in turn, may have influenced the selling of some captured African Americans in Pennsylvania.[33]

Ultimately, in a proclamation passed on May 1, 1863, the Confederate Congress left many of the details up to Davis, authorizing him to cause "full and ample retaliation" for the outrages of the enemy and the arming of black soldiers. Still, it was not until the Gettysburg campaign that Lee's soldiers could defiantly mock Lincoln's proclamation that Confederate slaves were "forever free" by capturing fugitive slaves and even free blacks in a Northern state.[34]

The 1863 slave raids, then, were not just a case of renegade soldiers or private individuals independently capturing African Americans. Senior leaders such as Longstreet, Pickett, and Rodes were involved, and the evidence also clearly implicates junior officers and senior noncommissioned officers. Isaac Reynolds, whose "boys" were "capturing negroes and horses," was a sergeant in the 16th Virginia Cavalry. Thomas Feamster, who "captured several Negroes and was sending them back," was a lieutenant in the 14th Virginia Cavalry. David Meade, who threatened to return to the Greencastle area and carry off African Americans, was a captain (he was also the nephew of the late Episcopal bishop of Virginia). The capture of fugitives, then, does not appear to have been a spontaneous activity of the soldiers, but one in which they were supervised by officers. This makes sense, as the gist of Lee's General Orders No. 72 was to keep the army from indiscriminate plunder and demoralization. It was hoped that oversight by officers would restrain the soldiers. In fact, many African Americans were probably captured during supervised foraging expeditions in which cattle and horses were also taken.[35]

This attempt to restrain mayhem through supervision was not always successful. McNeill's Rangers threatened to burn Mercersburg unless every gun and every African American in hiding were surrendered. At Greencastle, local residents had overpowered a guard and freed a convoy of captured African Americans. Confederate soldiers threatened arson unless the African Americans were surrendered—and they were supported by General Rodes, who, according to one Southern correspondent, appeared personally and vowed to have every building in the town leveled if they were not.[36]

Once captured, in some cases the black prisoners appear to have been particular targets of Confederate animosity. While pursuing Lee's army after Gettysburg, Union Lt. Chester Leach of the 2nd

Vermont reported finding a black man who had been tortured, muti-
ated, and murdered by Southern troops. The Vermont troops heard
that he had refused to cross the Potomac with the retreating Confederate army.[37]

This shocking incident—where a civilian, perhaps a prewar resident
of the Shenandoah Valley, chose torture and death rather than return
to slavery in Virginia—only underscores the unsettling nature of all
the captures. Even while underestimating their scope, historians have
struggled with these events for decades. Were they widespread, had
they had been sanctioned by Confederate command, and how typical
were they in the invasion? The answer to all of these questions appears
to be, more so than previously thought.

Retaliatory responses centered around the issue of African American soldiers were being actively debated in the Confederate government at the same time that many of Lee's soldiers burned for revenge
against the North. The slave raids in Pennsylvania were a continuation of similar practices that had occurred in 1862 in the Shenandoah
Valley, at Harpers Ferry, and even in Pennsylvania. Most soldiers who
participated in the raids appear to have been supervised by their officers, who encouraged or at least acquiesced in the activity. The actions
of General Rodes (who threatened to destroy a town to recapture
African Americans), and especially the order to General Pickett,
makes it very likely that the highest ranks of the Army of Northern
Virginia were aware of the raiding, and wanted to maintain control of
the captives.

It now appears that the Pennsylvania slave raids were not an aber-
ration, but an extension of Confederate warfare in the bitterly contested Virginia-Maryland-Pennsylvania theater. They were just a part
of the efforts of a resolute army that was retaliating against a determined foe, repudiating the Emancipation Proclamation, recapturing
a labor force, and fighting to preserve a way of life based on mastery
over African Americans.

Notes

1. W. P. Conrad and Ted Alexander, *When War Passed This Way* (Shippensburg,
Pa., 1982), 137.

2. Isaac Reynolds to wife, 9 August 1863, Isaac V. Reynolds Papers, DU; also available at http://rhobard.com/russell/letters/reynolds2.html, transcribed and edited by Greg Lepore; S. W. N. Feamster to Mother, 23 June 1863, Feamster Family Papers, Container 2, LC. "Back" in this sense means the rear of the Confederate army in the Shenandoah Valley.

3. Capt. W. S. How to Mr. Wills, 31 August 1865, in "Letters from Captain W. S. How in relation to Colored people at White Post," Freedmen's Bureau Records RG 105, NA, Virginia: Winchester 1865–67, Box 64. It is not clear whether the captain's threat referred to all local African Americans or just to the remaining "family slaves" he believed were in the area.

4. On retaliation and the Civil War, see Mark Grimsley, *The Hard Hand of War: Union Military Policy toward Southern Civilians, 1861–1865* (Cambridge, UK, 1995), and Charles Royster, *The Destructive War: William Tecumseh Sherman, Stonewall Jackson, and the Americans* (New York, 1991).

5. James Mohr and Richard Winslow III, eds., *The Cormany Diaries: A Northern Family during the Civil War* (Pittsburgh, 1982), 328–30 (16 June 1863); also available at the Valley of the Shadow project (hereinafter VS), http://valley.vcdh.virginia.edu/personalpapers/collections/franklin/rcormany.html.

6. Jane Dice Stone, ed., "Diary of William Heyser," *Papers Read before the Kittochtinny Historical Society* 16 (1978): 54–88 (18 June 1863), reprinted at VS, http://valley.vcdh.virginia.edu/personalpapers/collections/franklin/heyser .html; Peter C. Vermilyea, "The Effect of the Confederate Invasion on Gettysburg's African American Community," *Gettysburg Magazine* 24 (January 2001): 112–28.

7. The captures were widely reported in the *New York Times* (with at least seven mentions in articles from 18 June 1863 to 28 June 1863) and also reported in newspapers in Philadelphia, Harrisburg, and Baltimore. Wilbur S. Nye, *Here Come the Rebels!* (Baton Rouge, La., 1965), 144–45; Edwin B. Coddington, *The Gettysburg Campaign: A Study in Command* (New York, 1968), 161; James M. McPherson, *Battle Cry of Freedom* (New York, 1988), 649; Alan Nolan, *Lee Considered* (Chapel Hill, N.C., 1991), 16–18; John W. Schildt, *Roads to Gettysburg* (Parsons, W.Va., 1978), 106. Exceptions to this limited discussion include Ted Alexander, "A Regular Slave Hunt," *North & South* 4:7 (September 2001): 82–89; James F. Epperson, "Lee's Slave Makers," *Civil War Times* 41:4 (August 2002): 44–51; Vermilyea, "Confederate Invasion"; and Margaret S. Creighton, "Living on the Fault Line: African American Civilians and the Gettysburg Campaign," in *The War Was You and Me*, ed. Joan E. Cashin (Princeton, 2002), 209–36.

8. Grimsley, *Hard Hand of War*; Maj. Gen. Robert Patterson, "To the United States' Troops of this Department," 3 June 1861, *OR*, ser. 1, vol. 2, p. 662, cited by Edward H. Phillips, *The Lower Shenandoah Valley in the Civil War* (Lynchburg: H. E. Howard, 1993), 110; Benjamin Quarles, *The Negro in the Civil War* (Boston, 1953); Ira Berlin, Barbara J. Fields, Steven F. Miller, Joseph P. Reidy,

and Leslie S. Rowland, *Slaves No More: Three Essays on Emancipation and the Civil War* (New York, 1992), 1–76.

9. George M. Neese, *Three Years in the Confederate Horse Artillery* (New York, 1911), 61, and Phillips, *Lower Shenandoah Valley*, 114, 118 (Winchester); R. Channing Price to Ellen Price, 25 September 1862, in Robert J. Trout, *With Pen and Saber: The Letters and Diaries of J. E. B. Stuart's Staff Officers* (Mechanicsburg, Pa., 1995), 101 (Harpers Ferry); Jedediah Hotchkiss to Sara Hotchkiss, 17 Sept. 1862 and 14 October 1862, *Letters of Jedediah Hotchkiss, 1860–1865*, at VS, http://valley.vcdh.virginia.edu/personalpapers/documents/augusta/p2hotchkissletters.html (Harpers Ferry and Stuart's Raid).

10. W. H. Taylor to General[s], 21 March 1863, Orders and Circulars Issued by the Army of the Potomac and the Army and Department of Northern Virginia, C.S.A., 1861–65, NA Microfilm M921, reel 1, frame 1391. Also see Orders and Circulars, Rodes and Battle's Brigade, Army of Northern Virginia, 1861–65, NA, RG 109, chap. 2, vol. 66, pp. 175–76. Lee's order directed the army to comply with an early March directive by the Confederate Adjutant General (General Orders No. 25, Adjutant and Inspector General's Office, 6 March 1863, in *OR*, ser. 2, vol. 5, pp. 844–45).

11. P. W. Alexander, 27 June 1863, in *Writing and Fighting the Confederate War: The Letters of Peter Wellington Alexander, Confederate War Correspondent*, ed. William B. Styple (Kearny, N.J., 2002), 156.

12. Diary entry of Rev. Philip Schaff, 27 June 1863, in "The Gettysburg Week," *Old Mercersburg* (Williamsport, Pa., 1949), 169.

13. Richard O'Sullivan, *55th Virginia Infantry*, 2nd ed. (Lynchburg, Va., 1989), 1–2.

14. Lonnie R. Speer, *War of Vengeance* (Mechanicsburg, Pa., 2002).

15. See Section X of the "Lieber Code," General Orders No. 100, War Department, Adjutant General's Office, 24 April 1863, in *OR*, ser. 2, vol. 5, pp. 681–82.

16. See Articles 27, 28, 58, and 68 of the "Lieber Code," *OR*, ser. 2, vol. 5, pp. 672–75, cited by Speer, *War of Vengeance*, xi, 141.

17. Louis A. Brown, *The Salisbury Prison*, rev. ed. (Wilmington, N.C., 1992), 38–41; Grimsley, *Hard Hand of War*, 62–78, 85–92; Horace Kellogg to Job Parsons, 27 November 1862, *OR*, ser. 3, vol. 2, p. 944.

18. Lynda Lasswell Crist, Mary Seaton Dix, and Kenneth H. Williams, eds., *The Papers of Jefferson Davis*, vol. 9 (Baton Rouge, La., 1997), 37 nn. 1–2; R. E. Lee to James Seddon, 29 December 1862, *OR*, ser. 1, vol. 21, p. 1079; Lee to Maj. Gen. H. W. Halleck, 10 January 1863, *OR*, ser. 3, vol. 3, pp. 10–11; Halleck to Lee, 14 January 1863, *OR*, ser. 3, vol. 3, pp. 15–16; Lee to Jefferson Davis, 25 June 1863, in *The Wartime Papers of Robert E. Lee*, ed. Clifford Dowdey and Louis H. Manarin (Boston, 1961), 530–31.

19. William A. Blair, "'Barbarians at Fredericksburg's Gate': The Impact of the Union Army on Civilians," in *The Fredericksburg Campaign: Decision on the Rappahannock*, ed. Gary W. Gallagher (Chapel Hill, N.C., 1995), 113–41; G. M.

Sorrel to Col. J. B. Walton, 23 December 1862, *OR*, ser. 1, vol. 51, pt. 2, p. 666 J. H. Chamberlayne to Martha, 25 June 1863, in *Ham Chamberlayne — Virgin ian* (Richmond, 1932), 189; Heyser diary entries, 26–27 June, 30 June 1863.

20. Lafayette McLaws to his wife, 15 June 1863, in *A Soldier's General: The Civi War Letters of Major General Lafayette McLaws* ed. John C. Oeffinger (Chape Hill, N.C., 2002), 190.

21. Douglas Southall Freeman, *R. E. Lee: A Biography* (New York, 1934–35), 3:57 Coddington, *Gettysburg Campaign*, 154–55.

22. Heyser Diary, 22 June 1863; TNS (T. N. Simpson) to C. V. T. Miller, 28 June 1863, in *"Far, Far from Home": The Wartime Letters of Dick and Tally Simpson*, eds Guy R. Everson and Edward H. Simpson (New York, 1994), 251–52. 1860 cen sus data from the Historical U.S. Census Browser, http://fisher.lib.virginia .edu/collections/stats/histcensus; Vermilyea, "Confederate Invasion," 112–28

23. A Georgia soldier remarked that much of the retaliation came from Virginian avenging destruction in their home state (Styple, *Writing and Fighting*, 161).

24. "Jenkins's Raid into Pennsylvania: Chambersburg *Repository* Account," in *The Rebellion Record: A Diary of American Events* (1863), ed. Frank Moore (New York, 1863), 197; Reynolds to wife, 9 August 1863; Jeffrey D. Wert, *Mosby's Rangers* (New York, 1990), 91; James J. Williamson, *Mosby's Rangers* (New York 1896), 80; *Mercersburg Journal*, 17 July 1863, p. 3, col. 1 (first page is dated 26 June 1863).

25. "Movements of the Rebel Cavalry," *New York Times*, 30 June 1863, p. 1, col. 4 G. W. Beale to Mother, 12 July 1863, published in "A Soldier's Account of the Gettysburg Campaign: Letter from George W. Beale," *Southern Historical Society Papers* 11 (1883): 321–22; "Movements of the Rebel Gen. Stuart," *New York Tribune*, 1 July 1863, p. 1.

26. Julia Chase diary, 23 June 1863, in *Winchester Divided: The Civil War Diaries of Julia Chase & Laura Lee*, ed. Michael G. Mahon (Mechanicsburg, Pa., 2002), 96; A. A. Anderson to C. Anderson, 8 July 1863, in Patrick H. Cain Letters, DU; George W. Davis to Family, 7 July 1863, Rebecca Pitchford Davis Papers, SHC; Peter W. Alexander, 28 June 1863, in Styple, *Writing and Fighting*, 158.

27. *Rebellion Record* (1864), vol. 7, ed. Frank Moore (New York, 1864), 325; see also Alexander, "A Regular Slave Hunt," 87; O'Sullivan, *55th Virginia Infantry*, 52–53.

28. G. M. Sorrel to George Pickett, 1 July 1863, in *OR*, ser. 1, vol. 51, pt. 2, pp. 732–33; Alfred A. Nofi, *The Gettysburg Campaign* (New York, 1986), 37.

29. *Richmond Daily Whig*, 22 October 1862, cited in E. Merton Coulter, *The Confederate States of America, 1861–1865* (Baton Rouge, La., 1950), 266.

30. P. G. T. Beauregard to W. Porcher Miles, 13 October 1862, *OR*, ser. 2, vol. 4, p. 916, cited by William Buck Yearns, *The Confederate Congress* (Athens, Ga., 1960), 164.

31. Brown, *Salisbury Prison*, 51–54; James Seddon to Beauregard, 30 November 1862, *OR*, ser. 2, vol. 4, p. 954, cited by Brown, *Salisbury Prison*, 85 n.68; http:// www.history.umd.edu/Freedmen/pow.htm.

32. "Congressional," *Richmond Whig*, 22 February 1863, p. 2, col. 1; "Negroes in the Yankee Army," ibid., p. 1, col. 4.

33. Regarding the selling of African Americans at or shortly after capture, see Creighton, "Living on the Fault Line," 218; P. W. Alexander, 27 June 1863, in Styple, *Writing and Fighting*, 156; [Joseph Arnold], "Belle Island," in Bernhard Domschcke, *Twenty Months in Captivity* (Rutherford, N.J., 1987), 135–36.

34. Brown, *Salisbury Prison*, 54–56; James M. Matthews, ed., *The Statutes at Large of the Confederate States of America*, Third Session, First Congress, 1863 (Richmond, 1863), 167–68.

35. Isaac Reynolds makes this connection explicitly by describing his men capturing African Americans and horses in the same sentence (Reynolds to wife, 9 August 1863).

36. "The Late Rebel Invasion," *Mercersburg Journal*, 17 July 1863 (front page dated 26 June), p. 3, col. 1, reporting on events of June 1863; Schaff, 25 June–27 June 1863, p. 169; W. P. Conrad, "Gloryland: A History of Blacks in Greencastle Pennsylvania" (Shippensburg, Pa., 1983), 8, available at VS, http://valley.vcdh .virginia.edu/personal/gloryland.html; Alexander in Styple, *Writing and Fighting*, 158.

37. Letter from 1st Lt. Chester K. Leach, Company H, 2nd Vermont Infantry, 15 July 1863, in Alexander, "A Regular Slave Hunt," 87.

Queen Victoria's Refugees

───────── ⟨⟩ ─────────

Afro-Virginians and Anglo-Confederate Diplomacy

ERVIN L. JORDAN JR.

"I could fill pages with my griefs and misfortunes," wrote a Virginia slave woman shortly before the Civil War. "No tongue could express them as I feel." Approximately 6,000 published slave narratives, "written or dictated autobiographies and oral testimonies by escaped or freed slaves," appeared between the eighteenth century and the twentieth. Nearly two hundred book-length autobiographies by escaped Southern slaves were published in America and Great Britain between 1760 and 1947. Harvard black studies impresario Henry Louis Gates Jr. contends that African Americans are "unique in the history of world slavery because they were the only enslaved people to produce a body of writing that testified to their experiences."[1]

Two Afro-Virginian exiles in Great Britain published memoirs that may have contributed to the moral authority of the Emancipation Proclamation and helped deter Great Britain from a formal alliance with the Confederate States of America. Both were published in London in 1863. One was Dinah Browne's story, as edited by John Hawkins Simpson: *Horrors of the Virginian Slave Trade and of the Slave-Rearing Plantations, The True Story of Dinah, an Escaped Virginia Slave, Now in London, on Whose Body Are Eleven Scars Left by Tortures Which Were Inflicted by Her Master, Her Own Father, Together with Extracts from the Laws of Virginia, Showing That against These Barbarities the Law Gives Not the Smallest Protection to the Slave, But the Reverse.* The other was Francis Fedric, *Slave Life in Virginia and Kentucky; or, Fifty Years of Slavery in the Southern States of America.*[2]

The reminiscences of Browne (Simpson) and Fedric are not comparable in influence to Harriet Beecher Stowe's *Uncle Tom's Cabin* (1852), an international best seller, or to the *Narrative of the Life of Frederick Douglass* (1845). Moreover, their 1863 narratives were overshadowed by the publication, in that same year, of Fanny Kemble's *Journal of a Residence on a Georgian Plantation in 1838–1839.* Her reminiscences demonstrated how public denunciations of slavery by white abolitionists often received more publicity and credibility than did those of former slaves. A celebrated actress and writer, formerly married to Pierce Butler, a Georgia planter and America's largest slaveholder, Kemble was an abolitionist and advocate of equal rights for women at the time of their 1834 marriage, and the more she was exposed to American slavery, the more she came to hate it. The Butlers divorced in 1849; Kemble settled in Massachusetts until her return to England in 1862. Her diary, reworked into a series of letters to a female friend, was published in London in May 1863 and in New York City two months later. It championed the Emancipation Proclamation and sought to influence British public and political opinion against an independent Confederate nation. She has been credited for almost single-handedly preventing Britain from extending full diplomatic recognition and direct military assistance to the Confederacy. Nevertheless, the narratives of Browne (Simpson) and Fedric are significant, in that they were among the last of a distinguished legacy of African American voices giving powerful testimony against slavery. Theirs were secondary but supporting contributions to the Confederacy's defeat in the propaganda war for diplomatic recognition and political independence.[3]

Although most runaways who reached freedom prudently disappeared from public view, some boldly publicized their escapes by publishing their account. In doing so, they demonstrated their continued resistance to slavery. Beginning in the late eighteenth century, several former Afro-Virginian slaves had, like other American slaves, produced autobiographical accounts of their lives under slavery and demanded its abolition. The written testimony of ex-slaves has long served as powerful repudiation of the Peculiar Institution's racial propaganda. Throughout the antebellum period, it had been vocally audacious ex-slaves such as Frederick Douglass, in published narratives and public addresses at home and abroad, whose demands for slavery's abolition and graphic descriptions horrifically instructed Northern and European audiences.

Yet the antebellum and wartime slave narratives, like their postwar counterparts, were largely ignored, or their validity denied, by white scholars into the second half of the twentieth century. Meanwhile, few white scholars had questioned the validity of white Confederates' memoirs. Historian C. Vann Woodward reflected an important re-evaluation of both sets of sources in a 1974 review of *The American Slave: A Composite Autobiography*, when he observed that slave narratives were just as reliable as diaries, and newspapers, and just as subject to flaws, propaganda, and falsehoods. The use of slave narratives required, he said, "caution and discrimination . . . with necessary precautions . . . no more elaborate than those required by many other types of sources."[4]

According to slave scholar John Blassingame, "the fundamental problem confronting anyone interested in studying [antebellum] black views of bondage is that the slaves had few opportunities to tell what it meant to be chattel. Since antebellum narratives were frequently dictated or written by whites, any study of such sources must begin with an assessment of the editors. An editor's education, religious beliefs, literary skill, attitudes toward slavery, occupation all affected how he recorded the account of the slave's life." White abolitionists undoubtedly acted as ghostwriters for these fugitive slaves, few of whom were more even modestly literate. Although white amanuenses were responsible for much of the language, the narrative autobiographies reflected the sentiments of the escaped slaves. As Blassingame and other slavery scholars have noted, if we wish "to know the heart and secret thoughts of slaves," we must methodically study their testimony. Questions about slavery can best be answered by those who experienced it.[5] Slave narratives are among the best sources for understanding the history of slavery in the United States. Without them, we would be limited to slaveholders' side of the story, an inequity comparable to describing World War II concentration camps only from a Nazi perspective.

The narratives by Browne (Simpson) and Fedric emphasized slaves as people, not things, and America's mistreatment of blacks as contradictory to its assertions of Christianity and democracy. Theirs were the last of a long tradition of ex-Virginia slaves who published in Great Britain dating back to Olaudah Equiano (ca. 1745–97), *The Interesting Narrative of the Life of Olaudah Equiano, or Gustavus Vassa, the African* (1789). Equiano's autobiography is the only known published account by an African enslaved in Virginia, and he was the first Virginia slave to publish in Britain an account of his enslavement and escape. David Holmes (b. 1824), a tobacco field hand, was interviewed in London in 1852 by a member of the British and Foreign Anti-Slavery Society. After his owner's sympathetic sister warned that he was about to be sold "down South," Holmes fled Mecklenburg County and, with the assistance of Quakers and Northern abolitionists, made his way to New York, Canada, and eventually Great Britain, where his story appeared in the *Anti-Slavery Reporter*. During the Civil War, a few other Virginia slaves succeeded in transatlantic escapes. Henry Jarvis (b. 1832), for example, fled Northampton County in 1861 from an owner whom he characterized as "the meanest man on the Eastern Shore." Jarvis made his way to Liberia by way of Cuba but returned to America and enlisted with the Union army in 1863 with the all-black 55th Massachusetts Infantry Regiment.[6]

British public opinion was deeply divided over race, slavery, and the American Civil War. Thousands of factories employed hundreds of thousands of workers processing raw cotton into textiles. Therefore, the Confederacy adopted a strategy of "Cotton Diplomacy" (similar but less successful than the Arab oil embargoes of the 1970s) in an effort to secure diplomatic and even military support against the Union. Yet many people in Britain and Europe, even if sympathetic to the South, were troubled when they read accounts of the sale and separation of slave families and other cruelties. At the same time, the Union imposed a blockade along the Confederate coast to prevent trade that would help the Rebel cause. Although a number of Confederate doomsayers and reformists warned that Britain would not support the South unless slaves were emancipated, at the end of 1861 the *London Weekly* was urging Her Majesty's government to break the Union blockade "for the preservation of our commerce from ruin, and our citizens from starvation."[7]

Southerners were encouraged by British remarks such as those which appeared in the *London Times* ridiculing blacks and declaring that they were designed to be "a servile race, peculiarly fitted by nature for the hardest physical work." Virginia, deemed a model in fair treatment of slaves, was sometimes characterized as a Christian commonwealth that had tried to abolish slavery but had been constantly thwarted by radical abolitionists and avaricious Yankee slave merchants in New York and New England. "It is well known that Northern agents are now in this country, without stint of money, hiring lecturers and attempting agitation," complained the *London Times* in January 1863. The *Comic News*, a humorous illustrated weekly, offered a bit of doggerel that in part caricatured blacks' hopes of British influence with a dialect reference to "white broders t'oder side Atlantic." By contrast, the London *Punch* satirized the Confederacy's defense of slavery in the poem "Rule Slaveownia," sung to the tune of "Rule, Britannia":

> When first the South, to fury fanned,
> Arose and broke the Union's chain,
> There was the Charter, the Charter of the land,
> And Mr. Davis sang the strain:
> Rule Slaveownia, Slaveownia rules, and raves
> "Christians ever, ever, ever shall have slaves."[8]

Throughout the war, British abolitionists mobilized huge public meetings, lectures, and petitions, something pro-Confederate Britons were unable (or unwilling) to accomplish with any regularity, especially in 1863–64, during the crucial period following the Emancipation Proclamation, a series of Northern battlefield victories, and Lincoln's reelection. Most pro-Confederate associations were not organized until late 1863 and held few public meetings to rally support for their cause. What is more, by 1861 *Uncle Tom's Cabin*, the most influential antislavery book ever published, had sold in excess of a million copies in Great Britain, and antebellum runaway slaves were lionized by British audiences as heroic freedom fighters and welcomed as fellow Christians. During 1851 several of these black American refugees were welcomed as celebrities during pubic receptions at the Great Exhibition's Crystal Palace in London's Hyde Park, Europe's first great international fair. Fugitive slaves who reached Canada or

Great Britain euphemistically characterized themselves as "under the protection of the British Lion," "between the lion's paws," or as having "shaken hands with the British Lion's paw."[9]

Of the two Virginia ex-slaves who published narratives in 1863, perhaps the first was Francis Fedric, who most likely dictated his testimony to a London abolitionist, Rev. Charles Lee. His 115-page narrative, *Slave Life in Virginia and Kentucky*, appeared in the spring of 1863 shortly after the issuance of the Emancipation Proclamation. Fedric's grandparents had been kidnapped in Africa and shipped to Virginia. On one sickening occasion, his grandmother was flogged for attending a prayer meeting; her son (Fedric's father), who also happened to be the plantation's slave driver, was forced to administer forty lashes on the back of his own mother.[10]

Fedric was born in Fauquier County as one of nine children. (He did not state his year of birth, which was sometime before 1830.) His master owned a hundred slaves on a tobacco plantation in Virginia. Fedric recalled how adult slaves ate from bowls, while children fed from troughs like pigs; this, he claimed, was done to brutalize them. When Fedric was fourteen, his master decided to move to Kentucky and sold his slaves separately, ignoring pleas that they be sold with their families. In Kentucky, Fedric became a house servant and a cook, after pretending to be too stupid around animals and tools to be a field hand.[11]

But Fedric craved freedom, especially after becoming a Christian when he was about thirty years old. His first escape attempt earned him 107 lashes; shortly thereafter, on the death of his owner, the slaves were sold to satisfy gambling debts. Fedric contended that his fellow bondsmen associated Canada and Great Britain with freedom. In particular, they spoke often of going to Britain and of their hopes to "be among the Britainers," whom they associated with abolitionism. He eventually absconded with the assistance of the Underground Railroad to Toronto, Canada, although his hands were paralyzed as the result of exposure suffered in swamps during his escape. In Toronto, he found employment with the city's antislavery society and married a Devonshire woman.[12]

The Toronto society sent him to Liverpool, England, where he became one of many African American lecturers who horrified audiences with firsthand descriptions of slavery. Safe in the United Kingdom, Francis Fedric neither forgot nor forgave the injustices against his family and race: "After so many years, their wailings and lamentations and piercing cries sound in my eyes whenever I think of Virginia."[13]

In 1863 a fugitive Virginia slave woman, Dinah Browne, also reached freedom in England. There, over a five-day period, she dictated to British abolitionist John Hawkins Simpson a grim narrative, *Horrors of the Virginian Slave Trade*. This slender monograph of sixty-four pages provided an explicit, eyewitness account of Virginia slavery, her former master, Henry Hope (a pseudonym), and his plantation near Petersburg. Unlike many slave narratives (but like Fedric's), Browne does not or cannot state the year of her birth, though internal clues suggest that she was born about 1815. Her earliest recollections included hunger and whippings. Long after her first flogging—for the crime of talking back to her master, who also happened to be her own father—she recalled how "the blood trickled down her back onto the soil, how her breath seemed to go from her, and how great was the pain when her bleeding back was washed in brine to prevent mortification."[14]

Dinah Browne of Virginia vividly testified on behalf of herself and fellow slaves on the injustices they had suffered. When she was young, sometime around 1830, a neighbor who happened to be an English doctor told Dinah about the availability of freedom in England, and when she tried to act on this knowledge, she was caught, flogged, and branded on her right shoulder and left instep. Later, her master permitted her to marry a field hand named Jem Browne, and the couple had fifteen children, including four sets of twins. When her first child, Priscilla, was sold, Dinah was callously informed of this by her master as she served tea to him and a visiting slave trader: "Di, your child is going. This gentleman is to take her." After Priscilla was dragged away forever, the plantation overseer consoled the grieving parents with brandy, saying, "Master has sent this to you to set you right, and you are to get to work [i.e., produce more children] again at once." With what happiness they could find in slavery, Dinah and Jem Browne lived together for twenty years, until his murder in 1855 by an overseer.[15]

Sold to a slave dealer in the autumn of 1860, Dinah soon escaped. At one point she bribed a ferryman to take her across a river, according to her narrative, in exchange for her wedding ring. She crossed the Shenandoah River, the Blue Ridge Mountains, and the Potomac River alone and on foot and made her way to Pennsylvania, where she was given sanctuary by a white family until March 1861. Because of the uncertainty of the times, it was decided she would be safer in England, and a white clergyman assisted in her passage. She traveled by ship to Philadelphia, New York, and Calcutta, India, after being befriended by the ship's captain and his wife. Dinah Browne arrived at Portsmouth, England, in March 1863 and later moved to London, where she earned a living through her needlework.[16]

Dinah Browne suffered nightmares about her life as a slave, and the scars on her back caused unending pain, but she had found safety and refuge. Her editor, Simpson, spoke for and addressed thousands of Britons when he expressed sympathy for Southern slaves and dashed cold water on the Confederacy's desire for recognition: "Whether the North restores the Union, or whether the South proves itself hereafter strong enough to establish an Independent Confederation, whether the area and power of slavery be or be not contracted at the end of the war, the interests of mankind in general, and of the slaves in particular, cannot but be greatly promoted by our Determination never at any time hereafter to receive and recognize a minister sent by a country calling itself a Christian country, in which . . . a slave-owner is permitted to buy and sell slaves."[17]

Only one review of these two narratives (Dinah Browne's) by a London reviewer has surfaced: "The narrative . . . may be accepted as a truthful illustration of a part of the 'horrors' of the . . . slave trade in the United States, although it is, more correctly speaking, a recital of the vicissitudes of a female slave's life. We have ourselves seen and interrogated Di, and have no reason to call into question the genuineness of her narrative which we found consistent in all its parts." This reviewer went on to say: "In addition to Di's history will be found numerous quotations from the Virginian slave code, under which many of the indignities inflicted upon Di and some of her fellow-slaves were absolutely legal. The volume is a useful addition to anti-slavery literature, and is calculated to expose some of the abominations of a system which has recently found advocates in this country, and to perpetuate which, with all its atrocities, was the sole purpose of the slaveholders' rebellion."[18]

The overall contemporary impact of these two particular narratives may well have been limited. Yet the language in the review—even the fact that there was a review—reveals the likelihood that the narratives played some role in shaping public opinion in Britain. Browne and Fedric were advised and assisted by local abolitionist societies and, as likely as not, by the British and Foreign Anti-Slavery Society. Both narratives were undoubtedly employed for abolitionists' public campaigns against the Confederacy, and some historians—among them R. J. M. Blackett, Robert Durden, Benjamin Quarles, Charles Douglas Stange, and myself—have suggested that by the end of 1863 the Confederacy had, in effect, conceded defeat in its overseas propaganda war largely because of living testimony by former slaves and—in part a consequence of that testimony—antislavery attitudes by the leading European powers. Confederate envoys found the official climate so unreceptive to the idea of Southern independence with the prolongation of slavery that the Confederacy formally ended its already-limited diplomatic relations with Britain.[19]

Whatever the influence the two narratives may have had during the Civil War, they have remained in the background as far as many historians have been concerned. Original copies are scarce in America and available chiefly at the Library of Congress and the Schomburg Center for Research in Black Culture (one of the research libraries of the New York Public Library). Such seminal studies as John W. Blassingame, *Slave Testimony* (1977), Blyden Jackson, *A History of Afro-American Literature* (1989), and the bibliographies for Charles T. Davis and Henry Louis Gates Jr., *The Slave's Narrative* (1985), and Alan Grovenar, *African American Frontiers: Slave Narratives and Oral Histories* (2000), do not provide any discussion of these narratives. They are also absent from a book-length history of the black Virginia experience, *The Negro in Virginia* (1940), and from the annotated bibliography for the foremost study of Virginia slave narratives, *Weevils in the Wheat: Interviews with Virginia Ex-Slaves* (1976).[20]

Yet some writers have drawn attention to both narratives. Monroe N. Work, *Bibliography of the Negro in Africa and America*, a pioneering 1928 reference source, extolled the Browne (Simpson) and Fedric slave narratives as among the best of the genre. Donaldson Jordan and Edwin J. Pratt, in *Europe and the American Civil War* (1931), labeled them as "works positively favoring the North." Characterized as "a good example of both the Northern and English Abolitionists' sympathies with the thousands held in bondage in the American South," an abridged version of Browne/Simpson's *Horrors of the Virginian Slave Trade* appeared in Maurice Duke's 1995 anthology *Don't Carry Me Back! Narratives by Former Virginia Slaves*.[21]

That same year, Sharon Harley, *Timetables of African-American History* (1995), included the two Afro-Virginians' narratives among what she characterized as the three most significant slave narratives of 1863. (The third was ex-Missouri slave John Anderson's *The Story of the Life of John Anderson*.) They also appeared in occasional endnotes for my *Black Confederates and Afro-Yankees in Civil War Virginia* (1995). Recently, the two Afro-Virginians' narratives have attracted growing international attention. Electronic text versions are available at the University of North Carolina at Chapel Hill Libraries' "Documenting the American South/North American Slave Narratives" Web site, and Fedric's narrative was the partial subject of a paper presented at a 2001 conference in London.[22]

Slave narratives have been critically evaluated and accepted as within the standards of historical evidence as cogent accounts by the best of all possible witnesses of slavery—the slaves themselves—and overwhelmingly confirmed by other primary sources in the form of newspapers, letters, diaries, and related documents. Benjamin Quarles postulates the major reason for the failure of Confederate diplomacy as the antebellum speeches, lectures, biographies, and autobiographies of Frederick Douglass and other escaped American slaves whose regular appearances in Britain with scarred backs and tales of brutality increased the influence of the British antislavery movement and kept Queen Victoria's military machine neutral by illustrating slavery as a system that brutalized and exploited human beings.

These "ambassadors without portfolios," as one historian has characterized them, helped initiate and sustain a process that squelched Confederate nationhood, destroyed American slavery, and cleansed American democracy.[23] In addition, written testimony of slavery survivors who bore witness to the institution—among them Dinah Browne and Francis Fedric—not only contributed in some measure to slavery's defeat. Such testimony also continues to contribute, in incalculable ways, to our understanding of the past.

Notes

I am indebted to Professor Constance Schulz, University of South Carolina, and, Professor Richard Blackett, then of the University of Houston and now at Vanderbilt, for their insightful commentary following the presentation of this essay at the conference.

1. Elizabeth Keckley, *Behind the Scenes, or, Thirty Years a Slave and Four Years in the White House* (New York, 1868), 42; Lisa Clayton Robinson, "Slave Narratives," in *Africana: The Encyclopedia of the African and African American Experience*, eds. Kwame Anthony Appiah and Henry Louis Gates Jr. (New York, 1999), 1717–19; John W. Blassingame, ed., *Slave Testimony: Two Centuries of Letters, Speeches, Interviews, and Autobiographies* (Baton Rouge, La., 1977), 681; John W. Blassingame, "Using the Testimony of Ex-Slaves: Approaches and Problems," in *The Slave's Narrative*, eds. Charles T. Davis and Henry Louis Gates Jr. (New York, 1985), 83. Approximately 35 percent of the narratives came from escaped slaves; the rest were by people who had gained their freedom either during the Civil War or by purchase or manumission before the war.
2. John Hawkins Simpson, *Horrors of the Virginian Slave Trade* (London, 1863); Francis Fedric, *Slave Life in Virginia and Kentucky* (London, 1863).
3. Harriet Beecher Stowe, *Uncle Tom's Cabin: Or, Life among the Lowly* (Boston, 1853); Frances Anne Kemble, *Journal of a Residence on a Georgian Plantation in 1838–1839* (London, 1863); Frances Anne Kemble, *Journal of a Residence on a Georgian Plantation in 1838–1839* (New York, 1863); Catherine Clinton, *Fanny Kemble's Civil Wars* (New York, 2000), 177–79.
4. C. Vann Woodward, "History from Slave Sources," *American Historical Review* 79 (April 1974): 475, 480, a book review of George P. Rawick, general editor, *The American Slave: A Composite Autobiography*, 19 volumes, series 2 (Westport, Conn., 1972); this review is reprinted in Davis and Gates, *The Slave's Narrative*, 48–58.
5. John Hawkins Simpson, review of *Di, or Horrors of the Virginian Slave-Trade*, in *The Anti-Slavery Reporter*, n.s., 12, no. 3 (1 March 1864): 71; Blassingame, "Using the Testimony of Ex-Slaves," 79–83, 94.
6. Olaudah Equiano, *The Interesting Narrative of the Life of Olaudah Equiano, or*

Gustavus Vassa, the African, 2nd ed. (London, 1789); David Hackett Fischer and James C. Kelly, *Bound Away: Virginia and the Westward Movement* (Charlottesville, Va., 2000), 59; [Louis Alexis Chamerovzow], "I've Quit Smoking It," *The Anti-Slavery Reporter,* n.s., 1, no. 2 (1 February 1853): 25–28 (Holmes interview), also in Blassingame, *Slave Testimony,* 295–302 and 606–11 (Jarvis 1872 interview). Chamerovzow, an abolitionist journalist and editor of slave narratives, was secretary of the British and Foreign Anti-Slavery Society (Davis and Gates, *The Slave's Narrative,* 80, 164, 165).

7. John Bright, *Speeches of John Bright, M. P. on the American Question* (Boston, 1865), 94–96, 154–58; "A Slave Marriage Law," *Southern Presbyterian Review* 16 (October 1863): 145; *London Weekly* as quoted in the Richmond *Daily Dispatch,* 28 December 1861.

8. George McHenry, *The Cotton Trade: Its Bearing upon the Prosperity of Great Britain and Commerce of the American Republics, Considered in Connection with the System of Negro Slavery in the Confederate States* (London, 1863), 60, 213; *London Times,* 16 January 1863 ("It is well known" quote); *Comic News* (London), 5 September 1863, 58, as quoted in Gary L. Bunker, *From Rail-Splitter to Icon: Lincoln's Image in Illustrated Periodicals, 1860–1865* (Kent, Ohio, 2001), 232, 366 n.16; "Rule Slaveownia: The National Hymn of the Confederated States," London *Punch* as quoted in *Douglass' Monthly,* June 1861, 471.

9. Richard Cobden and John Bright, *A Friendly Voice from England on American Affairs* (New York, 1862), 14–15; Donaldson Jordan and Edwin J. Pratt, *Europe and the American Civil War* (Boston, 1931), 87, 125–88; William Still, *The Underground Rail Road: A Record of Facts, Authentic Narratives, Letters, &c.* (1872; rept. Chicago, 1970), 34, 128, 141, 143 (fugitives' euphemisms), 389–91 (African Americans at the 1851 Great Exhibition); James Brewer Stewart, *Holy Warriors: The Abolitionists and American Slavery* (New York, 1976), 162 (*Uncle Tom's Cabin* sales in Great Britain); Brian Jenkins, *Britain and the War for the Union* (Montreal, 1980), 2:209–34. See also Harold Hyman, ed., *Heard Round the World: The Impact Abroad of the Civil War* (New York, 1969); Sheldon Vanauken, *The Glittering Illusion: English Sympathy for the Southern Confederacy* (Worthing, U.K., 1988); and R. J. M. Blackett, *Divided Hearts: Britain and the American Civil War* (Baton Rouge, La., 2001).

10. Fedric, *Slave Life in Virginia,* 4, 6.

11. Ibid., 1, 7–8, 14–23, 38.

12. Ibid., iv, 41–44, 51–56, 75–87, 100–112.

13. Ibid., 14–15, 111–13.

14. Simpson, *Horrors of the Virginian Slave Trade,* 6–8, 15–18.

15. Ibid., 9, 12–18, 27–36, 46–47.

16. Ibid., 50–58.

17. Ibid., 58, 60–61.

18. John Hawkins Simpson review of *Di, or Horrors of the Virginian Slave-Trade,* in *The Anti-Slavery Reporter,* n.s., 12:3 (March 1, 1864): 71.

19. Jenkins, *Britain and the War,* 2:206; Benjamin Quarles, *Black Abolitionists* (New York, 1969), 141; Robert F. Durden, *The Gray and the Black: The Confederate Debate on Emancipation* (Baton Rouge, La., 1972), 17–18, 19–21; Charles Douglas Stange, *British Unitarians against American Slavery, 1833–65* (Rutherford, N.J., 1984), 205–7; Eli N. Evans, *Judah P. Benjamin: The Jewish Confederate* (New York, 1988), 234–37; Benjamin Quarles, *Black Mosaic: Essays in Afro-American History and Historiography* (Amherst, Mass., 1988), 90–91; Blackett, *Divided Hearts,* 74–88, 230; Ervin L. Jordan Jr., *Black Confederates and Afro-Yankees in Civil War Virginia* (Charlottesville, Va., 1995), 239; David S. Heidler and Jeanne T. Heidler, *Encyclopedia of the American Civil War: A Political, Social, and Military History* (New York, 2000), 600, 876, 1138. A long, detailed search of British biographical dictionaries, directories, encyclopedias, and newspaper indexes did not uncover any biographical information concerning Francis Fedric, Dinah Browne, or John Hawkins Simpson.

20. Blassingame, *Slave Testimony;* Blyden Jackson, *A History of Afro-American Literature,* vol. 1, *The Long Beginning, 1746–1895* (Baton Rouge, La., 1989); Davis and Gates, *The Slave's Narrative,* 327; Alan Grovenar, *African American Frontiers: Slave Narratives and Oral Histories* (Santa Barbara, Calif., 2000), 522–23; Virginia Writers' Project, *The Negro in Virginia* (1940; rept. Winston-Salem, N.C., 1994); *Weevils,* 391–94; Robinson, "Slave Narratives," 1717–19. The subject of slave narratives is barely discussed in the magisterial *Africana,* which mentions neither the Browne/Simpson narrative nor Fedric's.

21. Monroe N. Work, *A Bibliography of the Negro in Africa and America* (New York, 1928), 311, 313; Jordan and Pratt, *Europe and the American Civil War,* 279, 282; Maurice Duke, ed., *Don't Carry Me Back! Narratives by Former Virginia Slaves* (Richmond, 1995), 97–110.

22. Sharon Harley, *The Timetables of African-American History: A Chronology of the Most Important People and Events in African-American History* (New York, 1995), 147–48; John Anderson, *The Story of the Life of John Anderson, The Fugitive Slave,* ed. Harper Twelvetrees (London, 1863); Jordan, *Black Confederates and Afro-Yankees,* 33, 332 n. 42, 333 n. 22, 335 n. 43, 347 n. 39, 348 n. 50; University of North Carolina at Chapel Hill Libraries' "Documenting the American South/North American Slave Narratives," http://docsouth.unc.edu/neh/simpson/simpson.html and http://docsouth.unc.edu/fedric/menu.html; Lyn Innes, "Narratives of Refugees from American Slavery: Moses Roper, John Brown, William and Ellen Craft, and Francis Fedric," paper presented at "Discourses of Slavery and Abolition: Writing in Britain and Its Colonies, 1660–1838—An International Conference," University of London, Institute of English Studies, School of Advanced Study, 7 April 2001. Anderson, who killed a white man during his escape to Canada, later lived in Great Britain until emigrating to Liberia in December 1862 (*Life of John Anderson,* 15–17, 24–27, 30, 37–38, 147–79).

23. Quarles, *Black Mosaic,* 80–91 (chapter 5, "Ministers without Portfolio").

Reading Marlboro Jones

A Georgia Slave in Civil War Virginia

LUCINDA H. MACKETHAN

There are four—at least four—different ways to tell the story of Marlboro Jones, a slave and later freedman born in Liberty County, Georgia, around 1817. The first is through a picture, an enlarged reproduction of a small ambrotype on display in Richmond at the Museum of the Confederacy. This ambrotype tells two stories, one through the photographic likeness on the front and quite a different one through the inscription on the back. The other three source structures that inform us about Marlboro Jones are just as contradictory within themselves or measured against one another. Within each class of information are competing versions of a narrational identity bearing the name, but hardly resolving "the meaning" or "reality," of Marlboro Jones.

If ever a man was only a construct, or only "almost a man," it is Marlboro, yet he has left many traces of himself for us to ponder. First, Marlboro appears in his seven-inch-high ambrotype, in a glass display case, at the Museum of the Confederacy. Second, he is documented in court and census records for Liberty County, Georgia, between 1851 and 1872. Third, and rather remarkably, he makes an appearance in not one but three memoirs written by white plantation owners to describe what happened to them when a cavalry wing of Sherman's army invaded Liberty County in December 1864. And fourth, he is the hero of an 1898 novel called *Lyddy*, written by a woman from Liberty County, Eugenia Jones Bacon.

From Liberty County, to Trevilian Station near Charlottesville, Virginia, then back to Liberty County, and finally back to Virginia—

to the Confederate capital, in fact, that his master had died to protect—the journeys of Marlboro Jones are traceable now. Two of the
places that Marlboro knew, the battlefield of Trevilian Station and the
LeConte gardens in Liberty County, are today being reconstructed to
look as they would have looked to him in his time. Through these
restorations we can in a way see what Marlboro saw, but the man himself still eludes us, in spite of an astonishing amount of documentation—some of it labeled fact but serving the cause of fiction, some of
it called fiction but bearing more of the weight of certain realities than
the facts of the case reveal.

First, the ambrotype. This compelling image of a black man wearing
a Confederate uniform, posed with great dignity and authority, has
made Marlboro Jones the poster boy for the Neo-Confederate argument that slaves identified themselves with the Confederacy, and in
particular served the army, taking their masters' cause as their own.
The ambrotype's image has been reproduced in Ervin L. Jordan's
book, *Black Confederates and Afro-Yankees in Civil War Virginia;* in an
article in the Columbia (South Carolina) *State* about the Confederate
flag flying over the South Carolina capitol; and perhaps most emphatically, on the cover of an issue of the *Journal of Confederate History* devoted to proving the significant presence of loyal slaves within the
Confederate army. The ambrotype was donated to the Museum of the
Confederacy by a direct descendant of Marlboro Jones's last owner,
Laura Jones Camp, of Liberty County, Georgia.

We now know, although not from the ambrotype itself, that Marlboro himself was donated, after a fashion, to Laura Jones Camp's
brother, Randal Fleming Jones, to be his "body servant" during Captain Jones's service as a cavalry officer in the 7th Georgia Regiment
eventually attached to Wade Hampton's Cavalry as it moved into Virginia in the early summer of 1864. Randal Fleming Jones fought in the
battle of Trevilian Station and returned mortally wounded to Savannah. His remains, according to one source, were returned to his plantation home in Liberty County.

The ambrotype does not tell us this—and the silent portrait has
become window dressing for a different story that the editors of the
Journal of Confederate History want to tell. The special 1995 issue for

which Marlboro Jones appears as a striking "cover" is called "Forgotten Confederates: An Anthology about Black Southerners." Its prologue's announced agenda is to recognize the significant role that black slave soldiers played in the Confederate army, a warrant forwarded to support an even larger claim, that "deep devotion and affection [in many instances] transcended the master-slave relationship and [were] not destroyed by the divisive wedge of Federal reconstruction."[1]

The editors of the *Journal* speak of the need for a corrective vision of "Truth," in the matter of slave service in the Confederate army, and Marlboro's portrait, displayed both on the cover and inside the journal, acts as exhibit A. The editors do not, however, factor in the inscription that appears on the back of the ambrotype. There, in a clear

Marlboro Jones, Georgia slave in a Confederate uniform at a Virginia battle site.
THE MUSEUM OF THE CONFEDERACY, RICHMOND, VIRGINIA

hand, an unidentified writer left these words for posterity: "Marlboro the—faithful slave—who protected the women of the family while their husbands were in service—the Civil War. He wears the Confederate uniform." This writer does not recognize Marlboro's service to the Confederate army, indeed emphasizes that while he *wears* the Confederate uniform, his important service was as a slave protecting the women left behind while their husbands were off fighting. Most of the white men of Liberty County joined cavalry units; they were avid horsemen who participated in equestrian competitions, and many of them ended up in the greatest cavalry battle of the Civil War, Trevilian Station, June 14, 1864. Marlboro was there, probably wearing the Confederate uniform. The nature of his service is impossible to glean, while the inscription on the back only deepens the mystery of the man it describes.

A second way to tell the story of Marlboro Jones is through court and church records connected to the white families of Liberty County, Georgia. These families were a remarkable group of wealthy rice planters, many of whom had originally come to this seacoast area of Georgia as a group united by their religion. Their forebears, who became known in history as "Southern puritans," had arrived in Massachusetts from England in the 1630s, had moved to Dorchester, South Carolina, during the time of the witch trials, and founded their most permanent settlement thirty miles below Savannah, in an area known as Midway, as soon as slavery was legalized in the colony of Georgia through a series of legislative acts beginning in 1750.

They were remarkably industrious, as well as pious, and as we know from Robert Manson Meyers's *Children of Pride*, they were unusual as slave owners because of the extraordinary mechanisms they put into place to "direct" the spiritual welfare of their large slave workforce. Meyers's three-volume collection of letters concerns the Reverend Charles Colcock Jones family, who are no direct relation to Laura Jones Camp's family. Nonetheless, in the *Children of Pride* letters and in Meyers's notes, there are several references to Laura and her brother Randal—and indeed, as we shall see, to Marlboro himself.

Both the Charles Colcock Jones and the Laura Jones families, and Marlboro too, attended the Congregational church built in 1792 and still standing at Midway, Georgia, off Highway 17, thirty miles below Savannah. Laura Jones's great grandparents had been among the more prominent of this church's first families. Her father, Moses Liberty Jones, was a selectman for the church, as well as one of the six wealthiest planters in Liberty County in the late 1840s. He was also—until his sudden death in 1851—the owner of Marlboro Jones. Liberty County Court and Midway Church records document the extensive history of Marlboro's owners in this famous county, which is one secondary way to track Marlboro's history as well. Yet he appears as subject, and perhaps agent, in three of his own crucial government records as well: first—in the fascinating document, on file at the Hinesville courthouse, dealing with the distribution of Moses Liberty Jones's estate. Here, in a neatly organized chart, we find how the more than one hundred slaves of Moses Jones were divided among his eight children according to "Lots" that each child, or the child's legal guardian, drew. Laura Jones, at nineteen, was the oldest child—her mother had died a year before her father, leaving her in charge of two brothers and five sisters. She drew Lot One, and among the slaves listed in Lot One as it appears in the court record was Marlboro, carriage driver—estimated worth, $1,000.

The second important reference to Marlboro Jones is not in Hinesville, but in the U.S. Census for Liberty County, Georgia, 1870, the first census in which Marlboro Jones could appear as a free citizen. And there is his name, listed in the MacIntosh District, marking him as colored, illiterate, laborer, age fifty-three. A third Liberty County Court record is perhaps the most revealing. On October 25, 1872, Marlboro Jones petitioned the court for the right to buy land on which he had been living—land formerly known as Syphax, a plantation owned by Joseph LeConte, next-door neighbor to Moses Liberty Jones before the Civil War. Joseph LeConte was an absentee planter much better known for his academic credentials, first as professor at the University of South Carolina in Columbia, and afterwards at the University of California in Berkeley, where he and his brother John had distinguished careers as administrators and faculty of the new university. The LeConte brothers were first cousins of Moses Liberty Jones.

In his petition to the court to buy property that we know Joseph

LeConte had abandoned by the early 1870s, Marlboro's assets are listed as $472—less than half of his worth as chattel in 1851, yet not at all inconsiderable during the Reconstruction period. Obviously, Marlboro's activities, after virtually all of the white Joneses and LeContes left Liberty County, offered him a brief window of opportunity to realize the dream that Sherman had held out to the slaves of this area—forty acres and a mule—although Marlboro, according to the document, owned not a mule but an ox. Thus the same charming little courthouse that fixes Marlboro's function and value as slave also contains his petition as a free man to claim the land that had once claimed him.

A third way to tell Marlboro Jones's story is through several Georgia memoirs, one of them written by Joseph LeConte, who had returned to Liberty County in December of 1864 to rescue his sister and daughter, trapped alone at Halifax, one of the family's plantations. The plantation where he found them, and then ended up having to hide from Yankee foragers, bordered Moses Liberty Jones's estate, Green Forest, where Laura Jones Camp and several of her sisters were also alone and "unprotected," except for their slaves. LeConte related his account of Liberty County's darkest hour in journals that became a book entitled *'Ware Sherman*, first published in 1937. The events he describes spelled a cataclysmic end to the way of life of the rice planters in Liberty County.

Meyers's *Children of Pride* has since 1972 been another key source of information concerning this period. Yet even before Meyers published his edition of the Charles Colcock Jones letters, an account written jointly by his widow, Mary Sharpe Jones, and their daughter, Mary Jones Mallard, told of how the women and children were terrorized by Yankee troops on their Liberty County plantation during that December. Their memoir, called *Yankees A'Coming*, came out in 1959.

Finally, a third memoir, dictated by Laura Jones Camp's first cousin Cornelia Jones Pond, was privately printed—in excerpted form, in 1983, and was published in its entirety by the University of Georgia Press in 1999. Between 1899 and 1903, Pond had shared with one of her daughters the romantic story of her girlhood in Liberty County. The dramatic core of Pond's story is—not surprisingly—the time she and her young children spent on her father's plantation in 1864, while her husband, with many of her other male relatives, was in Virginia with Wade Hampton. At Hawes Shop, she tells us, her brother-in-law was shot in the windpipe. At Trevilian Station, her husband Thomas's horse was killed, but he himself never suffered even a scratch in all the battles that decimated his battalion, the 20th of Georgia, which was nearly wiped out during the June fighting in Louisa County.

Marlboro Jones is discussed in LeConte's *'Ware Sherman*, in the Jones women's *Yankees A'Coming*, and in Cornelia Jones Pond's recollections. He is called by name in the Pond and LeConte accounts. Cornelia Pond recollects how Marlboro, the coachman, usually drove her grandmother to Midway church from her uncle's plantation, Green Forest, and seated her in her own chair in the front of the church. LeConte tells how "the faithful Marlboro," reconnoitering for his mistress at Green Forest in the winter of 1864, brought him messages that helped him to escape the Yankees. In the C. C. Jones women's account, Marlboro is not named but is referred to as "a servant of Captain Randal Jones, who had been with him in Virginia." Mrs. Jones tells of how, on the fateful night of December 14, she was trying to make her way back to her plantation, alone after dark with only a slave boy to drive her wagon. Miraculously, a "manservant" of Captain Jones appeared, and guided her through the Yankee-infested territory.[2]

The inscription on the back of the museum's ambrotype is certainly borne out by these references. We know through other sources that Marlboro Jones had been with Randal Jones in Virginia, and we know through Joseph LeConte that by this winter, he was moving freely around the county, scouting for his mistress, Laura Jones Camp, and, not inauspiciously, aiding her prominent neighbors as well. Once home from Virginia, he obviously became one of the few able-bodied and trustworthy men of the county. Cornelia Pond says that most of her family's male slaves, even the most trusted, around this same time betrayed her father to the Yankees and stole valuables he had asked them to hide. Marlboro seems to have made a different choice, but perhaps he became "all things to all people" for a not dissimilar motive, pure self-preservation.

The three memoirs of prominent Liberty County planters corroborate details of one more work that announces itself as a novel, but which clearly is a closely autobiographical narrative related by yet another Jones of Liberty County: Laura Jones Camp's younger sister and Cornelia Jones Pond's first cousin, Eugenia Jones Bacon. In 1873 Bacon had been left childless and widowed by a typhoid epidemic in Atlanta that took the lives of both her husband and son. She turned to writing, painting, and chaperoning wealthy young women on trips to Europe in order to support herself. She had grown up in Liberty County at Green Forest, and like her sister Laura had received her share of her father's slaves. At the distribution of his estate, she drew Lot Four, included in which—as listed in the court record and described in the novel—was a thirty-eight-year-old slave by the name of Lydia, worth $850.

The novel that Bacon published in 1898 is entitled *Lyddy: A Tale of the Old South*, and its chief characters are a woman slave, Lydia or Lyddy, and a carriage driver or coachman named Marlboro, who is deeply in love with her. Marlboro the character is the close confidante of his gracious and deeply religious master, known as "Massa' Janes," who dies tragically one year after he has lost his wife, leaving eight children orphaned.

In the novel, Eugenia and her family, including Lyddy, become refugees in southwest Georgia during the Civil War, but Marlboro accompanies his mistress's brother, known as Mars Flem', to the "front"; near the end of the war, Marlboro returns his young master's body to Green Forest to be buried. Charles Colcock Jones, not so subtly renamed Parson C. C., makes a brief appearance in the novel to perform the marriage ceremony uniting Lyddy and Marlboro's brother, Robin, and Lyddy loves to quote from his sermons. Joseph LeConte is also mentioned, as "Joe LaMont," the owner of Flora, a woman slave whom Marlboro marries when he despairs of winning Lyddy. Bacon's double plot involves, on the one hand, Lyddy and Marlboro's hopeless love. Married to unworthy others, they are never allowed by their kindly master to divorce, although Marlboro passionately argues the case and even suggests to Lyddy that they should run away when Massa' refuses. The other plot is the story of Eugenia Jones and her siblings, their idyllic life before the war and their loss of home and loyal slaves after the war.

One of Bacon's sisters wrote to her when the novel was published that Bacon should not have bothered with pseudonyms, since everyone from Liberty County would recognize all the characters and events as real. Bacon wrote her story as a novel, she explained in its preface, to counteract the effect that Stowe's *Uncle Tom's Cabin* had wrought on the public's image of the antebellum South. Letters from friends compared her novel to works of Joel Chandler Harris, and it was briefly reviewed in many national papers, including the *New York Times.* Yet the most important, lengthy, and appreciative review was penned by Joel Chandler Harris himself in the *Atlanta Constitution.* The review is accompanied by a sketch—a clear copy of the ambrotype image of Marlboro in his Confederate uniform. The caption below it reads: "Old Marlboro: One of the characters in Eugenia J. Bacon's Story of the Old South."[3]

Lyddy, as a narrative construct providing an optional identity for Marlboro Jones, offers as clear and irreconcilable a contradiction between its covers as the front and back of the museum ambrotype, or as the 1851 and 1872 Hinesville court records, or as the Pond memoir's rebellious slaves versus the LeConte memoir's faithful ones. Eugenia Jones Bacon's Marlboro never grovels before his master, although it might be argued that the heavy, part Gullah dialect representation of his speech, grovels for him. He argues against his master's theological position on slave divorce quite forcefully, pointing out that "white folks breaks up marriages when dey sells niggers." He carries himself proudly as he travels with "our brother, the captain, in Virginia," and he is known in his master's cavalry unit as "Parson," because of his serious demeanor. We are told that he dressed fastidiously in a "military coat" and vest.[4] Yet we do not know if the uniform attests to his master's status or to his own preferences.

Bacon makes an attempt at understanding Marlboro's dissatisfaction with his status when she allows him to mutter bitterly to a horse he is grooming, "You and me is in bondage. Eat your corn, old fellow, wid a t'ankful heart, cause you ain't got no mind ter be cut up as I is. . . . Yonder, folks is eatin' sweet cake. I can't help myself caise I's a slave." Yet Bacon also makes him her chief spokesperson for the "good old times befo' dah wah" school of thought in the last chapter, where Marlboro tells a crude Yankee auctioneer that "de bes' victuals I ever eat an' de happiest days I eber lived was when I was coachman ter massa."[5]

Whoever Marlboro was, the contradictions within all the ways of representing his identity speak to the one capacity that might reconcile some of the paradoxes. He was quite clearly a negotiator, and what he was negotiating always was his own subject position within a system that had fewer hard and fast rules than we sometimes want to think. Constructed/Instructed to speak to competing ideologies, he is silent as himself. Those who speak for him for the record do not contain him, but nor do they free him.

In his slave narrative, *The Fugitive Blacksmith*, James Pennington might have been speaking for, if not of, Marlboro in 1849, two years before Marlboro's value was calculated at the breakup of Moses Jones's estate. Pennington writes that if a slave should want "to appeal to the history of his family, where will he find that history? He goes to his native state, to his native county, to his native town; but *nowhere* does he find any record of himself *as a man*. On looking at the family record of his old, kind, Christian master, there he finds his name on a catalogue with the horses, cows, hogs, and dogs."[6]

Pascal Buma, in an essay entitled "Being Black, Male, and African Alien in the United States of America," writes especially for the Marlboro of the ambrotype when he says, "The color of my skin is my label and like all labels, it is an open text that informs ordinary folk of what I am, what I am composed of. . . . Any sighting of me evokes images, feelings, desires, fears, and attitudes that the ordinary people have inherited almost as a matter of course. . . . They have become unwitting heirs to a way of life and a manner of dealing with black life that is backed and buttressed by four hundred years of history."[7]

Today, as well as a hundred years ago—or four hundred years— any sighting or citing of Marlboro that we make now is both smoke and mirror, for his record of himself *as a man* is nowhere, as well as everywhere, we look.

Notes

1. J. H. Segars, "Prologue," *Journal of Confederate History* 14 (1995): 4.
2. Cornelia Jones Pond, *Recollections of a Southern Daughter*, ed. Lucinda H. MacKethan (Athens, Ga., 1999); Joseph LeConte, *'Ware Sherman: A Journal of Three Months' Personal Experience in the Last Days of the Confederacy* (1937; rept. Baton Rouge, La., 1999), 20, 32; Mary Jones Mallard and Mary Sharpe Jones, *Yankees A'Coming: One Month's Experience during the Invasion of Liberty County,*

Georgia, 1864–1865, ed. with a prologue by Haskell Monroe (Tuscaloosa, Ala., 1959), 35.

3. Leonora Stacy to Eugenia Jones Bacon (private collection, Eugenia Barber Esham). For reviews, see *New York Times*, 18 February 1899; *Chicago Herald*, 28 December 1898; Joel Chandler Harris, *Atlanta Constitution*, 14 January 1900.

4. Eugenia Jones Bacon, *Lyddy: A Tale of the Old South* (1898; rept. [ed. Lucinda H. MacKethan] Athens, Ga., 1998), 87, 165, 187.

5. Ibid., 133, 276.

6. James W. C. Pennington, *The Fugitive Blacksmith* (London, 1849), in *Great Slave Narratives*, ed. Arna Bontemps (Boston, 1969).

7. Pascal Buma, "Mama, I'm Becoming a Black Man: Being Black, Male, and African Alien in the United States of America," *Jouvert* 6, nos. 1 and 2 (2001) http://social.chass.ncsu.edu/jouvert/v6i1-2/buma.htm.

Interracial Love, Virginians' Lies, and Donald McCaig's *Jacob's Ladder*

SUZANNE W. JONES

The Old South's taboo against love between blacks and whites has cast a long shadow. No cross-racial relationship has been so pathologized by American society.[1] Even in 1967, when the Supreme Court finally declared antimiscegenation laws unconstitutional in the case of *Loving v. Virginia*, sixteen states still prohibited interracial marriage, down from thirty states as recently as 1948.[2] Not until 1998 and 2000 did ballot initiatives in South Carolina and Alabama finally eliminate the last of the antimiscegenation laws, although no one had tried to enforce them for years. Recent U.S. census figures show interracial unions increasing—up from 3 percent in 1980 to 5 percent in 2000, or just over 3 million couples. But American inhibitions about black-white marriages still remain comparatively strong. The United States has the lowest black-white intermarriage rate among Western nations, and the 450,000 black-white couples make up only 14 percent of all interracial marriages in the United States, although the numbers are increasing among young people—young blacks are marrying across the color line at double the overall average, with 11 percent marrying outside their race. Although 40.1 percent of the black interracial marriages occur in the South (as compared to 19.3 percent in the Northeast, 21.3 percent in the Midwest, and 19.3 percent in the West), a 1997 survey by *Interrace* magazine does not list a single Southern city in its top ten cities most hospitable to interracial couples.[3] Contemporary Southern fiction is only somewhat more hospitable—even when the author's heart is in the right place—in large part because this fiction is almost always set in the past.

Although the burden of Southern racial history automatically pre-
cludes happy endings, these contemporary historical novels do complicate the regional story of race and sex as it has been traditionally
told. Contemporary writers are interested in the very stories that bell
hooks argues have not been told: stories that examine the conditions
under which interracial sexuality served "as a force subverting and
disrupting power relations, unsettling the oppressor/oppressed para-
digm."[4] These recent fictions, even though set in the past, explore interracial relationships of mutual desire and examine contemporary social
concerns without neglecting the exploitation of black women or the
demonization of black men that white prejudice both produced and
denied. This recent outpouring of historical fiction set in the South
expresses a deep need to recover repressed truths about past interracial
intimacy that a great many people, white Southerners especially, have
refused to acknowledge. Perhaps this fiction also reflects a need to
better understand the past before turning to the present or imagining
the future. Whether this focus on the past also betrays a reticence to
represent interracial love in the present is difficult to determine. What
is clearer, and perhaps more significant, is that readers of these historical Southern fictions—which invariably end in thwarted interracial
love, no matter the hope embedded in their plots—may find it surprising that today twice as many interracial couples in which one partner is African American live in the South as in any other region of the
country.

In the nineteenth century, both before and after the Civil War,
white novelists, though rarely from the South, employed the love affair between a white man and a black woman as a vehicle for illustrating the common humanity of blacks and as a hope for racial reconciliation, but many African American novelists treated interracial sex as
a sad fact of life or a threat to black solidarity. While events of the 1960s
released a flood of fiction examining black male-white female couples,
treatment of white male-black female couples, so prominent in nineteenth-century fiction, dwindled. But this tide seems to have turned at
the very end of the twentieth century. Interracial intimacy between
white men and black women has figured in much recent nonfiction
about the Old South. Among such works are Carrie Allen McCray's
Freedom's Child: The Life of a Confederate General's Black Daughter (1998),

Edward Ball's *Slaves in the Family* (1998), Henry Wiencek's *The Hair-stons: An American Family in Black and White* (1999), and most notably Annette Gordon-Reed's *Thomas Jefferson and Sally Hemings: An American Scandal* (1999), which ultimately argues that white male historians did a disservice not only to black Americans but to all Americans in re-fusing to see the truth of interracial intimacy. Twenty years after his-torian Fawn Brodie's speculations in *Thomas Jefferson: An Intimate History* (1974) and Barbara Chase-Riboud's fictional follow-up in *Sally Hemings: A Novel* (1979), Americans seemed more willing to accept a founding father's transgressions. As a result, popular culture could not get enough of this story, which many white male historians thought they had laid to rest in the 1980s. The lingering doubts about the story's veracity, which helped make the Merchant-Ivory film, *Jefferson in Paris* (1995), a flop at the box office, were much less in evidence four years and several DNA tests later, when the television miniseries *Sally Hemings: An American Scandal* (1999) made its debut.

Annette Gordon-Reed has said that Chase-Riboud's novel "has been the single greatest influence shaping the public's attitude about the Jefferson-Hemings story."[5] Contemporary fiction may have a similar effect in shaping future attitudes about interracial love, espe-cially if the stories are bought by Hollywood. In *Jacob's Ladder: A Story of Virginia during the War* (1998), Donald McCaig revisits Virginia's Civil War and its aftermath—not only to prod readers to rethink the war but also to reconsider interracial intimacy and racial identity in the Old South and perhaps, most surprising, to contemplate the social mobility afforded a few poor whites and some light-skinned African Americans. The plot of *Jacob's Ladder* is driven by the ironies gener-ated when Southern honor intersects with cross-racial desire, when the racial codes of Southern society conflict with traditional chivalric gender roles, and when reputations of racial identity belie the truths of racial genealogy.

In *Jacob's Ladder*, young Duncan Gatewood becomes intimately in-volved with the contradictions in Southern society after he falls in love with Midge, a mulatto slave, and conceives a child with her. His father a prominent landowner in the Shenandoah Valley, tries to erase this fact by marrying Midge off to a slave she does not love and by exiling Duncan to Virginia Military Institute. At the end of the college term

Duncan's father administers the ultimate final examination by forcing Duncan to meet Midge's new husband and to accept his own son Jacob as his slave. McCaig employs a familiar nineteenth-century trope, making Jacob "as white as" Duncan and forcing Duncan to contemplate his son's future as "a field hand perhaps, a woods worker like Rufus or a house nigger like Pompey."[6] Still in love with Midge and falling in love with their child, Duncan angrily raises his hand to strike his father. However, equally determined to be the Southern gentleman his father expects him to be, Duncan restrains himself only by biting his own hand so hard that blood spatters onto Midge and the child. Duncan's reflex reconsideration of his seemingly instinctual paternal response symbolizes both the contradictions inherent in the Southern code of honor and the epistemological problems of racial and familial identity in the nineteenth-century South. In protecting his father from the blow, Duncan has protected the Gatewood family reputation, but harmed himself. By honoring his father's desire that the Gatewood bloodlines remain pure, he dishonors the new family he has created with Midge—producing the very Southern family fictions that have turned contemporary Southern historians, both professional and amateur, into detectives.

When Duncan later fails to persuade his father to allow him to marry Midge and to recognize Jacob as his son, his father sells both Midge and Jacob. In doing so, Mr. Gatewood effectively banishes the muse who has provoked Duncan's preliminary but "imaginative" new thinking about Southern race relations (70). Duncan's inchoate questions about his society's racial code are not powerful enough to throw off the heavy mantle of Southern honor and the awful reality that the woman he loves is a slave. After a period of dissipation in which Duncan attempts to forget his sorrows by drinking and gambling, he joins the Confederate army, hoping that "Honor will be retrieved" (93). Although the war deprives Duncan of his youth, his good looks, and his right arm, he feels that courageous military service has restored his honor. He never once considers that a bolder move would have been to join the Union army and fight for Midge's freedom. McCaig suggests that even a sensitive, thoughtful, rebellious Virginia gentleman's imagination could not make such an enormous leap in the nineteenth century.

McCaig employs the women who love Duncan—Midge and Sallie—to reveal how Southern notions of both honor and racial identity have been deceptive. For Sallie, the white woman who nurses Duncan in a Richmond hospital, the war restores nothing, but rather takes away life and limb, health and well-being, all for an ignominious cause. To Sallie, honor is an empty abstraction that keeps men enthralled. She responds to Duncan's rhapsodies about Dixie, the Confederate battle flag, and General Lee's army by averting her face and declaring, "I have seen too much of honor" (305). For Midge, whom Duncan later meets by chance at a party in Richmond, "honor" is a commodity, which can be "preserved" only because "southern gentlemen . . . can sell their embarrassments" (335). For Donald McCaig, honor is a poignant metaphor for the sad charade that Southern white men lived. What the war has really done for Duncan is to restore his public reputation as a gentleman by allowing him to fight honorably for the Confederacy. But privately he finds that he must come to terms with his own guilty conscience for allowing his father to sell his son into slavery and for giving up the woman he loved. Guilt continues to eat away at Duncan, because during the war he sees, by chance, the beautiful Southern lady Midge has become—a fact that produces the change in ideology his youthful imagining failed to provoke. Slowly, Duncan realizes that the cause he has fought for was not just. Only then does Sallie consent to marry him.

In *Jacob's Ladder*, McCaig exposes racial identity as a charade as well. What the war has done for Midge is to establish her reputation as white. Eric Sundquist argues that under the Southern taboo of miscegenation, identity became "a radical act of imagination": "either in an act of self-recognition or in the attribution of identity to another."[7] McCaig employs this idea when Midge and Duncan meet in Richmond. Midge tells Duncan how she let her imagination run wild during their youthful affair. "I pictured us married! Me: the mistress of Stratford! Ignorant pickaninny playing the lady. Imagine!" (336). Although Duncan never acts on his own radical act of "imaginative" thinking, Midge does, but it takes a poor white partner who is also a Southern social climber to assist her. Silas Omohundru, the upwardly mobile slave trader who bought her from Mr. Gatewood, falls in love with her. Unlike Faulkner's Thomas Sutpen in *Absalom, Absalom!* (1936), Silas believes that what he can hide will not hurt him or his design. Silas proposes to Midge once they have left Virginia and moved to the more cosmopolitan port city of Wilmington, North Carolina. There Silas abandons slave trading for the lucrative and glamorous job of blockade running. Midge seizes this opportunity to pass as white and easily becomes Marguerite, Silas's beautiful Bahamian wife. Although she does not love Silas, marriage to him ascribes to her son, Jacob, the racial identity that his biological father Duncan denied him. This marriage also unexpectedly allows her to prove to Duncan, when she later encounters him at that Richmond party, that her Southern racial identity did not have to be her destiny. At first he does not recognize her, but then heartbreakingly he realizes that she has become "the lady" he once fleetingly imagined she could be. McCaig titles the chapter in which they meet "Charades" after the parlor game played that evening, but also to signify the racial masquerade that Marguerite has embarked on and that Duncan poignantly pledges he will not divulge—an illusion of white racial purity that many white Southerners still believe in, the Southern family fiction they have been reluctant to confront.

Although Marguerite cannot give Jacob the Gatewood family name, her choice to pass as white eventually makes Jacob the son of a Confederate war hero, if not a descendent of one of the First Families of Virginia (FFV). While Silas's blockade running in Wilmington makes him rich during the war, he cannot buy his way into Southern high society, because he is a bastard, so he enlists in the Confederate army to enhance his status. Eventually Silas posthumously earns his reputation as a Southern gentleman by dying for the lost cause—with the result that Marguerite's position in Richmond society is also secured. She becomes a wealthy, well-respected Confederate widow, and as a result she succeeds in making Jacob both a gentleman and a graduate of Harvard Law School. By the 1930s, when she chooses to end her masquerade, Marguerite Omohundru is the aging matriarch of a prominent "white" family, who lives in "one of the grandest homes" in Richmond (247) and who belongs to the Virginia Historical Society—not quite FFV, but not bad for a slave named Midge. Or so Donald McCaig seems to want his readers to think. And yet the narrative frame around his Civil War story suggests that he is striving for much more.

Unlike most African American novelists on the subject of passing, McCaig, who is white, does not ascribe guilt to Marguerite's masquerade, but he does register her anger at not having been able to fulfill her own potential without the white mask. As recompense he gives her pride of accomplishment in having given her child a better life, and no small amount of pleasure at having deceived Richmond aristocracy. The way McCaig frames Marguerite's story suggests that his ultimate target is really the contemporary white myth of racial purity, not the older story of blacks passing as white. McCaig registers the shock of realization that he must have hoped many white readers would experience through the perspective of his unnamed young white WPA worker, herself a member of Richmond high society. Expecting to talk with Marguerite's black servant Kizzy about her life as a slave, the young white woman is speechless, when she learns that it is Marguerite whose oral history she will be collecting. But she is willing to listen. Her family, however, pronounces Marguerite Omohundru "not herself" (247), and the young white woman's father urges her to read Thomas Nelson Page's short stories in order "to know" what Virginia's past was really like (295). The attempts by the woman's family to deter her from taking Marguerite's story seriously call attention to Southern white power in ascribing meaning to race and in controlling the South's interracial history.

Donald McCaig is a transplanted New Yorker who considers himself a Virginian after living twenty-five years on a farm in the Allegheny Highlands. He clearly sees himself as telling a different "Story of Virginia during the War" (the subtitle of his novel) than Virginia's nineteenth-century chronicler, Thomas Nelson Page, told.[8] In the collection *In Ole Virginia* (1887), Page blames Southern problems on Northern interference, rather than on slavery and the contradictions inherent in Southern racial codes and social customs. McCaig assigns blame very differently. His Confederate veteran Duncan Gatewood—eventually judging himself "a damned coward" (299) for allowing his son to be sold into slavery—subsequently views Virginia plantation society, the slavery that supported it, and the Confederacy that defended it as causing the South's demise. In this final reassessment, Duncan's position resembles Robert E. Lee's 1869 comment, which provides McCaig his "Afterword": "So far from engaging in a war to perpetuate slavery, I am rejoiced that slavery is abolished. I believe it will be greatly in the interests of the South" (527).

The difference between Page's and McCaig's choice of frame narrator for their Civil War stories is equally significant. In Page's "Marse Chan," a former slave tells a Northern tourist a fanciful story of happy darkies and genteel Southern families, a romanticized tale of Southern honor and Confederate glory. A century later, in *Jacob's Ladder*, a former slave who is passing as white tells a native Virginian a revisionary story of Southern dishonor and Civil War horrors, and a cautionary tale about the bloodlines of Virginia's finest white families. Page was trying to convince skeptical nonnatives that Virginia's way of life was honorable; McCaig is trying to convince skeptical native Virginians that stories like Page's have deprived them of the truth. By having the WPA worker choose Marguerite's oral history over Page's published stories, McCaig unseats Page as Virginia's Civil War chronicler and suggests that there is a hidden Virginia history that at least some white Virginians may be ready to hear.

McCaig's decision to create a light-skinned African American woman for his white male characters to fall in love with allows him to interrogate the social construction of racial identity. But it can also be read as reifying white definitions of female beauty. Aware that such a charge could be made, McCaig has Marguerite self-consciously assess this literary practice in historical terms: "'It is curious, is it not, that the lighter-skinned we are, the more anxious the dominant race is to mate with us. Those first white men to sleep with the dark-skinned daughters of Africa were such bold pioneers!' She raised her invisible eyebrows mockingly. 'I suppose it is more agreeable to make love with creatures that closely resemble oneself. Narcissism is one of the South's notable frailties'" (20). In some respects Marguerite can also be seen as a figure similar to nineteenth-century literature's "tragic mulatta": beautiful (according to white definitions), accomplished, moral, but mistreated.[9] However, McCaig does not fully follow nineteenth-century abolitionists' conventions. Although he does not shy away from depicting white racism's effect on African Americans, he is intent on showing how it deformed the lives and minds of his white characters as well. Marguerite is far from a tragic victim; she is depicted as strong, resourceful, and imaginative, unlike the weak white man Duncan Gatewood, who loves her.

Despite the difficulties of living in a racist society, Marguerite does not let her life slip totally out of her control. In *Jacob's Ladder*, true love is thwarted because of race, but McCaig uses this plotting device to begin his novel rather than end it, as was the custom with nineteenth-century novelists. McCaig makes Midge/Marguerite the mistress of her own fate, although her life never again includes romance. Significantly, McCaig represents the African American woman as initiating the interracial affair. Given the Southern history of white male aggression toward black women, he may be reluctant to have his white male protagonist make the first move in a novel of interracial attraction. In *Jacob's Ladder*, however, the end of the interracial affair is as heartbreaking for the white man, Duncan Gatewood, as it was for the black woman in nineteenth-century fictions.

In a published conversation with C. Vann Woodward, William Styron, and Robert Penn Warren, novelist Ralph Ellison argued that "one of the important roles which fiction has played, especially the fiction of southern writers," is "to tell that part of the human truth which we could not accept or face up to in much historical writing because of social, racial, and political considerations."[10] Donald McCaig is but one example of a growing number of Southern novelists, both black and white, who are telling the South's repressed stories. These historical novels about interracial intimacy not only revisit old taboos but also expose continuing psychic burdens. There are no happily-ever-afters in these novels. Given the preponderance of historical fiction about interracial love, it appears that serious literature about interracial intimacy in the contemporary South will be written only when the burden of Southern history does not weigh so heavily on novelists' imaginations.

Notes

Portions of this essay appeared in *Race Mixing: Southern Fiction since the Sixties* by Suzanne W. Jones, ©2004 The Johns Hopkins University Press, reprinted with permission of The Johns Hopkins University Press.

1. Robert P. McNamara, Maria Tempenis, and Beth Walton, *Crossing the Line: Interracial Couples in the South* (Westport, Conn., 1999); but also see Paul C. Rosenblatt, Terri A. Karis, and Richard D. Powell, *Multiracial Couples: Black and White Voices* (Thousand Oaks, Calif., 1995), which shows that the pathologizing occurs north of the Mason-Dixon line as well.

2. Peter Wallenstein, *Tell the Court I Love My Wife: Race, Marriage, and Law — An American History* (New York, 2002), and Robert E. T. Roberts, "Black-White Inter-marriage in the United States," in *Inside the Mixed Marriage: Accounts of Changing Attitudes, Patterns, and Perceptions of Cross-Cultural and Interracial Marriages,* eds. Walton R. Johnson and D. Michael Warren (Lanham, Md., 1994).

3. Statistics about intermarriage in this paragraph are from Darryl Fears and Claudia Deane, "Biracial Couples Report Tolerance," *Washington Post,* 5 July 2001, A1, 4; and Robert Suro, "Mixed Doubles," *American Demographics* 21, no. 11 (November 1999): 57–62. The region the U.S. government defines as the South includes Delaware; Maryland; Washington, D.C.; Virginia; North Carolina; South Carolina; Georgia; Florida; Alabama; Mississippi; Louisiana; Texas; Oklahoma; Arkansas; Tennessee; Kentucky; and West Virginia. For international comparisons, see Thomas F. Pettigrew, "Integration and Pluralism," in *Eliminating Racism: Profiles in Controversy,* eds. Phyllis A. Katz and Dalmas A. Taylor (New York, 1988), 26. Results of the *Interrace* questionnaire are reported in *Jet* 92, no. 20 (6 October 1997): 25.

4. bell hooks, *Yearning: Race, Gender, and Cultural Politics* (Boston, 1990), 57–58.

5. Annette Gordon-Reed, *Thomas Jefferson and Sally Hemings: An American Controversy* (Charlottesville, Va., 1997), 4. See also Jan Ellen Lewis and Peter S. Onuf, eds., *Sally Hemings and Thomas Jefferson: History, Memory, and Civic Culture* (Charlottesville, Va., 1999); Eugene A. Foster, M. A. Jobling, P. G. Taylor, P. Donnelly, P. deKnijft, Rene Mierenet, T. Zerjal, and C. Tyler-Smith, "Jefferson Fathered Slave's Last Child," *Nature* (5 November 1998); and the Thomas Jefferson Memorial Foundation's research report, made public 26 January 2000, which concluded that based on new research there is "a high probability that Thomas Jefferson fathered Eston Hemings, and that he most likely was the father of all six of Sally Hemings's children."

6. Donald McCaig, *Jacob's Ladder: A Story of Virginia during the War* (New York, 1998), 69. Subsequent quotations are identified parenthetically in the text.

7. Eric J. Sundquist, *To Wake the Nations: Race in the Making of American Literature* (Cambridge, Mass., 1993), 398.

8. McCaig gives this information in his acknowledgments, 522.

9. See James Kinney's definitions in *Amalgamation!* (Westport, Conn., 1985), 47, 90, 111, 194–95.

10. Ralph Ellison, William Styron, Robert Penn Warren, and C. Vann Woodward, "A Discussion: The Uses of History in Fiction," *Southern Literary Journal* 1, no. 2 (Spring 1969): 70.

PART THREE

AFTER THE WAR

The Freedmen's Bureau School in Lexington versus "General Lee's Boys"

JOHN M. MCCLURE

In November 1865 the American Missionary Association sent William L. Coan to western Virginia to organize new schools for African Americans. Coan left Richmond with his sights set on the small college town of Lexington in the Shenandoah Valley. Freedmen's Bureau agents warned Coan that "General Lee's boys" in Lexington would make it "a *hard* place for 'Nigger' Teachers." Before Coan reached the Valley, during a rest stop at a train station in Gordonsville, he was assaulted after confirming that he was a "meddling Yankee" en route to establish a freedmen's school. The man hit Coan several times in the head, while a small crowd of about twenty people stood by. Coan wrote later that the "'Southern Gentlemen' enjoy[ed] hugely seeing the damned . . . Yankee thus handled." The beating at Gordonsville failed, however, to stop Coan from continuing on to Lexington. Indeed, his resolve was strengthened. He looked forward to helping "God open up the fields, and prepare the soil to receive the seed" of freedmen's education. Coan opened the school in Lexington on December 12, 1865.[1]

Freedmen's Bureau commissioner Oliver Otis Howard pinned many of his hopes for the betterment of the freedpeople on their access to education, but the agency initially had little explicit authority and virtually no capital to engage in educational efforts. Northern missionary groups, which had taken up the cause of educating black Southerners while the Civil War was still being waged, provided the practical means for Howard's goals. Many of the groups that worked closely with the Freedmen's Bureau had originated in the abolitionist movement and consisted of evangelical Christian missionaries. Later, when Congress wrested Reconstruction policy away from President Andrew Johnson, Freedmen's Bureau coffers greatly expanded, enabling the agency to facilitate the construction and repair of schools and to supplement teachers' salaries.[2]

In Virginia the American Missionary Association (AMA) was the most active Northern aid society and worked closely with the Freedmen's Bureau. The AMA's wartime experience in eastern Virginia positioned the group to dominate postwar aid efforts in the state. Originally from Chelsea, Massachusetts, William Coan was a veteran of the abolitionist movement. He traveled in 1864 to Hampton, where he became an AMA school organizer and superintendent. Orlando Brown, who headed Virginia's Freedmen's Bureau for most of its existence, had become familiar with AMA officials and operations while serving in the Bureau of Negro Affairs in the tidewater area late in the war.[3] The two men's experience and familiarity with each other naturally expanded the linkage between the AMA and the Virginia Freedmen's Bureau. The cohesion between the two organizations in Virginia mirrored the relationship at the national level between O. O. Howard and top AMA officials.[4]

As Coan journeyed through the "Wicked Valley" in the fall of 1865, he corresponded regularly with Brown to update him on his progress. Lexington became an important goal for Coan, because he heard many boasts about Washington College, Virginia Military Institute, and the renewed vigor Gen. Robert E. Lee would lend to those institutions as the recently installed president of Washington College. Freedmen's Bureau agents throughout the Shenandoah warned Coan that whites would watch the freedmen's school closely, hoping for its failure. After Coan's arrival in Lexington, he described the town and its "defiant Rebels" as a "nest of Vipers, . . . the vilest of vile sinks of pollution."[5]

Lexington's blacks, by contrast, immediately embraced the school. Months before Coan's arrival, they had pooled their money to rent a room in anticipation of a school, and they had asked the local Freedmen's Bureau agent many times when a teacher would arrive. When Coan first met with many of the town's African Americans at their church on December 11, his announcement provoked "shouts of joy and many Hallelujahs." Within a week of the school's opening, more than three hundred students—ranging in age from very small children to grandparents in their sixties—nearly overwhelmed Coan and the one female teacher accompanying him. The classes soon became so large that the teachers began using the basement of their rented house to meet the demand. Night schools, because they permitted the students to keep their daytime jobs, especially flourished. The school progressed rapidly; the teachers were impressed with how quickly their scholars learned. Coan reported proudly to his superiors that "the Ice is *broken,* and . . . these *infernal Rebels* have [black schools] among them, and in their very midst."[6]

Whites, outraged that a school for blacks had opened in their town, vented their anger in myriad ways. Whites taunted black children as they walked to school; white employers warned their black workers "I don't need educated niggers." Some local merchants began to charge blacks higher prices than their white customers. The Northern teachers who arrived in Lexington met similar hostility. No one would rent lodgings to the missionaries except the Unionist Mrs. Archibald, and she soon left town to join her husband in the North, because she could no longer stand being treated like "a leper." The teachers met with epithets and silent glares on the town's streets; storeowners often refused to do business with them.

In addition to the townspeople, the students and cadets of local Washington College and the Virginia Military Institute added a strong element of young, white males who were proudly unreconstructed. Many of the students and cadets were veterans of the Confederate army, and many came from elite families. They responded to the freedmen's school by threatening to tar and feather William Coan and burn down the school building. Other warnings included the blunt promise that "'Nigger schools' shall not go on." The college students frequently threw stones at the school's windows and loudly sang "rebel songs" during impromptu evening "parades." Many of the young men boarded near the AMA mission house and encountered the teachers frequently on the street. Teachers were called "Yankee bitches" so often that the insult "hardly impress[ed]" them after the first few months. The female teachers contended that the physical encounters were more offensive. Men often stood in the women's path as they walked home from school in the evening, forcing the teachers to push past them. On several occasions the students jostled the women and made "vulgar suggestions"; the teachers reported smelling whiskey on the men's breath.[7]

Teachers' complaints about the college students provoked action by the local Freedmen's Bureau agents. Especially during the first year of freedmen's schools in Lexington, when the Freedmen's Bureau could offer little material aid to the missionaries, the agents provided a critical protective buffer between the teachers and hostile whites. Agent Lieutenant Tubbs sent written warnings to Lee and to Francis H. Smith, superintendent of Virginia Military Institute, in late January respectfully advising the leaders to curb their students' "rambunctious" behavior toward the "fine ladies" of the AMA school.[8] Tubbs warned a Washington College professor that continued harassment of the teachers could result in black troops being garrisoned in Lexington—a possibility that "horrified" the professor.[9] Agent Carse issued a public warning to the town. In April 1866, for the first time in Rockbridge County, a local magistrate considered a controversial case of assault and battery brought by a black man against three VMI cadets. The freedman had been on his way home from a night school session when he was attacked. The court ordered the cadets only to keep the peace; the magistrate decided that since the freedman "had given as good as he got" and had not been injured, the cadets had perhaps learned their lesson. The landmark case drew an overflow crowd to the courthouse, including a majority of the cadets of VMI and the students of Washington College. Carse took advantage of the opportunity to warn the students "unless they acted differently, the Government would [probably] close the college and Institute."[10]

The AMA teachers faced organizational hurdles in addition to a hostile environment. The teachers wrote to their superiors requesting supplies to be sent from New York in order to avoid inflated Virginia prices and surly white merchants in Lexington. The teachers soon expanded their idea of importing Northern goods. Julia Anne Shearman proposed to her AMA superiors in January 1866 the establishment of a store to cater to Lexington's black community; the enterprise would save the AMA money and would enable black residents and the teachers alike to largely avoid white storeowners. The Freedmen's Bureau agreed to provide free transportation of goods within Virginia, adding to the thriftiness of the plan. By the end of February, AMA teacher Erastus Johnston had rented a room for the business, hired an "intelligent black man who can read and write" to help run the store, and begun to stock goods. In addition to competing economically with white storeowners by reducing their monopoly on black customers, Johnston challenged Lexington's racial order by placing an African American man in a managerial position. Whites denounced the new store, and Johnston became a pariah to the white community.[11]

Despite financial support from the Freedmen's Bureau and continuing patronage from Northern missionaries, black contributions remained critical to the success of black schools in the region. Lexington's African Americans shrewdly prepared for emancipation's opportunities before the end of the war. They paid off the mortgage on their church building with Confederate currency in late 1864, because they knew that Union victory would render their dollars worthless. Yet they worried that Lexington bankers would dispute the balance remaining on the mortgage in the chaotic aftermath of war. In January 1866 local blacks established the "Freedman's School Society." The group collected donations to help pay "the expenses of the school rooms, rent, wood, [and] lights" and proposed to buy books for students who could not afford them.[12] African American financial support in the Lexington area grew throughout the Reconstruction period, and soon blacks ran schools themselves. Baptist reverend Milton Smith established the private "Lexington School" in December 1869. Blacks paid for the school wholly; they received no support from aid societies or the Freedmen's Bureau.[13] In rural areas outside of Lexington, African Americans initiated two schools in Rockbridge County in 1867, one in Brownsburg and the other at Natural Bridge.[14]

The AMA school in Lexington continued to enjoy a strong enrollment and the steady progress of its students. But the school remained at the center of combustible black-white relations—particularly when statewide political battles elevated local racial tensions. In March 1867, just after Virginia became officially known as "Military District Number One" in accordance with Congress's Reconstruction Acts, five white college students went to the schoolhouse likely planning to disrupt Republican speeches to the black audience. As they peered into the windows, a freedman told them to leave. One of the students proceeded to beat the freedman with his pistol, but caused only minor injuries. The perpetrator managed to escape after the brief altercation, but his four companions were arrested. News of the fight and arrests reached the Washington College campus quickly, prompting a large mob of students to march toward the center of town, planning to "rescue" their friends from jail. Givens Strickler, a college student and former Confederate captain, successfully appealed to the students to restrain themselves, invoking General Lee's name to implore the men not to storm the jail. Strickler's arguments convinced the mob to disperse. Lee expelled the student who committed the pistol whipping when he later admitted the deed in Lee's office. Bureau agent Captain Sharp told his superiors that, although a "major collision" was "narrowly avoided," the situation remained "highly volatile."[15]

Tensions were again high in early 1868 as the state constitutional convention meeting in Richmond vigorously debated the scope of political rights for black Virginians. Erastus Johnston was no longer teaching school in Lexington, but he continued to operate his store and organized the local "loyal league" in support of the Republican Party.[16] Such activities made him, as Douglas Southall Freeman described in an elegant understatement, "somewhat notorious and distinctly unpopular" among Lexington's whites. Agent Sharp reported bluntly that Johnston was "very obnoxious to the white citizens of the county with exactly no exception. They openly despise him and are incendiary." Conversely, and perhaps unsurprisingly, Johnston enjoyed "great popularity among the Freedpeople."[17]

On February 4, 1868, Johnston went skating at a popular spot on the North River just outside of Lexington. He met with the usual mix of glares and catcalls from the other skaters until a young white male (as young as twelve or as old as seventeen, according to various reports) approached Johnston and called him a "son of a bitch." Johnston drew his pistol; he later claimed he felt threatened by both the taunt and the crowd who were now closing in on him. White witnesses claimed that Johnston aimed the pistol at the boy and threatened his life. The crowd, with many college students among them, quickly became an outright mob, throwing rocks and chunks of ice at Johnston. Cries of "Hang him!" echoed after Johnston as he ran away from the river and returned to town. That night, after Johnston reported the incident to local authorities, a crowd gathered in front of his store. They loudly threatened his life and attempted to break into the building, but they dispersed without violence. Local white officials immediately downplayed the incident, but Freedmen's Bureau agent Douglas Frazar was concerned enough to call for troops from Major Willcox in Lynchburg. The incident brought national attention to Lexington when Johnston wrote to the New York newspaper *The Independent* about his experience, and AMA teacher Julia Shearman wrote to the same journal to discuss the "Rebel sentiments" of Lexington whites. Johnston, perhaps prudently, decided within a few days of the incident to move out of town.[18] Thus, through intimidation and violence, Lexington whites succeeded in removing the influential activist from their midst.

While these public acts of violence punctuated Lexington's Reconstruction experience, more private forms of violence also permeated the atmosphere. These interior battles pitted white men against black females. Some Washington College students and VMI cadets sexually abused black girls and young women, many of them students at the freedmen's school. The social stigmatization associated with sexual violence in the mid-nineteenth century ensured that these incidents were not always dealt with in an open manner, but there is strong evidence that some white men acted as sexual predators in Lexington. Bureau agent Captain Sharp reported that, on several occasions, college students attempted "to abduct . . . unwilling colored girls [for] readily divined purposes."[19]

In June 1866 a VMI cadet attacked a young black woman working as a chambermaid in the Lexington Hotel. The woman entered the man's room expecting him to be absent; he instead surprised her and attempted to rape her. The hotel's owner heard her screams and interrupted the attack before the cadet "ravished" her, but she was left "much bruised." Bureau agent Carse reported that he urged the woman's father to have the local magistrate issue a warrant for the man's arrest. But after ominous warnings from several students not to pursue the case, the family let the matter drop.[20] The family's reluctance to bring charges is perhaps explained by an incident in 1868. On that occasion a VMI cadet accused of raping a black woman avoided trial when Mayor Ruff "allowed and assisted" his escape from the military authorities investigating the crime.[21]

Other sexual encounters between the white college students and young black females were more complex. AMA teachers reported in the spring of 1866 that they expelled a "young colored girl" because she was pregnant; the girl implied that the father was a white student. The teachers believed that the unmarried girl's presence would be "a poor moral example" for the smaller children in the day school. Rather than slip away in shame, however, the expelled student angrily objected to the teachers' decision. The girl claimed that she—like many girls in the school, she said—was guilty only of "regular cohabitation with one white man, of which neither he nor she was ashamed." The girl's defense suggests that some college students engaged in relationships with black females that approximated prostitution. Johnston, at this time still a teacher at the school, confirmed that the student "supported" the girl, presumably in return for sex, and that such an arrangement was "sadly common."

Although some of these encounters may not have constituted rape in a legal sense, the inherent disparity in gender and race relationships in postwar Lexington, combined with the lingering effects of slavery-era sexual subordination of black women, guaranteed that such sexual relations were intrinsically coercive. Teacher Sarah Burt wrote that girls felt "helpless" when pursued by white men, and that many were simply forced to "succumb to the brutal desires" of the college students. Indeed, Johnston claimed "the chief amusement of many of the Students and [cadets] is to seduce young, colored girls" and that "there is scarcely a virtuous girl here over 16 years of age." The threat of violence was omnipresent in such encounters: black women and girls undoubtedly knew they risked being assaulted if they denied their aggressors' demands. Moreover, white men apparently faced little chance of prosecution for rape. Bureau agents usually mentioned such incidents in passing with little elaboration and generally did not follow through with investigations or arrests. Local white authorities either ignored the crimes or followed Mayor Ruff's example and abetted the men's escape from prosecution. Sexual violence constituted one of the more tragic aspects of Reconstruction in Lexington.

Throughout 1867 and 1868, relations between Lexington's blacks and whites grew ever more tense. In July 1868 a group of African Americans traveled from Lexington to Collierstown, a small village ten miles away, to make political speeches to black residents there about the elections that, it was expected, would soon be taking place. The speakers were "surrounded and chased" by a large group of white men. As Freedmen's Bureau agent Frazar reported, "so many men were hiding in the bushes and riding on the roads after dark that the Freedmen abandoned their [wagon] and took to the woods for safety." The mob searched for the black speakers as they fled back to Lexington— but failed to find them. Among the white men were several prominent Lexington residents, including W. W. Scott and future Virginia governor Charles T. O'Ferrall. According to Frazar's report, several blacks spotted O'Ferrall in the mob; he had recently taken over the Lexington Hotel, and he entered Washington College to study law in the fall of 1868. Scott vented his frustration by locking up the Lexington freedmen's school building with his own key. The school was soon reopened, but the incident shows that Lexington's whites understood the importance of the school to the black community. When unable to physically punish African Americans for asserting their political rights, whites attacked a symbol of blacks' nascent freedom—their school.[22]

In antebellum Virginia, a state law had outlawed schools for black residents. When the proscription ended with Union victory in the Civil War, freedpeople enthusiastically flocked to newly founded schools. Education was a practical goal, but it meant much more to Southern blacks than learning to read and write. Freedpeople's schools embodied one of the fundamental elements of emancipation: by attending school, freedpeople rejected the mental imprisonment attempted by their former owners. Moreover, black schools came to represent African Americans' agency and assertiveness. The Lexington school building became a focal point for the black community, where students of all ages received instruction, political meetings took place, and social events provided entertainment.

As a symbol of black independence, however, the school became a target for Lexington whites' angry—and sometimes violent—response to a new postwar reality. The last Freedmen's Bureau agent in Lexington, John W. Jordan, lamented the deteriorating state of race relations there in 1868. Jordan recognized "the deeply seated hatred

198 JOHN M. McCLURE

cherished toward the [black] race by these [students and cadets] and the *quiet* encouragement and support given it by the citizens residing here."[23] Moreover, the students received ambiguous signals from their beloved General Lee. Lee expelled violent students for personal and pragmatic reasons, and he genuinely cautioned them against "lawlessness." Yet he testified before the Joint Committee on Reconstruction that Virginia would be improved by the removal of its black population. While the general cultivated a conciliatory posture in the Northern press, he wrote to friends, family, and former comrades that the Confederate cause was just. Indeed, despite the contentions of Lee's hagiographers, the general remained an unreconstructed Southern nationalist after the war—and his opinions were widely circulated in the South.[24] Lee publicly denounced the intimidation of blacks and missionaries that occurred in Lexington, but his "boys" were almost certainly aware of his political views. And, despite Lee's protests, the students continued to deliver an emphatic message to the black community rejecting their civil and political rights.

Notes

1. W. L. Coan to Rev. George Whipple, 12, 25 December 1865, Virginia Field Records, American Missionary Association Archives, Amistad Research Center, New Orleans, Louisiana. The author consulted a microfilmed copy of the Virginia records of the AMA at the Library of Virginia in Richmond. Hereafter, these records will be referred to as "AMAA-VA" with writer, recipient, and date of the letter or report noted.

2. Eric Foner, *Reconstruction: America's Unfinished Revolution, 1863–1877* (New York, 1988), 144–46.

3. Joe Richardson, *Christian Reconstruction: The American Missionary Association and Southern Blacks, 1861–1890* (Athens, Ga., 1986), 3–5, 12, 95–96, 204–5.

4. The AMA and Freedmen's Bureau had many ties; both organizations were closely linked to the Congregational Church. Howard's superintendent of schools, John W. Alvord, was a Congregational minister. Rev. George Whipple, the corresponding secretary of the AMA, formed a close friendship with Howard, often advising him on a wide range of topics. See Ronald E. Butchart, *Northern Schools, Southern Blacks, and Reconstruction: Freedmen's Education, 1862–1875* (Westport, Conn., 1980), 102–3; Richardson, *Christian Reconstruction,* 76–77; and Robert C. Morris, *Reading, 'Riting, and Reconstruction: The Education of Freedmen in the South, 1861–1870* (Chicago, 1976), 48.

5. W. L. Coan to Rev. George Whipple, 12 December 1865, AMAA-VA.

6. Ibid.; E. C. Johnston, Teacher's Monthly Report for Jan. 1866, AMAA-VA.
7. W. L. Coan to Rev. George Whipple, 12 December 1865; E. C. Johnston to Rev. Samuel Hunt, 28 February 1866; J. A. Shearman to Rev. Samuel Hunt, 5 February, 31 March 1866, AMAA-VA; Michael Fellman, *The Making of Robert E. Lee* (New York, 2000), 250–51.
8. Lieutenant Tubbs to R. E. Lee, 27 January 1866, and to F. H. Smith, 27 January 1866, Letters Sent and Orders Issued, Lexington Office of the Bureau of Refugees, Freedmen, and Abandoned Lands, Record Group 105, Entry 4044, National Archives, Washington, D.C. (Hereafter, records from the Lexington Bureau office held in the National Archives will be referred to with appropriate designation of the type of record, followed by "Lexington Office, BRFAL, RG 105, Entry Number, NA.")
9. W. L. Coan to Rev. George Whipple, 12 December 1865, AMAA-VA.
10. Brevet Major Carse to Captain How, 1 May 1866, Reports of Operations and Conditions: Monthly Narrative Reports, January 1866–December 1868, Virginia records of the Bureau of Refugees, Freedmen, and Abandoned Lands, Record Group 105, National Archives Microfilm Publication 1048, roll 44, frames 692–93. (Hereafter, records of the Lexington Bureau office microfilmed by the staff of the National Archives will be referred to as "BRFAL-VA, RG 105, M-1048" followed by roll and frame number.)
11. W. L. Coan to Rev. Samuel Hunt, 9 December 1865; J. A. Shearman to William E. Whiting, 20 January 1866, E. C. Johnston to Rev. Samuel Hunt, 27 January, 28 February 1866, AMAA-VA.
12. W. L. Coan to Rev. George Whipple and Michael E. Strieby, 12 December 1865; E. C. Johnston to Rev. Samuel Hunt, 27 January 1866.
13. Teachers' Monthly School Reports, December 1869–January 1870, Records of the Superintendent of Education for the State of Virginia, Bureau of Refugees, Freedmen, and Abandoned Lands, 1865–70, National Archives Microfilm Publication 1053, roll 14, frames 143–44, roll 18, frame 370. (Hereafter, Virginia Bureau education records microfilmed by the staff of the National Archives will be referred to as "BRFAL-VA-ED, RG 105, M-1053" followed by roll and frame number.)
14. Captain Sharp to Gen. O. Brown, 31 May 1867, Unregistered Letters, April 1867–July 1868, BRFAL-VA-ED, M1053, roll 7, frame 177.
15. Captain Sharp to Captain Lacey, Monthly Narrative Report, 31 March 1867, BRFAL-VA, RG 105, M-1048, roll 44, frames 317–19, Douglas Southall Freeman, *R. E. Lee: A Biography* (New York, 1934–35), 4:316–17; Charles Bracelen Flood, *Lee: The Last Years* (Boston, 1981), 150–51.
16. E. C. Johnston wrote to Rev. Samuel Hunt on several occasions that a viable Republican Party was "absolutely necessary" for Virginia's blacks to gain political agency; he reportedly discussed politics with Lexington blacks many times. Additionally, Captain Sharp nominated Johnston as an electoral registering agent in 1867 upon Johnston's return from meetings in Richmond with

Republican officials, after being selected by Lexington blacks as their representative. See Johnston to Hunt, 30 April 1866, AMAA-VA; Captain Sharp to Captain Lacey, 29 May 1867, Press Copies, Lexington Office, BRFAL, RG 105, Entry 4046, NA; and the Lexington *Gazette and Banner,* 17 April 1867, 3.

17. Freeman, *Lee,* 4:346; Captain Sharp to Captain Lacey, 29 May 1867, Press Copies, Lexington Office, BRFAL, RG 105, Entry 4046, NA.

18. Douglas Frazar to Captain Lacey, Monthly Narrative Report, 29 February 1868, BRFAL-VA, RG 105, M-1048, roll 48, frames 746–47; Major Willcox to Douglas Frazar, 27 February 1868, Letters Received, Lexington Office, BRFAL, RG 105, Entry 4048, NA; Freeman, *Lee,* 4:345–48; and Flood, *Lee,* 176–78.

19. Captain Sharp to Captain Lacey, 28 February 1867, Monthly Narrative Report, BRFAL-VA, RG 105, M-1048, roll 48, frame 46.

20. Brevet Major Carse to Bvt. Maj. J. H. Remington, 14 June 1866, and endorsement by Inspector Neide, 26 June 1866, Letters Received, Lexington Office, BRFAL, RG 105, Entry 4048, NA.

21. Douglas Frazar to Captain Lacey, 31 August 1868, Monthly Narrative Report, BRFAL-VA, RG 105, M-1048, roll 49, Frame 588.

22. Douglas Frazar to Captain Lacey, 31 July 1868, ibid., frames 496–498; Lexington *Gazette and Banner,* 25 March 1868, 3; Minor T. Weisiger, "Charles T. O'Ferrall: 'Gray Eagle' from the Valley," in *The Governors of Virginia, 1860–1978,* eds. Edward Younger and James Tice Moore (Charlottesville, Va., 1982), 135–37. Elections to choose the governor, lieutenant governor, and attorney general were anticipated in Virginia in 1868, as well as a referendum on the state constitution written by the Underwood Convention, but Congress failed to authorize the contests until July 1869. See Richard Lowe, *Republicans and Reconstruction in Virginia, 1856–70* (Charlottesville, Va., 1991), 148–55, 172.

23. John W. Jordan to Captain Lacey, 31 October 1868, Monthly Narrative Report, BRFAL-VA, RG 105, M-1048, roll 49, frame 901.

24. The most cogent discussion of Lee's complex postwar mind-set is found in Fellman, *Making of Robert E. Lee,* 249–94; see also Alan T. Nolan, *Lee Considered: General Robert E. Lee and Civil War History* (Chapel Hill, N.C., 1991), 134–52.

Contested Unionism

⟋ᜤᜤ⟍

William Pattie and the Southern Claims Commission

SUSANNA MICHELE LEE

William Pattie, a white storekeeper living in Warrenton, Virginia, submitted a claim to the Southern Claims Commission for horses, cattle, wood, corn, and hay, property amounting to about $1,700 in his estimation. Congress established the commission in 1871 to compensate Southerners for their wartime losses. To qualify for an award, the commissioners required Southerners to prove their loyalty to the Union. In his defense, Pattie testified that he opposed secession and then, after the war, supported the Republican Party. Political rivals, however, challenged Pattie's claims to loyalty. In their decision, the commissioners applied their own standards of Southern loyalty. Their attempts to sort out Pattie's loyalty reveal the clash between Southern and Northern understandings of loyalty in the post–Civil War South.

After Confederate armies surrendered in the field, new battles emerged over the terms upon which Southerners would reenter the Union. Northern Democrats favored a policy of forgiveness for former Confederates, but Northern Republicans, who controlled Congress until after the 1874 elections, feared the return of their former enemies to power. For that reason, Congress limited the full benefits of citizenship to Unionists in the postwar South. Only Union soldiers and their dependents received pensions from the federal government. During Reconstruction, military commanders and congressmen routinely restricted local, state, and federal offices to Southerners who swore loyalty oaths to the U.S. government. Congress reserved compensation for wartime property losses to Southerners who proved their loyalty to the Union. In sum, bearing the reputation of a loyal citizen carried both economic and political benefits in the postwar South.

What constituted a loyal citizen in the South? Northerners and Southerners frequently disagreed over the line between loyal citizens and disloyal rebels. Claims by Southerners for compensation for property taken by the Union army during the Civil War offer an excellent opportunity to examine the differing conceptions of loyalties held by Northerners and Southerners. In establishing the Southern Claims Commission, Congress specifically limited compensation to "loyal citizens."[1] The task of defining loyalty was left to the three Northern men who presided over the commission.

The commissioners understood the "late rebellion" as an unconstitutional attempt by secessionists to overthrow the Union. They judged Southerners as traitors, whites guilty of disloyalty by virtue of their residence in the "so-called Confederate States."[2] Placing the burden of proof on Southerners, the commissioners required claimants to present evidence to refute their automatic categorization as disloyal. In addition, the commissioners employed a specific definition of loyalty, known as "iron-clad" Unionism, which required the claimant's support of the Union from secession to surrender. In cases where investigators uncovered evidence inconsistent with their version of loyalty, the commissioners quickly discerned fraud or fabrication. They denounced the impudence of rebels posing as Unionists to cheat the federal government.

While the commissioners understood the Union war effort primarily as a repudiation of secession, Southerners offered alternate interpretations of the war. White women indicted the war for its tragic death toll, among which numbered their husbands, sons, friends, and neighbors. Former slaves and free blacks identified the Civil War as a war for their freedom and the abolition of slavery. Some nonslaveholders depicted the war as a continuation of their ongoing conflict with wealthy slaveholders. Moving beyond a simple determination of guilt or innocence, clashes between claimants and commissioners reveal divergent understandings of loyalty. The commission therefore operated as a forum for debate over Northern and Southern definitions of loyalty.

Most historians turn to the records of the commission as sources on the war and only situate the records in the postwar period as a caution against the biases of the testimony as accurate depictions of the war. Yet the "biases" of the sources can serve as opportunities as well as problems. The commission's records reveal the interaction between wartime and postwar perspectives. Commissioners questioned claimants and witnesses on events after the passage of five, ten, even twenty years, a stretch long enough to strain the recollections of even the most diligent diarist. As a result, wartime memories carried their own history, as the passage of time adapted old perspectives to new circumstances and brought new significance to formerly inconsequential events.

Iron-clad loyalty to the Union was nearly impossible to maintain in many areas of Virginia. In fact, strongly secessionist communities rarely tolerated dissent from the Confederate cause. As a consequence, many Virginians who had initially opposed the war felt obliged to hide their opposition to the war and render aid to the Confederate cause. Maintaining steadfast loyalty to the Union was particularly difficult in heavily contested areas that alternated between Union and Confederate command.

Many Virginians who could not meet the standards of iron-clad Unionism nonetheless still felt justified in making claims of loyalty. Because Virginia had been reluctantly drawn into the war, many Virginians did not need to invent conversations or events to make their claims to loyalty. Claimants remembered their skepticism of the success of the Confederacy, their dissatisfaction with the Davis government, and their frustration with the casualties of the war. They remembered feeding hungry Union soldiers, nursing their wounded, and aiding Confederate deserters and forgot their resentment toward the imposition. In comparing their positions with those of the devoted secessionists in their neighborhoods, Virginia's claimants felt they could present a compelling case for their loyalty.

Because Virginians blurred the lines between loyalty and disloyalty, both during the war to survive Confederate and Union hostility and after the war to reap the benefits of postwar citizenship, their state presents an intriguing opportunity to explore definitions of loyalty in the postwar South.[3] The claim of William Pattie reveals the extent to which Northern commissioners altered their definitions of loyalty to accommodate Southern perspectives, but it also reveals the continuing disjunction between perspectives. The complicated notions of loyalty in the South did not fit within the confines of "iron-clad" Unionism.

Like many claimants, Pattie testified that he "vehemently opposed . . . secession and the war," that he "spoke against it as long as it was safe for me to speak," and that he "exerted all my influence in favor of the preservation of the union." Pattie's assertions amounted to the routine assertions of hundreds of other self-identified Unionists in Virginia. Had the commissioners decided Pattie's case on that basis, they could have readily approved his claim.[4] But Pattie encountered several obstacles in prosecuting his claim.

First, the poll books for Fauquier County listed Pattie as approving Virginia's Ordinance of Secession, even though he insisted that he had not voted on the question at all. Pattie argued that, though he did not approve of secession, the hostility generated by a vote consistent with his principles would have been of such proportions that "I doubt if I could have remained in the community." During the war, Warrenton had been a strong secessionist community. For this reason, he asserted that he voted neither for secession nor against it.[5]

Even a vote for secession would have been a familiar story and forgivable circumstance to the commissioners.[6] Stories from claimants revealed the atmosphere of terror within which white Virginians made their decisions regarding loyalty. For many whites, the question of loyalty was more than a matter of a simple vote for or against secession. Over and over again, claimants from Virginia argued that it would not have been safe for them to speak, let alone act, against secession or the war. Virginians testifying before the commission vividly detailed the difficulties awaiting those who openly supported the Union. Confederates threatened to hang Unionists and would-be Unionists, to burn their homes and destroy their possessions, and to drive them from the community.

Stories of the harassment experienced by Unionists in Virginia forced the commissioners to recalibrate the standard of loyalty they could reasonably expect a Southern Unionist to meet. The commissioners originally had little sympathy for excuses by claimants that hostile Confederates had forced them into disloyal acts. But with only a year's experience with the claims, the commissioners realized that Confederates plagued some areas with "so much terrorism and intimidation that loyal men felt a constant and oppressive apprehension of lawless violence." To escape these dangers, the commissioners concluded, "men who were at heart true friends of the Union felt compelled to appear friendly to the confederate cause and to do disloyal acts."[7] In accordance with this new realization, the commissioners occasionally excused a vote for secession or conscription in the Confederate army and, more often, excused contributions of food, clothing, or money to the Confederate cause.

The commissioners' broadened definition of coercion meant that poll books showing Pattie's vote for secession did not necessarily brand him as disloyal if he could provide an adequate excuse. Pattie offered a complex explanation as to why his recorded vote for secession should not be viewed as evidence of disloyalty to the Union. According to Pattie, as he left the polling place after voting on another measure, William Gaines, one of the judges of the election, detained him and demanded to know why he had not voted on the secession question. Pattie replied that he did not believe in the right of secession. When asked what he did believe in, he told Gaines that he believed in what he called "the right of revolution if a man or a party felt oppressed." Though Pattie advocated revolution, he cautioned that in exercising their "inherent right," revolutionaries "must take the consequences." Pattie told the commissioners that disunion carried too great a cost. He testified that "no man, nor set of men, had any legal right to destroy the government."[8]

In advocating revolution, Pattie attempted to manipulate Gaines and other secessionists. "Revolution" had been a word on the lips of many Virginians, particularly secessionists. A letter reprinted in the Warrenton newspaper just before the vote invoked "revolution" in support of the secessionists' cause: "Many of our people do not believe in what is called the 'right of secession,' but they all maintain the right of revolution, and they are all agreed that the time has come to exercise it."[9] With this argument, the letter writer supported the vote for the separation of Virginia from the Union, reframing this act, not as an act of "secession," but an act of "revolution." Invoking the patriotic actions of the founding fathers, secessionists hoped to portray separation from the Union as less unprecedented than the word "secession" seemed to suggest. Pattie's private understanding of revolution, however, did not coincide with the letter writer's, because he did not view secession as an acceptable form of revolution. In using the word "revolution" without clarifying his definition, Pattie hoped to mislead secessionists. Pattie's carefully chosen words during the secession vote and his subsequent explanation of them before the commission suggest that he attempted to capitalize on semantic differences to maintain simultaneously his principles and his safety.

During the war, this strategy succeeded. Pattie certainly had confused Judge Gaines, who provided his own account of the vote. In his deposition before the Southern Claims Commission, Gaines testified that he had asked Pattie if he wished to vote for secession. According to Gaines, Pattie avoided his question by responding that "I vote for revolution." Gaines replied that he considered secession a "minor offence compared with revolution." Gaines then offered that "I should enter his vote for the ratification of the ordinance of Secession," to which Pattie "made no objection." Gaines admitted that Pattie had not asked for his vote to be recorded as favoring secession, but that Gaines had entered Pattie's vote for secession "with his assent, as I supposed." When pressed upon his logic in recording the vote, Gaines explained that the "vote on the question of Secession was taken 'for' or 'against'" and that the "question of revolution was not a question voted; and no one voted for it but Mr Pattie at the Warrenton precinct." Gaines allowed Pattie to leave without further harassment.[10]

Special Commissioner Isaac Baldwin weighed in on behalf of Pattie. Though their primary duty consisted of taking depositions in a claimant's locality, special commissioners occasionally forwarded their recommendations regarding loyalty to the commissioners in Washington, D.C., who then ruled on the claims. Special Commissioner Baldwin granted Pattie's account of May 23 the "fullest credit," but found Gaines's testimony "evasive" and "ambiguous." Noting that Gaines "appeared very fearful of saying something that would reflect on his official action as Judge of the election," Baldwin concluded that the judge had recorded the vote for secession without Pattie's authorization. Such an occurrence had not been unusual in the Warrenton polls, Baldwin informed the commissioners, as "Several others who are recorded for Secession (who have no claims before the commission) declare emphatically that they did not vote at all." Baldwin identified Pattie as "among the first and highest with the loyal element" and praised him as a "Sterling Loyalist."[11] In this way, the special commissioner advised the commissioners to excuse the first obstacle to the successful prosecution of Pattie's claim.

Pattie encountered a second obstacle in the complications of postwar Virginia politics, however—in rivals in the postwar grab for political power. John S. Mosby and his associates in Warrenton charged Pattie with disloyalty to the Union. The dispute between Pattie and Mosby represented a postwar battle for control over the direction of Virginian politics fought within the Southern Claims Commission.

During the war, Mosby had gained fame as the commander of a Confederate guerrilla force known as the Rangers. Virginians remembered Mosby's wartime activities well. Some claimants identified him as the commander ordering their arrest during the war. Others cited his confiscations as evidence of Confederate harassment. Following the war, Mosby returned to Warrenton to resume his antebellum law practice and participate in local, state, and national politics. Unfortunately for William Pattie, part of Mosby's political dealings included giving the Southern Claims Commission the benefit of his opinion on the loyalty, or in Pattie's case, the disloyalty of claimants.[12] In his testimony, Pattie had accused Mosby of targeting him for harassment on account of his Unionist principles. In a deposition taken by a special investigator, Mosby asserted that his confiscation policies targeted both Union and Confederate sympathizers. During the war, he impressed crops from a large number of men who were as earnest Confederates as himself. Regardless, said Mosby, he could not have targeted Pattie for his political sympathies, for he had never heard of Pattie as a Union man. To further undermine Pattie's claims of Unionism, Mosby reported that Pattie's iron-clad oath generated great surprise in the community.[13]

In response, Pattie and his witnesses charged that Mosby's insinuations of disloyalty were politically motivated. Pattie wrote to the commissioners that a "*few* men here who have a dislike for me, on account of my being before and during the War, in favour of the Union and since the War . . . fully identified with the Republican party." Pattie stressed, "It has cost me *no little* to occupy my present position—as a Republican in this County and State."[14] According to John Withers, Mosby first attempted control of the Conservative faction.[15] Withers believed that, when unsuccessful in that effort, Mosby "undertook to engineer the republican party" but "found Mr Pattie in his way." James Chilton credited Pattie as "the first man who made any move to organize the loyal element into a party after the war, and that whatever was done was effected through his instrumentality; and that he is, and has ever since been, the organized head of the republican party in this county." Mosby unsuccessfully attempted to oust Pattie from his position as chairman of the Republican county committee.[16]

The end of the war brought a struggle for political power in communities across the South. In Virginia, Unionists rallied around the "Union Republican" party, while former Confederates constituted themselves under the banner of the Conservative party. Considerable internal disagreements characterized each party. Republicans in Virginia soon lost control of the state government. In 1870 a compromise between Virginia Conservatives, congressmen, and President Ulysses S. Grant allowed Virginia to reenter the Union with a constitution that mandated full manhood suffrage, including blacks and former Confederates alike.[17]

Though Republicans had lost control of their state government, they continued campaigning and organizing, hoping for a resurgence for their party. They fought for a revolutionary settlement to the Civil War and for a genuine reconstruction of Virginian society. Antebellum Virginia had benefited wealthy slaveholders. In postbellum Virginia, Pattie wanted to bring a new elite to power. He sought to redeem the South from the grasp of former slaveholders and secessionists.

An exchange between Pattie and one of Mosby's political allies in Warrenton reveals Pattie's struggle to effect a transformation in Southern society. William Bootwright told an investigator for the commission that at the outset of the war, the community regarded Pattie as "a good southern man," but toward the end Bootwright heard talk "on the street that he had changed his sentiments." Pattie responded that "I did mingle with the rebels while waiting for news, and

I was a good southern man." But Pattie employed an altogether different definition than the one used by his challengers: "I was a good
southern man but not a southern sympathizer, nor a rebel." As Pattie's
attorney explained, "he evidently does not mean by this anything
more than that he considered himself a friend to the . . . true interests
of the South."[18]

So what *did* Pattie consider to be the true interests of the South? In
his claim, Pattie suggested that nonslaveholders like himself had been
oppressed by the slaveholding elite. Though the vote on the Ordinance of Secession has garnered the most attention during the election on May 23, 1861, the Virginia Convention submitted another
vote to the people that day. Pattie braved the polls on May 23 to redis-
tribute the balance of power between nonslaveholders and slaveholders. For taxation purposes, the 1851 Virginia constitution had ex-
empted slaves under the age of twelve and had specified a maximum
valuation of $300 on nonexempted slaves. Rising slave prices meant
that slaveholders accumulated wealth without a proportionate increase in taxes. Nonslaveholders, especially those in the neglected
northwestern region, expressed increasing dissatisfaction with the in-
equitable tax system. Slaveholding whites, by contrast, opposed tam-
pering with tax provisions, which combined with Virginia's mixed system of representation, provided slaveholders a disproportionate
amount of economic and political power.[19]

The taxation measure passed by the Virginia Convention of 1861,
the so-called "Secession Convention," addressed the longstanding
grievances of nonslaveholding westerners. The proposed amendment
declared: "Taxation shall be equal and uniform throughout the Commonwealth, and all property shall be taxed in proportion to its value."[20]
While other opponents of secession remained safely at home, Pattie
risked going to the polls, not to vote on the Ordinance, but to shift the
burden of taxation toward the slaveholding elite.

White witnesses did not offer much comment on Pattie's views
toward slaveholders and the institution of slavery. This aspect of Pattie's claim was clearest in the testimony of his black witnesses, who
were accustomed to thinking in these terms. Even though the commissioners asked no questions about the institution of slavery,
black Southerners emphasized its role in the war. For blacks in post-

war Virginia, the Civil War was more about slavery and race than secession or state's rights. Ex-slaves told agents of the Southern Claims Commission that they believed that a Union victory would bring their freedom and that they regarded Union soldiers as their friends. Blacks favored the Union side, because they believed that the Union army would end slavery and bestow the rights of citizenship.

Though white witnesses mentioned Pattie's abolitionist reputation, black witnesses identified specific incidences as evidence of Pattie's loyalty.[21] Lawson Craig told the special commissioner that Pattie and his family were called "bad names on account of not having slaves and for speaking against slavery." Another black witness, Thomas Hudnall, related that Pattie "was called an Abolitionist before the war by the southern people," but more important, "proved himself such" to the satisfaction of "the colored people." According to William Patterson, Pattie gained the confidence of the black community with "the way he treated me & other colored people." Patterson testified that during the war Pattie warned blacks about impending threats from white Southerners. He credited Pattie with saving him from white retaliation for using his livery business to aid escaping slaves. Hudnall regarded Pattie as "about the only white man we could go to in confidence for information and advice" about the war.[22]

Much of the testimony from blacks followed these lines—hostility from whites for his "abolitionist" sentiments and gratitude from blacks for his advice. Had the commissioners asked the black witnesses about their postwar relations with Pattie, they may have been able to make a stronger case for Pattie's Unionism. Because the commissioners didn't ask about the postwar period, the only information from these years came from one witness who fit it in himself. William Patterson testified that he had heard that Pattie protected black men when they registered for the vote.[23] Of course, the commissioners were interested primarily in wartime Unionism and not postwar Unionism. But Pattie's wartime Unionism may not have meant as much to the black community as his postwar efforts on their behalf. In all likelihood, Pattie's reputation for Unionism among the black community became most established after the war.

Despite stories of antebellum abolitionism and postbellum Unionism, the commissioners decided Pattie's case solely on the issue of secession. Despite the assertions of Pattie, his attorney and witnesses, and even the special commissioner, the commissioners remained skeptical of Pattie's opposition to secession. Without additional indications of disloyalty, the commissioners might have ruled in Pattie's favor as they had in many other cases, but the charges of Mosby and his political allies cast an impression of suspicion on the whole claim. The commissioners noted: "We must regard the record as true, and regard him as properly recorded as voting for secession."[24] Pattie's postwar Republicanism, often cited by individuals within the Warrenton community as the culmination of his wartime loyalty, was completely ignored by the commissioners. After all, the case of John S. Mosby, who had famously cast his loyalties with the Republican Party, demonstrated that even the most devoted Rebels could experience a change of heart.

The case of William Pattie reveals the disjunction between claimants and commissioners over the characteristics of the Southern Unionist. In his claim before the commission, Pattie made a case for understanding the Civil War as the culmination of an ongoing political struggle between the nonslaveholding majority of whites and a slaveholding elite. In choosing sides in this struggle, Pattie befriended slaves and free blacks before the war and promoted the interests of the Republican Party after the war. In the reconstruction that followed, with the slave power finally crushed, Pattie hoped to emerge with the political clout he had previously been denied. Though the commissioners adapted their questions to include unexpected categories of Southern Unionists and to account for intimidation by secessionists, they retained their basic framework for understanding the Civil War and Southern Unionism. The commissioners conceived of the war as a conflict to defeat Southern secession rather than to overthrow the Southern slave power. With this understanding, the commissioners ruled Pattie disloyal to the Union and disallowed his claim.

Pattie's plight mirrored the fate of many white Republicans across the South. Only a few Northern Republicans extended substantial support to their Southern brethren. Republican congressmen from the North had little confidence in their Southern colleagues in the House and Senate. Republicans from the South occupied few influential leadership positions in Congress. Most Northern Republicans believed that Unionists, an implicitly white group, constituted only a small minority in the South that would never attain power in the South without the collaboration of blacks. By 1877, when the commissioners finally ruled on Pattie's claim, President Rutherford B. Hayes removed the support of the army from the last remaining Republican governments in the South. Long marginalized as members of the Republican Party, Southern Republicans felt abandoned by the federal government.[25] In losing his case before the Southern Claims Commission, in being ruled "disloyal," Pattie lost another battle for the Union he envisioned.

Though ostensibly a forum for uncovering wartime sentiments and activities, the operation of the Southern Claims Commission cannot be extracted from its context in the postwar South. In bringing together Northerners and Southerners, blacks and whites, and Confederates and Unionists into the same forum, the commission allows historians to uncover the process of reunion in intimate detail.[26]

Virginians continued wartime conflicts over loyalty to both community and nation into the postwar period. As these conflicts demonstrated, the Confederate surrender at Appomattox and the restoration of Virginia to the Union did not settle the meaning of the war or the course of reunion. Even as former Confederates took control of state politics in Virginia, former nonslaveholders still hoped that the failed rebellion of the secessionist and slaveholding minority would bring the loyalists to power. At the same time, former slaves and free blacks spoke of the Civil War as a war for freedom and wanted Confederate defeat to bring their full rights of citizenship. In the years after the Civil War, Virginians continued their struggles to effect their own versions of reconstruction in line with their interpretations of the war.

Notes

1. On the creation of the Southern Claims Commission, see Frank W. Klingberg, *The Southern Claims Commission* (Berkeley, Calif., 1978), the only book-length treatment. Congress limited compensation to commissary and quartermaster stores and excluded claims for damages, rent, and other kinds of property.

2. The commissioners of the Southern Claims Commission referred to the "late rebellion" and "so-called Confederate states" throughout their questionnaires

for claimants and witnesses. The questionnaires are reprinted in U.S. Congress, House of Representatives, First General Report of the Commissioners of Claims, 42nd Cong., 2nd sess., 1871, H. Doc. 16; Second General Report of the Commissioners of Claims, 42nd Cong., 3rd sess., 1872, H. Doc. 12; and Fourth General Report of the Commissioners of Claims, 43rd Cong., 2nd sess., 1874, H. Doc. 18.

3. As the major battleground of the Civil War, Virginians had encountered more than their share of hungry Union as well as Confederate soldiers. Almost four thousand Virginians submitted petitions to the commission for these supplies, the second largest group of claimants following Tennesseans. Virginians submitted 3,731, though Congress barred 534 claims for which the claimants had not submitted evidence. Of the 3,197 claims prosecuted by Virginians, the commissioners allowed approximately 907, or 28 percent—not far from the 30 percent for the Southern states as a whole. See tables 7 and 8 in Klingberg, *Southern Claims Commission*, 174–75.

4. Example are the claims of John Brown of Culpeper County, Jesse Butler of Clarke County, David M. Firestone of Botetourt County, John Haley of Culpeper County, Thomas Harmon of Alleghany County, James B. Kirk of Culpeper County, and Archibald Shaw of Culpeper County, all in Allowed Claims, Southern Claims Commission, RG 217, NA (hereafter cited as Allowed Claims).

5. William A. Pattie deposition, 18 November 1873, William A. Pattie Claim, Disallowed Claims, RG 217, NA (hereafter WPC/DC).

6. Example are the claims of Sam Lipes of Botetourt County, Hugh Morson of Caroline County, and William F. Stolle of Clarke County, all in Allowed Claims. Very much like Pattie, Lipes asserted that the poll books incorrectly listed him as voting for secession; had two sons in Confederate service against his advice; suffered from Confederate harassment; harbored Union men; served in the Reconstruction government; and took the iron clad oath. The commissioners found Lipes loyal the year after they ruled on Pattie's claim.

7. Second General Report of the Commissioners of Claims, 42nd Cong., 3rd sess., 1872, H. Doc. 12, p. 5.

8. William A. Pattie deposition, 18 Nov. 1873, WPC/DC.

9. "Patriotic Letter," Warrenton *Flag of 98*, 21 May 1861.

10. William Gaines deposition, 18 November 1873, WPC/DC.

11. Special Commissioner Isaac Baldwin Remarks, n.d., WPC/DC.

12. See James L. Gardner Claim, Loudoun County, Va., Allowed Claims. Mosby's dealings with the Southern Claims Commission are also mentioned in "Personal," *Harper's Weekly*, 10 May 1873, 387.

13. John S. Mosby deposition, n.d., WPC/DC.

14. William A. Pattie to the commissioners of Southern claims, 23 July 1875, WPC/DC.

15. John Withers deposition, 21 September 1876, WPC/DC. Withers may have

been referring to Mosby's support of James Lawson Kemper of Orange County for governor of Virginia in 1873. He and James Barbour, a prominent lawyer from Culpeper, encouraged Kemper to ally with the Grant administration after his victory. Under pressure from Democrats, Kemper abandoned plans for coalition. After this defection, Mosby never spoke with Kemper again. Virgil Carrington Jones, *Ranger Mosby* (Chapel Hill, N.C., 1944), 293–94; Jack P. Maddex Jr., *The Virginia Conservatives, 1867–1879* (Chapel Hill, N.C., 1970), 135–38.

16. James Chilton deposition, 21 September 1876, WPC/DC.

17. Louis Moore, "The Elusive Center: Virginia Politics and the General Assembly, 1869–1871," *VMHB* 103 (April 1995): 210–12; Maddex, *Virginia Conservatives*, 57–60.

18. William Bootwright deposition, 15 July 1875; George C. Round brief on loyalty, 25 November 1876, WPC/DC.

19. For taxes on slaves, see Daniel W. Crofts, *Reluctant Confederates: Upper South Unionists in the Secession Crisis* (Chapel Hill, N.C., 1989), 159–60. William Shade argues that "in the short run the greatest threat posed to planter power was not the abolition of slavery but the taxation of their slave property" (*Democratizing the Old Dominion: Virginia and the Second Party System, 1824–1861* [Charlottesville, Va., 1996], 286).

20. For mention of the taxation amendment, see "Ordinance," Warrenton *Flag of 98*, 9 May 1861. Pattie submitted a notarized copy of the amendment in his claim. For the importance of the slavery issue at the Virginia convention in 1861, see William W. Freehling, "The Editorial Revolution, Virginia, and the Coming of the Civil War: A Review Essay," chapter 1 in his *The Reintegration of American History: Slavery and the Civil War* (New York, 1994).

21. For white witnesses who mentioned Pattie's reputation for abolitionism, see Edward Cologne deposition, 21 September 1876, and Holland George deposition, 18 November 1873, WPC/DC.

22. Lawson Craig deposition, 18 November 1873; Thomas Hudnall deposition, 21 September 1876; William Patterson deposition, 29 March 1877, WPC/DC.

23. William Patterson deposition, 29 March 1877, WPC/DC.

24. Summary Report, 1877, WPC/DC. In making their decision, the commissioners ignored Pattie's stories of his role within the African American community, his white witnesses' evaluations of his sentiments, and his postwar Unionism. Although the commissioners acknowledged that Pattie nurtured abolitionism, they did not find such sentiments sufficient to prove his Unionism; they disregarded the black witnesses who testified to Pattie's stalwart Unionism in favor of white government witnesses like William Bootwright and John S. Mosby.

25. Richard H. Abbott, *The Republican Party and the South, 1855–1877* (Chapel Hill, N.C., 1986).

26. On reunion and the meaning of the Civil War, see David W. Blight, *Race and*

Reunion: The Civil War in American Memory (Cambridge, Mass., 2001); Paul Herman Buck, *The Road to Reunion, 1865–1900* (Boston, 1937); Jim Cullen, *The Civil War in Popular Culture: A Reusable Past* (Washington, D.C., 1995); Gaines M. Foster, *Ghosts of the Confederacy: Defeat, the Lost Cause, and the Emergence of the New South, 1865 to 1913* (New York, 1987); Rollin G. Osterweis, *The Myth of the Lost Cause, 1865–1900* (Hamden, Conn., 1973); Kirk Savage, *Standing Soldiers, Kneeling Slaves: Race, War, and Monument in Nineteenth-Century America* (Princeton, N.J., 1997); and Nina Silber, *The Romance of Reunion: Northerners and the South, 1865–1900* (Chapel Hill, N.C., 1993).

Navigating Modernity

The Bible, the New South, and Robert Lewis Dabney

MONTE HAMPTON

Robert Lewis Dabney died on January 3, 1898, and was buried at Hampden-Sydney College in Virginia, adjacent to the Presbyterian seminary where he had spent the better part of a lifetime. His professional life spanned the birth and death of the Confederate nation, and through the post–Civil War decades, he worked as an apprehensive midwife to its attempted cultural rebirth. The words his widow had inscribed on his monument attested to his importance in a land where the Bible, Confederate memory, and catastrophic change were among the fundamental verities of life: "Minister of the Gospel, Professor of Theology in Union Seminary, and of Philosophy in the University of Texas, Major in the Confederate Army, and Chief of Staff to Stonewall Jackson."[1]

As a seminarian, Dabney had trained numerous ministers, who, in turn, influenced whole congregations and Southern society. As a well-read theologian and intellectual, he had sought safely to steer two generations of Southerners through the treacherous currents of modern thought. Given his intimate association with sainted Stonewall Jackson—as his chaplain and also as his hagiographer—Dabney ostensibly wielded the cultural authority to pontificate on the bewildering multitude of questions relating religion, modern thought, and Southern culture. The last line of Dabney's epitaph—"Prove all things, hold fast to that which is good"—reminded the world that he had not shrunk from the task of navigating modernity.

For nearly half a century, Dabney tested modernity through the pages of scripture, and he found much of it wanting. He was, as his biographer put it, "at war with much in his age."[2] An alternate epitaph—suggested by his son but declined by his mother—summed up not only his characteristic pugnacity, but also his generally negative judgment of his times: "He was what he was. Let the Heathen rage."[3] Perhaps Dabney's oppositional bent and the long list of contemporary developments he resisted should suggest "antimodern" as a more fitting label than a navigator of modernity. Part of the problem lies in the definition of modernity, a word that has been defined with such variety as to render it an almost hopelessly vague term. Marshall Berman's analysis of the culture of modernity provides a useful starting point for studying the Southern experience of modernity. According to Berman, nineteenth-century modernism neither simply opposed nor favored the changes of modern life. Instead, it had a dynamic and dialectical relationship with these changes, alternately, often simultaneously, embracing their possibilities and regretting their dislocations. Modernists ambivalently longed to be "rooted in a stable and coherent personal and social past" while at the same time feeding their "insatiable desire for growth," whether personal, intellectual, or economic.[4]

Southern Presbyterians—like most Calvinist communities—had such an ambivalent relationship with modernity from the start.[5] They adhered to the Reformed doctrine of the perspicuity of the scriptures, which had legitimated the individual's questioning of papal tradition, thereby elevating the role of human reason in the acquisition of Bible knowledge. Moreover, since this conviction of perspicuity—implying as it did that all honest readers of the Bible would accede to its clear truths—collided with various forms of skepticism through the seventeenth, eighteenth, and early nineteenth centuries, a hallowed apologetic tradition had developed that further emphasized the importance of squaring reason and revelation. At the same time, however, the doctrine of *sola scriptura* (scripture alone) meant that the Bible was to be the rule of all faith and life, so the faithful must always vigilantly guard against modern, human encroachments on an ancient, divine standard.

This tension between the certainty and absolutism inherent in a book of eternally valid principles and the contingency and particularity inherent in apprehending and applying those principles by historically situated readers vitalized much of Southern Presbyterian thought, and it was alive and well in the mind of Robert L. Dabney.

While he might advise his readers to reject much of nineteenth-century philosophy, for instance, the rejection was accompanied by tedious (if sometimes tendentious) analysis of Comte, Mill, Darwin, and Spencer. Dabney's many responses to the late nineteenth-century South's diverse developments—social, intellectual, and theological—cast light on the ways educated Southern white believers thought. How they thought affected how they debated issues, and how they debated issues determined the way many well-informed religious Southerners would enter the twentieth century. In addition, Dabney's herculean effort to bring the Bible to bear on the society, culture, and thought of the late nineteenth-century South may serve as a case study on a hermeneutical challenge faced by nearly all Reformed communities—all the theological descendants of John Calvin—at any time: how to apply a revelation believed to be eternally and universally true to particular historical situations that differ from those in which it was first communicated.

While many other intellectual communities had affirmed the harmony of reason and revelation, for Southern Presbyterians this bedrock conviction had never faced a more serious challenge than in the turbulent decades after the Civil War. Indeed, the many late nineteenth-century conflicts within Southern Presbyterianism—in many ways coming to a head in the Southern Presbyterian evolution controversy of the 1880s—may represent the first full-fledged modernity crisis experienced by Southern intellectuals. While the earlier debates over slavery and scripture could certainly contend for this designation, few Southerners opposed proslavery orthodoxy. This near unanimity hindered genuine engagement, allowing for the facile dismissal of divergent views as so much alien fanaticism. By contrast, many of the late nineteenth-century developments Dabney addressed—such as novel scientific theories, the expansion of democracy, the rise of commerce, and public education—had garnered the support of fellow Southerners, even Southern Presbyterians who professed faithfulness to scripture as vociferously as Dabney did. Therefore, greater engagement was required, and these engagements exposed the latent tension between faithfulness to holy writ and reasonableness to human wit. Dabney saw these postbellum developments as nothing more than new manifestations of the same rationalistic spirit that vitalized abolitionism. To him, they were all of a piece.

Regarding the Southern experience of modernity, David Joseph Singal, in his excellent study of early twentieth-century Southern culture, argues that Southern intellectuals did not embrace modernity until the period between World War I and World War II. He maintains that, unlike the rest of the nation, modernity was delayed in the South by the New South program. Revitalizing the Cavalier myth, this movement gave new life to Victorianism, thereby postponing the Southern experience of modernity until the twentieth century, a full fifty years after Dabney's response to the New South. But the list of intellectuals whom Singal studies—literary figures, historians, and sociologists—is curiously free of theologians and preachers. Surely, one might legitimately question whether an average Southerner might have been more likely to read Faulkner or listen to an evangelical preacher. At the very least, it would certainly not be unreasonable to include religionists in a study of Southern culture.

Such an inclusion in a study of Southern modernity places the key historical moment about fifty years earlier. To be sure, Singal's chosen topic determines his subjects and his definition of modernity—the shift from Victorian innocence with its moralistic insistence upon "civilization" over against "savagery" toward the Modernist erasure of the distinction and its eagerness to "plumb the nether regions of the psyche." Robert Lewis Dabney probably qualifies as a good Victorian, but rather than *embrace* the New South program as a deterrent to the eclipse of Victorianism—as Singal's thesis would suggest he should— Dabney *opposed* it as a threat to the biblical civilization he defended.

A more promising basis for a definition of modernity than the "savagery" versus "civilization" dichotomy upon which Signal extensively relies is the epistemological clash between universality and particularity at work in the late nineteenth century. Singal himself notes that a shift from notions of solidity to notions of change and plasticity accompanied the shift from Victorianism to Modernism. The Southern Presbyterian experience shows that, for many Southerners, this tension between certainty and flux played out in the process of reading and applying the Bible. As old as the Protestant Reformation itself, the smoldering difficulties inherent in appealing to a universally applicable standard whose principles can only be appropriated by historically situated readers now erupted through the fractured world of late nineteenth-century Southerners.[6]

Many Americans—even many white Southerners—did not always find Dabney convincing. But he did speak for a number of influential conservative Southern Presbyterians—men like Benjamin M. Palmer and John L. Girardeau—who had augmented their cultural influence through their earlier defenses of the South and who linked all that was good in Southern culture with biblicism. From 1853 until 1883— when he left Union Seminary for a professorship in philosophy at the University of Texas[7]—Dabney's professorial chair at Union was the fount of perhaps the most elaborate postwar defense of Southern conservatism to claim the very word of God as its basis. As if replicating the reputed battlefield steadfastness of Stonewall Jackson, Dabney committed most of his mature years to the erection of a stonewall of Southern-biblicist apologetics. Though other Southern theologians also examined modernity through the prism of their religious convictions, Dabney perfected an apologia that identified biblical orthodoxy as the basis of Southern culture, and Southern culture as the protector of the authority of scripture. In doing so, he engaged such diverse concerns as racial amalgamation, Yankee commercialism, radical democracy, women's rights, public schools, philosophical empiricism, higher criticism of the Bible, and modern science.

According to Dabney, these disparate, dangerous aspects of modernity arose from deserting the Bible as the infallible standard of belief and practice. In the crucible of sectionalism and war, Dabney believed, only the South had remained faithful to Christianity. As each decade brought new threats, including—to Dabney's mind—the treasonable cry for a "New South," the role of theologian-apologist grew more critical. As a person entrusted with the training of future ministers, Dabney viewed his profession with gravity. A sound theological education, he would remind his fellow divines in 1883, conferred skill in detecting "error and sophism in false doctrines" and instilled "the Presbyterian and orthodox idiosyncrasy of mind."[8] Indeed, Dabney personified a Southern-biblicist apologia that developed among Southern Presbyterians from the sectional debates of the 1850s through the late nineteenth-century defenses of the Lost Cause as an attempt to restore to modernity its biblical bearings.

While historians have documented various forms of Southern opposition to the New South program, few have appreciated the strength and significance of this theological critique personified by Dabney. Eugene Genovese, for example, has minimized the importance of theological orthodoxy in the late nineteenth-century South altogether. While he eloquently stresses the importance of biblical orthodoxy in the antebellum period—seen by Southern theologians as the last, best hope for maintaining a Christian society that could enjoy all the blessings of modernity without being destroyed by its curses—Genovese minimizes the significance of biblical orthodoxy in Southern theologians' handling of modernity after the war. He argues that the South's defeat and assimilation into the larger transatlantic capitalist culture precipitated a retreat from orthodoxy in the postbellum decades.[9] While there can be little doubt that, between the Civil War and the turn of the twentieth century, theological orthodoxy declined, or was diluted, in the South much as throughout the trans-Atlantic Protestant world, the war hardly destroyed Southern orthodoxy. Rather, it augmented the already developing Southern-biblicist apologetic and, at least for a while, intensified orthodoxy. Southern Presbyterian theologians like Dabney, Palmer, and Girardeau went to their graves in the years around the turn of the century as both orthodox theologians and unreconstructed Southerners.

For other historians, like C. Vann Woodward, Paul Gaston, and Gaines Foster, religion—orthodox or otherwise—has been peripheral to the main sources of opposition to the New South ideology. Although Woodward acknowledges the pervasive religiosity of the South, his treatment of religious critiques of the New South is cursory, and, rather than exploring the theological dimensions of Dabney's work, dismisses him as a relic of the eighteenth century who was swept into "dustbin of the eighties." Charles Reagan Wilson does treat numerous Southern ministers of various denominations who opposed the New South movement from a religious perspective. His emphasis on a Southern civil religion does not, however, specifically account for the element of biblicism.[10]

From Dabney's perspective, the problem with most of modernity stemmed not from its newness but from its lack of biblical warrant. Since the theological debates over slavery and the Bible in the 1850s—when antislavery theologians had demurred on accepting the verdict of a commonsense, literalist reading of scripture—Dabney had viewed virtually every issue in terms of a stark dichotomy: rationalism versus revelation. An increasing trust in human reason was eclipsing the authority of scripture, and more often than not, this wicked hubris originated outside the South. This hardly meant, however, that none of the South's sons were culpable. In December 1886 Henry W. Grady, the Georgia-born editor of the *Atlanta Constitution-Journal*, delivered a speech before the New England Club of New York entitled "The New South." Grady was but one of a number of advocates of this ideology of the same name that had divided Southern intellectuals by the 1880s. The debate revolved, in part, around the values of the Old South. Though a love for the South animated both sides, the architects of the New South program advocated novelties such as commercialization, sectional reconciliation, public education, and racial harmony. Opponents, among them Dabney, held that such departures constituted an utter rejection of the eternally valid principles of the Old South.

Grady addressed his Northern audience from the same dais from which Daniel Webster had addressed it forty years earlier. And though a bloody, sectional war had intervened between the two speeches, Grady believed that Webster's antebellum call for reconciliation was as relevant as ever. "Standing hand to hand and clasping hands, we should remain united," he quoted Webster, "citizens of the same country, members of the same government, united, all united now and united forever." Grady affirmed one of the central planks of the New South platform when he declared Southern sectionalism moribund. "We have learned that one *Northern* immigrant is worth fifty foreigners," he assured them, "and have smoothed the path to Southward, wiped out the place where Mason's and Dixon's line used to be, and hung out the latchstring to you and yours." In place of a "dead" South of sectionalism, slavery, plantations, and oligarchy, he declared "living, breathing, growing every hour" a South of union, racial cooperation, commerce, and "perfect democracy." The hoary distinction between "Cavalier" and "Puritan" had terminated in the rise of "the American," of whom the ideal type was—of all people—Abraham Lincoln.[11]

Lincoln, Webster, the facile erasure of the Mason-Dixon line—such talk would have mortified the likes of Robert L. Dabney. Four years earlier, before the graduating class of Hampden-Sydney College, he had delivered a commencement address also entitled "The

New South." While he acknowledged that a new South was inevitable in the wake of military defeat and, therefore, must be accepted, Dabney hardly endorsed the tenets of Grady's discourse. For instance, he warned the students about the very expansion of democracy that Grady championed—a "new-fangled republicanism" that had been on the rise since the French Revolution and had incarnated itself across the Atlantic in the form of abolitionists, Yankee troops, the rise of "King Mob," and now black suffrage.[12]

Dabney's opposition to black suffrage (and blacks' education at public expense) doubtlessly flowed from a visceral commitment to white supremacy that—as Mark Noll has observed—Dabney scarcely attempted to support with scripture.[13] But the most fundamental divergence between the vision of Grady and that of Dabney—especially from the perspective of the latter—lay not in differences on any specific questions so much as in the role each allotted to God and the Bible in the postbellum South. While Grady certainly alluded to the divine, God appeared in his address mainly to bless the destruction of the old system. Indeed, Grady measured the worth of the New South not by anything like allegiance to a divine plan so much as the region's economic progress and independence.[14]

Dabney, by contrast, measured developments in the contemporary South by the degree to which they conformed to the word of God. Even in his speech on "The New South"—treating an ostensibly less theological topic than was the case in most of his other work—he challenged the listener to remember scripture. After cautioning against too hasty an adoption of novel political notions, for instance, he concluded, "Here in one word, is the safe pole-star for the 'New South.'" He went on, "let them adopt the *scriptural* politics, assured that they will ever be as true and just under any new regime as under the one that has passed away."[15] Whether he was addressing political economy; "women's rights"; the epistemology of Mill, Spencer, and Comte; or schemes to reconcile the book of Genesis with modern geology, Dabney's ratiocinations often finally appealed to a text of scripture.[16] He pointed his young Virginians back to the Bible, whence, he believed, all that was good in their section derived.

Although in Dabney's hands allegiance to scripture meant opposition to the New South creed, emphasizing God's will and God's role in Southern culture could also lead in a quite different direction. Atticus Haygood—Southern Methodist bishop, president of Emory College, and the "evangelical echo" of Henry Grady—espoused the New South in the name of God.[17] Two years before Dabney gave that commencement address at Hampden-Sydney, Haygood also delivered an oration entitled "The New South." But whereas Dabney extolled the Old South and rebuked its too hasty doomsayers, Haygood celebrated the end of sectionalism and slavery, which he regarded not as the biblically grounded social system but "an incubus upon every white man, woman, and child in the South." He called on white Southerners to aid downtrodden blacks and to develop the traits of "social toleration," hard work, and "industry."[18]

The difference between his assessment of the New South and that of Dabney could not have been greater; yet, Haygood's vision for the South hardly excluded God. Indeed, the healing of national wounds, already under way, was owed to the "Protestant religion." Hardly claiming that the Southern past was the apogee of divine approbation, Haygood pointed his audience forward: "We are to do the work of today, looking forward and not backward. We have no divine call to stand eternal guard by the grave of dead issues. Here certainly we may say, 'Let the dead bury their dead.'"[19] Such language bordered upon sacrilege in the mind of Dabney. Indeed, he may have been responding directly to Haygood's words when, approaching the conclusion of his own speech, he warned against those who say, "Let us bury the dead past. Its issues are all antiquated, and of no more practical significance. . . . We are in a new world. Its questions alone concern us." To these Dabney responded, "Be sure that the former issues are really dead before you bury them."[20]

For Dabney, many of these "issues" concerned faithfulness to the Bible, but the differences between Dabney and Haygood—both of whom revered scripture—stemmed in large part from different conceptions of what it *meant* to be faithful to scripture.[21] It was not so much Dabney's resolute adherence to the Bible but his hermeneutical assumptions—how its texts were to be interpreted and applied to modernity—that facilitated the Southern-biblicist conception of orthodoxy. Scripture, he told his Hampden-Sydney audience, was "the safe pole-star for the 'New South.'"[22] Of course, nearly all Protestants regarded the Bible as the Christian's guiding standard, but this choice

of metaphor did more than merely adorn the ubiquitous Protestant af-
firmation of *sola scriptura*. Rather, it manifested Dabney's assumption
that the truths of scripture were not conditioned by the vantage point
of the reader. No matter where he stood, the pole star would be as un-
varying to the theologian as the North Star appeared to the wander-
ing navigator. Differences between the historical context of an original biblical text and the sociocultural milieu of the modern believer
were virtually irrelevant. The questions facing the modern South may
have changed, but the answers were timeless.

Dabney's opposition to the establishment of the Virginia "common schools" in the 1870s illustrates this hermeneutical conviction. In
a written debate with William H. Ruffner, the superintendent of the
incipient public school system, Dabney made no allowances for social,
political, and pedagogical differences between the ancient Hebrews
and first-century Christians, on the one hand, and the modern American South, on the other. While Ruffner based his defense of public
education in part on general Protestant Christian sensibilities such as
the need for literacy to render scripture directly accessible, the broth-
erhood of all mankind, and Christian sympathy, Dabney argued that
the Bible plainly placed the responsibility of educating children on the
parents, not the state. It was as simple as that. He flatly declared, "Such
is the Protestant doctrine, the Bible doctrine." "It is the teaching of the
Bible," he said, "that the education of children belongs to the sphere of
the family."[23]

To be sure, the historically situated nature of biblical documents
was too obvious completely to escape the notice of Dabney's keen
theological eye. Indeed, he occasionally based his positions on nuanced
distinctions between the historical contexts, and therefore modern
applicability, of different biblical texts. In his opposition to the use of
instrumental music in Christian worship, for instance, he took pains
to point out that the Old Testament instances of such music did not
apply to Christian worship. "God set up in the Hebrew Church two
distinct forms of worship," Dabney wrote. One was "spiritual and universal, and therefore perpetual in all places and ages," while the other
(inclusive of instrumental music) was "peculiar" and "local."[24]

In his urgency to effect social, cultural, and intellectual compliance
with the universal standard of holy writ, Dabney often lost this dis-

tinction between the "universal" and "perpetual," on the one hand, and the "peculiar" and "local," on the other. This collapsing of herme-neutic distance between the original biblical context and the modern American South appeared first in Dabney's response to the crisis over antislavery. In reply, Dabney argued from the Old Testament record of slavery among the Hebrews, together with the absence of its repeal in the New Testament, that slavery could not be a *malum in se* (evil in and of itself). But he scarcely addressed differences between slavery as practiced in the nineteenth-century South and slavery as practiced among the ancient Hebrews, not least of which, as Mark Noll has noted, was the racial basis of American slavery.[25]

Neither did differences between the ancient contexts of the Bible and the modern South count for much in Dabney's numerous post-bellum political statements. An erstwhile admirer of John C. Calhoun and an advocate of limited government and circumscribed democratic participation, Dabney found the postwar expansion of democracy very disturbing. Referring to incessant "mob" calls for expanded suffrage as "Jacobin," "ultra-democratic," and "new-fangled republicanism," Dabney advocated a return to "scriptural politics." While it may be true that the Bible contained no accounts of the gaining of political franchise by the masses or by women, Dabney did not deign to explain why it also provided no precedent for anyone—male or female, elite or commoner—to vote in the first place.[26] Whether addressing poli-tics, the "peculiar institution," public education, or a host of other par-ticulars, Dabney tirelessly tried to hold his contemporaries to the uni-versal standard of the word of God. But in such efforts a stubborn irony emerged. The greater his ardor to universalize the biblical text—to diminish or deny its historical particularity—the more likely he was unwittingly to render it a captive of his own particular culture. In Robert Lewis Dabney's hands, the Bible often became South-bound.

Notes

Beth Barton Schweiger and Mitchell Snay contributed valuable critical insights that are reflected in the revised version of this paper.

1. Thomas Cary Johnson, *The Life and Letters of Robert Lewis Dabney* (Richmond, 1903), 539. The last line of the epitaph quoted 1 Thessalonians 5:21. In re-

sponse to my thesis that Dabney's theology was an attempt safely to "navigate modernity," Beth Barton Schweiger has suggested that it would be more accurate to say that Dabney "never left the dock." While I argue that Dabney and his ilk were but the ultraconservative wing of late nineteenth-century Southern Presbyterians—all of whom should be seen not as obscurantists, but as theologians laboring to engage modernity through the lens of scripture—Schweiger's eloquent comment captures Dabney's typical disapproval of his age.

2. Johnson, *Life and Letters of Robert Lewis Dabney*, 568.

3. David Henry Overy, "Robert L. Dabney: Apostle of the Old South" (Ph.D. diss., Univ. of Wisconsin, 1967), 322. William O. Harris and Paul Kemeny brought this alternate epitaph to my attention.

4. Marshall Berman, *All That Is Solid Melts into Air: The Experience of Modernity* (1982; rept. New York, 1988), 16, 35, 36.

5. I am indebted to Michael O'Brien, who in a private communication reminded me that Calvinism, from its inception, had taken modernity seriously.

6. See David Joseph Singal, *The War Within: From Victorianism to Modernism in Southern Thought, 1919–45* (Chapel Hill, N.C., 1982), 1–10, 94–96, 103, 202.

7. At the University of Texas, Dabney continued his apologetic work, though less prolifically.

8. Robert L. Dabney, "Thoroughly Educated Ministry," *Southern Presbyterian Review* (April 1883), reprinted in *Discussions Evangelical and Theological*, ed. C. R. Vaughn, vol. 2 (1890; rept. London, 1967), 676.

9. Eugene V. Genovese, *The Slaveholders' Dilemma: Freedom and Progress in Southern Conservative Thought, 1820–1860* (Athens, Ga., 1992), 6, 7; Genovese, *A Consuming Fire: The Fall of the Confederacy in the Mind of the White Christian South* (Athens, Ga., 1998), 79–89, 120, 121; and Genovese, "Religion in the Collapse of the American Union," in *Religion and the American Civil War*, eds. Randall M. Miller, Harry S. Stout, and Charles Reagan Wilson (New York, 1998), 80, 81.

10. C. Vann Woodward, *Origins of the New South, 1877–1913* (Baton Rouge, La., 1951), 172–74; Paul Gaston, *The New South: A Study in Southern Myth-Making* (Baton Rouge, La., 1970); Charles Reagan Wilson, *Baptized in Blood: The Religion of the Lost Cause, 1865–1920* (Athens, Ga., 1980), 79–99; Gaines Foster, *Ghosts of the Confederacy: Defeat, the Lost Cause, and the Emergence of the New South, 1865 to 1913* (New York, 1987), 48–62, 74, 75, 87. Foster classes Dabney with other "irreconcilables" who wielded little influence by the 1880s. Foster also sees a shift in the 1880s and 1890s in the way the Confederate Tradition was defined—from an earlier focus on the war itself and the heritage of Confederate military efforts to a later concern about commercialization, populist radicalism, racial liberals, and integration into national society. Foster recognizes Dabney's role in the earlier phase, but Dabney, in fact, combined both types of concerns and tied each to Southern faithfulness to scripture (Foster, *Ghosts*, 48–62, 74, 75, 87).

11. Henry Woodfin Grady, *The New South and Other Addresses* (1904; rept. New York 1969), 23, 27, 28, 32, 41, 42.

12. Robert L. Dabney, "The New South," in *Discussions by Robert L. Dabney,* ed. C. R. Vaughn, vol. 4 (1897; rept. Harrisonburg, Va., 1994), 10, 11, 17, 18.

13. Noll, "The Bible and Slavery," in Miller, Stout, and Wilson, *Religion and the American Civil War,* 64. Similarly, Genovese notes the general tendency of late nineteenth-century Southern preachers to resort to secular arguments—rather than scripture—to sustain racial segregation (*Consuming Fire,* 86, 120).

14. Grady, *New South and Other Addresses,* 38, 39.

15. Dabney, "New South," 16. The emphasis is mine.

16. His characteristic approach to the "theory of 'Women's Rights'" was to refer readers to numerous biblical passages he regarded as proof texts, and then to deduce that anyone "who reverences the Christian scriptures" could see that such theorizing is "sheer infidelity" (Dabney, "Nature Cannot Revolutionize Nature," *New York Independent,* 1 October 1873, in *Discussions* 4:471). In a book-length critique of the more doctrinaire expressions of nineteenth-century empiricism—*The Sensualistic Philosophy of the Nineteenth Century, Considered* (New York, 1875)—Dabney attacked all epistemologies denying humans innate ideas and asserting that all genuine knowledge was acquired via the senses alone. If sense perceptions were the only valid knowledge, Dabney reasoned, then all abstractions—even causation, which undergirded the biblical doctrine of teleology—were dubious. Such a positivist approach, he believed, lay at the bottom of many of the nefarious developments of modern times. Significantly, he stressed its contradiction of *biblical* doctrines regarding the human soul, eternal life, and divine design (ibid., 110, 112, 337, 338). And, though Dabney reiterated the standard disclaimer that the Bible was not written to teach natural science, his response to the numerous nineteenth-century schemes of accommodating the language of Genesis to the latest geological findings also revealed his conviction that the Bible should be taken for an authority in such matters. "Can the Scriptures," he asked, "be shown plastic enough to be remolded, without total fracture of their authority, into agreement with all these views?" See Dabney, "A Caution against Anti-Christian Science Criticized by Dr. Woodrow," in *Discussions* 3:119.

17. "Evangelical echo" is Harold W. Mann's appellation in *Atticus G. Haygood: Methodist Bishop, Editor, and Educator* (Athens, Ga., 1965), 109.

18. Atticus G. Haygood, *Sermons and Speeches* (Nashville, 1883), 116, 122, 123. The "incubus" comes from another speech by the same title, delivered in Boston in 1881 (ibid., 360).

19. Ibid., 123.

20. Dabney, "New South," 20, 21.

21. Haygood also attempted to ground his reasoning in scripture. Addressing the question of what constituted criteria for truth, he said, "'Search the Scriptures,' says our Lord, 'for they are they which testify of me.' If the prophets do not

speak according to this word, we must reject their message" ("Prove All Things," *Sermons and Speeches*, 303).

22. Dabney, "New South," 16.

23. William Henry Ruffner, *Public Free School System*, 5, 7, 8, 9; Charles William Dabney, *Universal Education in the South*, vol. 1 (Chapel Hill, N.C., 1936), 155, 159; Robert L. Dabney, *Discussions* 4:191–224 (quote 194). After an opening shot by Robert Lewis Dabney in the *Southern Planter and Farmer*, he and Ruffner exchanged volleys in the *Richmond Dispatch* and the *Richmond Enquirer*, each contributing eight articles. Ruffner excoriated Dabney's lack of sympathy for the postwar plight of Southern blacks, but neither man questioned the propriety of segregation. Indeed, to placate fears that public education for blacks would be the first step toward racial amalgamation, Ruffner assured Dabney that a separate public school system for blacks would instead shore up the social separation of the races: "Of all the public arrangements of Southern society, the school system alone renders a bold, emphatic testimony to the immiscibility of the races. We find Negroes in our churches, our theatres, our courthouses, our rail-cars, our halls of legislation; but there is one place where no negro enters, and that is a white public school house" (Ruffner, *Public Free School System*, 10).

24. Dabney, "Instrumental Music in Public Worship," *Discussions* 5:324 (reprinted from *Presbyterian Quarterly* 3 (July 1889): 462–69). This article very favorably reviewed *Instrumental Music in the Public Worship of the Church* by John Girardeau, who essentially shared Dabney's views on this issue.

25. See Dabney's *A Defense of Virginia, and through Her, of the South* (1867; rept. Harrisonburg, Va., 1991), 94–208, and his *The Practical Philosophy* (1897; rept. Harrisonburg, Va., 1984), 404–8, for two among many instances; see also Noll, "Bible and Slavery," 64.

26. For "scriptural politics" and criticisms of ultrademocracy, see Dabney, "New South," 5–16. When, in his arguments against the participation of women in American politics, Dabney offers more than vague *assertions* that scripture supports his contention, he mainly cites biblical texts that deal with female subjection in domestic and ecclesiastical situations. He does not explain how these apply to modern political questions, nor does he address the greater question of why—given the absolutist political environment of the Roman Empire in which New Testament Christians lived—*any* Christian may participate in a democracy ("The Public Preaching of Women," *Discussions* 2:117; "Women's Rights Women," *Discussions* 4:499; "Woman Suffrage," *Discussions* 5:422).

Surviving Defeat

The Trials of "Mrs. Ex-President Tyler"

THEODORE C. DELANEY

Life in the Reconstruction South was an alarming challenge for elite white widows. They quickly discovered that prior social status guaranteed neither adequate resources nor access to men who held political power. Among those who had to face this predicament was Julia Gardiner Tyler. She had always relished her status as "Mrs. Ex-President Tyler," and her prewar position had seemed permanently assured. Although Julia eventually achieved a partial return to antebellum wealth, social standing, and ease of mind, she spent years in improvident denial. In the period from the end of the war until the 1880s, she led a life of negation, as if circumstances should never modify her desires or interfere with her dreams. In this respect, Julia Tyler was probably not alone. So many plantation widows found it psychologically difficult to surmount the trials of genteel penury and diminished social position.

In her early years, Julia had been a wealthy New York socialite before her wedding with President John Tyler in 1844 during the last months of his presidency. It was nearly two years after the death of his first wife, Letitia Christian Tyler, and only Alice, the youngest, was still a teenager. Julia, though only twenty-four years old at the time of her marriage to the fifty-four-year-old president, quickly demonstrated superb political skills and proved an able asset to her husband. For instance, she hosted lavish parties designed to secure the annexation of Texas. Julia was a worldly-wise woman, often very outspoken about politics and the character of politicians. When British abolitionists decided to join their voices with Harriet Beecher Stowe in

1852, Julia quickly responded with a carefully argued defense of slavery. She was also such a staunch defender of the Confederacy that one Union soldier believed she deserved the title "Her Secession Ladyship."[1] But political acumen and pro-Confederate sympathies had not prepared Julia for a world in which she would have to focus on the mundane concerns of daily life—survival, education of her children, restoration of her war-torn property, and adjustment to a new social order.

Before the war, John Tyler had sheltered his wife from day-to-day decisions involving the family's financial resources. Often his efforts had not been sufficient, and Julia's wealthy mother, Juliana Gardiner, had supplemented the family income. Juliana also provided a comfortable inheritance to support Julia and the Tyler children during the years following the war. Yet Julia had difficulty managing a household budget and living within it. John Tyler died in 1862, at age seventy-two, while attending a meeting of the Confederate Congress in Richmond. His death had left the widow and their seven children isolated at Sherwood Forest, their James River plantation. It proved to be a vulnerable location as Union troops massed for George McClellan's Peninsula Campaign. The Tyler family remained at the plantation until October 28, 1863, when Julia finally sought refuge at her mother's New York home. Life there was relatively secure, but then Juliana Gardiner died on October 4, 1864. Julia inherited her mother's home and initially continued to live in it, preferring to manage her Southern affairs from a safe distance.

Julia did not abandon her Southern principles and, along with other elite white women, retained the hope that white superiority and antebellum class status would prevail in the long run. Although her husband had died of natural causes rather than wounds sustained in combat, Julia shared many traits with other white Southern widows in 1864 and 1865. Like many others, Julia had had neither the opportunity to learn the technical or financial intricacies of running a plantation nor the skills needed for making important financial decisions that affected the family's future. Few others, of course, were as privileged as she in keeping a residence in the North. Important matters nonetheless required immediate attention, and no one other than she could address those matters.

Julia Tyler identified restoration of Sherwood Forest as her first priority. To her mind, its immediate return to antebellum productivity would aid her in caring for the children. Located in Charles City County, Virginia, along the James River, Sherwood Forest displayed wartime neglect and the ill effects of military occupation during the latter part of the war. The plantation house remained standing, but much of its furniture had been carried away. Opposing armies had trampled the yard and fields, and outbuildings had "been pulled down and burnt."[2] During Julia's stay in New York, the former slaves had drifted away, and she needed laborers to cultivate crops. But she planned neither an immediate return to Virginia nor the return of black laborers to Sherwood Forest. Instead, she would become an absentee landlady and employ Swedish laborers. Julia's residency in New York enabled her to recruit Swedish farmers and send them to her Virginia plantation. Such an experiment with European immigrants had not been tried on a James River plantation since the days of indentured servants, and Julia's plan was scarcely without problems.

John C. Tyler, an elderly cousin of President John Tyler, resided at Sherwood Forest, and he wryly concurred in the arrangement Julia had made, because "the negroes . . . are perfectly worthless." She hired Sievert von Oertzen, and he began managing Sherwood Forest on July 3, 1865. He resolved to plant crops as quickly as possible, but early July was far too late in the season. According to John C. Tyler, Julia agreed to "furnish each family with a few acres of ground for their own use," and, in exchange, "they [were] to give four days labour . . . and [have] two days for themselves." Julia would "provide for them until they shall have made the first crop—then they are to provide for themselves without . . . assistance, and continue the remainder of three years to perform the same proportion of labour as above mentioned." The agreement was in the form of a written contract. Tyler cautioned her about "the cost of keeping these families so long before they would be able to relieve you of the expense of providing for them."[3]

Julia persisted with her experiment, however, and Oertzen made an earnest effort to rework the fields at Sherwood Forest. John C. Tyler reported that Oertzen "purchased two condemned Army horses" and began to plow in preparation for planting "turnips, beans and potatoes, . . . the only crops now offering any chance to bring to perfection."[4] Tyler also asked Julia for thirty bushels of wheat seed, if she could find a place to purchase it. But Julia was not ready to take on the responsibility of being an absentee planter. Once Oertzen arrived at Sherwood Forest, she rather neglected the duties that an absentee landowner had to bear. Julia wanted to see it make profits, but she had no appetite for direct involvement. She seemed to have forgotten the many times during the 1840s and 1850s that her mother had extended generous loans to John Tyler as he struggled to make ends meet between harvests. She also failed to understand that July was far too late in the season to begin plowing and planting. Moreover, a drought in eastern Virginia made success even less likely.

By early September, Oertzen admitted failure. "It is so very dry here," he wrote, "that everything is dying away, the ground so hard that not two horses are able to get a plough through the ground, and so we are waiting for rain or money or both, but I fear we have waited to long already, the time for the wheat is here." Additionally, Oertzen was unable to feed his laborers. He reported that, except for a little meat and flour, food supplies were all expended. They had to live on "milk and peaches and peaches and milk mornings, noons and nights."[5] Oertzen's situation annoyed Julia, and she failed to provide the needed money.

Despite nearly twenty years of residence on a Virginia plantation, Julia was unprepared to deal with perceived impertinence from a manager on her farm. Yet, Oertzen persisted in his complaints and displayed far more dignity than Julia did. She fired him and ordered him to leave Sherwood Forest. Oertzen wrote:

> I am very sorry, that our engagement has lasted such a short time. What your son told me about my bill is insulting, but I do forgive him he does not know better. So far as I know the world I always found that the expences of a man engaged on a place are paid by the owner. I am sorry to see that that offended you. Please reduce the bill to that you think proper and send the money to me here, as soon as possible. I am quit out of funds and wait for the money to move.[6]

Oertzen was at Sherwood Forest five months, and he calculated Julia's debt to him to be $100, or $20 per month, for the time he had already worked. When she did not pay, Oertzen decided to sue Julia. Historian Robert Seager reports that the suit was eventually thrown out of court, but not before Julia had expended nearly the amount of Oertzen's claim in legal fees. Perhaps Julia's apparent selfishness and indifference resulted from circumstances beyond her control. Her mother's estate had not yet been settled, and Julia's brother contested a will that favored her. Julia's own resources were limited. Nonetheless, some explanation or even apology to her manager was called for. In any event, she backed away from the scheme of using immigrant laborers and instead employed black sharecroppers to tend her fields. Whatever the labor force, she did what she could, she claimed. "I want to do something for myself on the farm if I have the power in order to lengthen out my purse which you can imagine with all these children to look after & educate requires it to be of some length. I feel the loss of all assistance from my Virginia property severely. . . . suppose my mother had left me nothing . . . what would have become of us?"[7] Problems at Sherwood Forest, however, were nearly insurmountable for a woman with limited funds and little understanding of farming.

A number of small bills totaling approximately $1,000 encumbered Julia's plantation. Many dated from the 1850s, and each had grown from accrued interest. Julia's Virginia creditors all desperately needed money and were anxious to collect. Indeed, historian Allen Moger has written that "the most impoverished areas in Virginia" after 1865 "were the same areas where wealth in slaves had been greatest before the war."[8] Financial problems for Sherwood Forest and Julia would persist into the 1870s and would not end until her son David Gardiner Tyler (hereafter called "Gardie), diligently restored the plantation's productivity. Unlike his mother, David was willing to reside there and learn through trial and failure.

Sherwood Forest was not the only Virginia property that commanded Julia's attention. She also owned a summerhouse called Villa Margaret in nearby Hampton. After the war, the American Missionary Association sent teachers into the area to work with freed slaves, and Freedmen's Bureau officials had assigned the house to them. Julia's Charles City County neighbors, John and Lu Clopton, kept a keen watch on the villa and were quick to pass information to Julia about the condition of the property. Charles B. Mallory, a Hampton attorney, advised Julia to write directly to Gen. Oliver O. Howard, who headed the Freedmen's Bureau, to beg him "to have this property returned to you."[9]

Getting the property back proved no problem. But the federal government was unwilling to compensate Julia more than four dollars per month rent for the time it had been used—far too little money to restore Villa Margaret to its antebellum condition. In June 1874 Julia sold it for $3,500, less than a third of its antebellum value. The Bank of Virginia, which held a lien against it, had sued in 1873, and Julia's lawyer, Richmond attorney Thomas J. Evans, was quick to discover that collecting his own fee was no easy matter. "I regret that you have not been able to send me the ($85) amount of my fee," he wrote. "It has put me to some inconvenience, I am dependent entirely upon my profession for a support and a mother, sister, wife and seven children are dependent upon me."[10] Julia needed legal assistance but seemed indifferent to the fact that other Southerners—like Evans—were having a difficult time, particularly during the depression year of 1873. Unlike most Southerners, she had an inheritance to serve as a buffer against the depression, but it was mostly rental properties in Manhattan that provided her monthly income.

In spite of economic hard times, Julia faced the task of educating seven Tyler children and serving as legal guardian for her orphaned nephew, Harry Beeckman, who, like Julia, had received a generous share of her mother's estate. Although a New Yorker, Harry identified with his Tyler cousins in many ways, including political ideology. Julia's oldest son, Gardie, had just begun studies at Washington College in Lexington, Virginia, during the early weeks of the Civil War. Unlike his mother, Gardie was loath to accept the Confederate defeat in 1865. He and his brother Alex were very unhappy with the Reconstruction, and Julia suggested they go to school in Germany. She urged Harry to do the same. Additionally, she decided to send her daughter Julie to Halifax, Nova Scotia, to study in the Convent School of the Sisters of the Sacred Heart.[11]

Julia's plans for educating her children abroad were consistent with her determination to live according to antebellum economic standards. She neither comprehended the expense an education abroad entailed, nor did she care. Once the young men were in Germany, she seemed aloof from the difficulties they encountered. Within weeks of their arrival in Germany, Gardie complained of their "want of the *almighty dollar.*" To make matters worse, only Alex had an aptitude for the German language and the ability to take formal classes in it. Julia decided to bring Harry back home and place him in Washington College. Shortly thereafter, Gardie assessed his own situation. He explained that "the yearly expenditures of a gentleman's son who goes to the Polytechnic School here is, as my landlady . . . tells me, about on an average of 1500 guldens, that is $600 gold." Gardie decided to return home and join Harry at Washington College. Julia might have saved herself a few headaches by bringing Alex home as well, but he remained in Germany and trained as an engineer. Julia's purse remained far too small to meet his needs, and Alex's extravagance made matters worse. In 1874 a German attorney contacted Julia "in respect to some of [Alex's] unsettled bills," amounting to about 1400 gilders.[12]

Julie Tyler's situation in Halifax was similar. Like many teenagers, she alternated between love for the school and lamentation about being too far from home. She did not return to Halifax after the first year, probably because of Julia's strained finances. During her time there, however, Julie required clothes and other items befitting a prominent and extravagant young woman in boarding school. Bills from Halifax required immediate attention, and when Julia did not meet these obligations, the debts became a source of embarrassment for Julie's guardian in Canada, John Taylor Wood. He had perhaps unwisely authorized the purchases. Wood instructed the merchants to press their claims against Julia, but he paid the bills himself to avoid continued annoyance by the creditors. When he finally billed Julia for the amount in 1869, the sum, including interest, came to $370.

The four other Tyler children attended schools in the United States. Julia's son Lyon (called Lonie) attended the University of Virginia, and his complaints about the lack of spending money were as intense as those of his older brothers. Many of his letters from college displayed little sympathy for his mother's financial difficulties. Gently Julia tried to keep him in line:

> You have read me a quite nice lecture my dear little Lonie upon the subject of my wishing you to keep an account to all your expenditures. Why shouldn't you? Your brother Gardie did so before you—& so did your Mama do so before you at your age. However if it is so *mortifying* and it seems to imply my want of faith in you—a very mistaken notion—I won't press it any further—though I must *impress* it upon you *to be very careful in everything*—no matter what *other* boys do . . . some boys at college injure their parents very much.[13]

Julia persisted in her attempt to teach her children frugality, but she failed to set a very good example herself. Tyler family collections at both Yale University and the College of William and Mary contain bills demonstrating that Julia's clothing expenses reached far beyond her means, as she continued to clothe herself in the same manner to which she had been accustomed before the war. Julia understood her financial limitations, but she spent lavishly regardless. When a physician pressed for payment of an old bill, Julia provided a clear statement of her financial situation. "I seem to have completely succumbed to the disturbed financial state of the times," she wrote. "As you must have observed in the course of the dreadful shrinkage of value of late years those who thought themselves well off . . . suffer more deeply than those who apparently have no property."[14] But Julia did experience profound change in her life during those years following the war—change precipitated by the hard realities of life.

Perhaps nothing affected her more than the loss of her twenty-one-year-old daughter Julie, who married in 1869 and died after giving birth to a daughter on May 8, 1871. Will Spencer, the baby's father, became a drifter, moving first to Colorado and then to California in search of his fortune. During the mid-1880s, the Tylers lost contact with him forever.[15] Will left the child for Julia to rear. Nicknamed "Baby," the child was a great joy to Julia but did not distract her from the pain of Julie's loss. As she attempted to deal with her grief, Julia turned to prayer and sought consolation through religion. Throughout her life, she had been a marginal Episcopalian. Now she began to make inquiries about Roman Catholicism. After Julie's death, she moved to Washington, D.C. There she placed her two youngest children in Catholic academies. Perhaps Julie's brief experience at the Convent School of the Sacred Heart in Halifax had inspired this decision. In any event, the children's enrollments in Georgetown College and Georgetown Academy of the Visitation enabled Julia to acquaint herself with the priests and nuns and the faith they espoused.

Jesuit Father Patrick Francis Healy had the greatest effect on her spiritual life. He was a philosophy professor who became dean of studies at Georgetown in the early 1870s. By 1873 Father Healy had become acting president of the college. The Jesuits confirmed him in that role in 1874.[16] Julia and Father Healy developed a close friendship, and whenever she traveled outside of the city, they corresponded. Kindly and tenderhearted, Healy was a fair-skinned mulatto son of a Georgia slave, far different from other people with whom Julia had ever associated. She had always boasted about the high social rank of her friends and acquaintances and was quick to give details of their genealogy. Oddly, this very Southern ex-Confederate seemed totally unconcerned about Father Healy's ethnicity or lineage. One wonders if she ever thought about the contradictions involved in their friendship.

Whatever prompted her breaking of the racial divide, her religious journey with Father Healy became particularly important to Julia. He smoothly guided her though the conversion process and served as godfather at her baptism. Strong willed as she was, Julia met the church on her own terms. She would continue to enjoy the world's pleasures but in a manner that she thought did not offend God. "I do not think that I am bound to lead the life of an ascetic," she reasoned without a shred of irony. "There is nothing in a good play or opera criminal in itself. On the contrary, some of them constitute the highest evidence of genius of taste and moral[s]. Like everything else they are liable to abuse. So of music and dance [and] all amusements of life, all the good gifts of Providence may be abused," she reflected. "*Use but not abuse* would seem to me to be a sound maxim, which conflicts not with but is recommended by the Christian precepts."[17]

Julia took great comfort in her new religious faith in spite of a multitude of criticisms from family and friends. The Roman Catholic Church hardly enjoyed widespread popularity in the nineteenth-century United States. Julia's son Lonie was quick to scold his mother for her decision: "Well done! What must happen next?" he chided sarcastically. "Now that Mrs. Ex-President Tyler has changed from Episcopal—from the Protestant Church of her fathers to the Roman Catholic, the relentless and persecuting enemy in former times of her national church! And pray for what reason have you taken this course?" he asked rhetorically. "Because 'there is unity and system in it,' you say. Fine unity and system indeed! If you consider that there is a *true* unity and system in superstitious beliefs."[18]

Lonie had voiced his anger more vividly than others who merely grumbled and gossiped. Yet, Julia would not be swayed. She had never done anything radical and had always presented herself as a conven-

tional member of the American elite. Now she needed spiritual consolation and a fresh source of inner strength. At this point in her life,
she was far more willing to put the sectional conflict behind her and
accept the new realities of postwar United States. Julia's conversion
upset her children almost as much her social call to the White House
in 1872 had. Lonie expressed outrage that his mother had "forgotten
yourself so much as to pay a cordial visit to Mrs. Grant." Julia was ready
to put the war behind her. In one letter addressed to President Ulysses
S. Grant requesting compensation for federal use of her Hampton
property, Julia expressed admiration of "your kind & liberal course in
the political matters of the country."[19] The letter was self-serving, but
Julia's compliment was unmistakable, and perhaps a part of her religious journey.

Indeed, money troubles did not submit to the same transformation
that her religious faith had undergone. Desperate, she applied in 1878
for a federal pension. Lonie had alerted her about how veterans of the
War of 1812 and their widows were being given such funds. He suggested that she might well be eligible, too. "It provides for the widows
of any *volunteers or militiamen of the War of 1812* that served for 12 days,
and provides too the land warrant such soldier received for services in
such war shall be evidence of his service," Lonie explained. He urged
his mother to claim the "pension of $8 a month and if you don't care
for such pittance, pass it over to me." Congress had enacted the statute
in 1862, and Julia pressed for retroactive pay. The federal government
was not that generous, but she did begin receiving the modest pension
in 1879.[20] Eight dollars per month was not enough to solve her financial problems. Yet, she was relieved to get whatever she could. Success
with this effort may have emboldened her to begin a more ambitious
campaign to obtain a presidential widow's pension.

The struggle to obtain such a federal stipend helped restore Julia's
confidence in her own personal skills and her status as Mrs. Ex-
President Tyler. Congress had granted Mary Todd Lincoln a pension
in 1870 that paid $3,000 annually. Other surviving widows at that time
included Sarah Childress Polk and Caroline Fillmore. Completely
optimistic about her chances for success, Julia submitted her petition
to Congress. But on the advice of friends, including Virginia Democratic congressman John Goode, she withdrew it. Goode did not

believe that economic and political realities of the 1870s would permit the petition to go forward. After deciding upon a temporary delay, Julia noted that her "chief hope [is] that Congress will feel a President's widow should not petition in vain!"[21] Acting on the counsel of her friend and personal attorney, William M. Evarts, who was also the U.S. secretary of state, Julia resubmitted her petition in 1879.

This time, Lonie urged his mother to be firm in her resolve to win. "I really believe you will succeed," he wrote, "for I don't think Congress would have the face to refuse. If you propose to petition take the step firmly and openly and advisedly and don't back down as you did before. Just think what a nice little pension of $3000 would do for you! To let the widow of a President petition in vain when so many hundreds have succeeded and are now living comfortably on a fat little income at the public expense would be a shame."[22]

Two Democrats from Virginia—Senator John W. Johnston and Congressman J. Randolph Tucker—agreed to support Julia's petition. She sensed, however, that neither possessed much energy, interest, or political influence. Julia confided to Lonie that she viewed both men as "awful old foggies," and added, "I selected these two to act for me because I could hardly do otherwise as they were the ones who represent Virginia. I really think I could have obtained a greater interest from some others though I hope it may not prove so."[23] Unwilling to entrust the matter completely to this Virginia congressional pair, Julia lobbied any congressman or journalist she could reach by letter or by personal confrontation. No matter the length of presidential service or the political revolution that the Civil War had wrought, she insisted that she should be treated as Mary Todd Lincoln's equal. Congress approved the pension in 1881 but set the amount at $1,200 per year.

Unwilling to tolerate such unequal treatment, Julia pressed for a much larger stipend. The editor of *The Jeffersonian*, a Charlottesville newspaper, agreed and sent her a copy of his editorial. Convinced that Senator Johnston needed to see the editorial more than she did, Julia forwarded it to him.[24] Soon Julia received unexpected political assistance that came in the form of a national tragedy. The assassination of President James Garfield resulted in widespread sympathy for his widow, Lucretia Randolph Garfield. Congress approved a $3,000 annual stipend each for Julia, Sarah Polk, and Lucretia Garfield (Caroline Fillmore had since died). Yet, even this sudden windfall did not satisfy Julia. She argued, "They ought to go back to the deaths of our husbands for Mrs P[olk] and me."[25]

At last Julia's persistence paid off. She secured an increase in the stipend, though not back payments. In late April, Senator Johnston informed her that a bill to increase her pension had passed. "Your name will be placed on the roles at the rate of $5000 a year and you will be paid hereafter just as you have been heretofore," he confided.[26]

When the pension checks began coming in 1882, Julia's children had already completed their formal education. The money was nevertheless a most welcome resource. At last she had found a way of "lengthening her purse." The pension would provide financial security in the years to come. It would also rescue her from the worry and humiliation of delinquent bills and angry creditors. And after all of the years of chiding her children to be careful of expenses, they had learned the importance of budgets and now aided their mother in governing her finances.

What Julia Gardiner Tyler had been unable to accomplish through farming at Sherwood Forest, Mrs. Ex-President Tyler finally achieved through political means. No ordinary nineteenth-century Southern woman, she demonstrated considerable talent as a politician and far less skill at managing a household. So few women of her generation in the South would have had the same good fortune and pluckiness that she enjoyed, even if financial security and the increased social status it conveyed had been a long time reaching her doorstep.

Notes

1. J. C. Thompson to Gen. Benjamin F. Butler, 22 January 1864, in *Private and Official Correspondence of General Benjamin F. Butler*, vol. 3 (Norwood, Mass., 1917), 327.

2. David Gardiner Tyler to Julia Gardiner Tyler (hereafter JGT), 28 November 1864, Tyler Family Papers, CWM (hereafter TFP).

3. John C. Tyler to JGT, 10 July 1865, TFP; Robert Seager II, *And Tyler Too: A Biography of John and Julia Gardiner Tyler* (New York, 1963), 513.

4. John C. Tyler to JGT, 10 July 1865, TFP.

5. Sievert von Oertzen to JGT, 3 September 1865, Gardiner-Tyler Papers, Yale University (hereafter GTP).

6. Sievert von Oertzen to JGT, 23 September 1865, GTP.

7. J. Buchanan Henry to JGT, 20 December 1865, GTP; Seager, 515; JGT to Mr. Lyons, n.d., TFP.

8. Allen W. Moger, *Virginia: Bourbonism to Byrd, 1870–1925* (Charlottesville, Va., 1968), 80.

9. Seager, *And Tyler Too*, 516; Charles B. Mallory to JGT, 2 August 1866, Gardiner-Tyler Family Papers.

10. Seager, *And Tyler Too*, 516; Thomas J. Evans to JGT, 11 February 1873, GTP.

11. Historian Jane Turner Censer demonstrates that, like Julia Tyler, some plantation women found cities far more inviting than rural plantation life after the war, and she suggests that many Southern women reconceived the future that they wanted for their children (*The Reconstruction of White Southern Womanhood, 1865–1895* [Baton Rouge, La., 2003], 138–43, 276). Julia's children were not the only Southerners to flee the United States; many headed for Brazil and elsewhere. Julia lent an unspecified amount of money to former Confederate first lady Varina Davis as she made plans to take her children to Canada (Varina Davis to JGT, 12 February 1866, TFP). In spite of her failure to honor financial commitments to Sievert von Oertzen, Thomas J. Evans, and others, Julia could not resist aiding Varina Davis, a woman she viewed as her social equal.

12. David Gardiner Tyler to JGT, 15 June, 28 August 1866, TFP; A. Baudmare [Geissenhainer Brothers, Attorneys and Counselors at Law] to JGT, 6 April 1874, GTP.

13. JGT to Lyon Gardiner Tyler, 19 April 1870, TFP.

14. JGT to Dr. Clark, n.d., TFP.

15. Seager, *And Tyler Too*, 537.

16. R. J. Henle, *Patrick F. Healy, S.J.: A Black Man's Dream Come True* (Washington, D.C., n.d. [pamphlet]), 9; Albert S. Foley, *Dream of An Outcast: Patrick F. Healy* (Tuscaloosa, Ala., 1989), 135. In general, Foley's book is the best source of information on Patrick Healy's life, but its information on Julia Tyler's conversion is unreliable.

17. Julia Gardiner Tyler's response to a church inquiry about her faith; undated and unsigned, TFP.

18. Lyon Gardiner Tyler to JGT, 16 May 1872, TFP.

19. Ibid.; JGT to General Grant, n.d., TFP.

20. Lyon Gardiner Tyler to JGT, 13 March 1878, TFP; Seager, *And Tyler Too*, 547.

21. JGT to John Goode, n.d., TFP; John Goode, *Recollections of a Lifetime* (New York, 1906), 107.

22. Lyon Gardiner Tyler to JGT, 6 March 1879, TFP.

23. JGT to Lyon Gardiner Tyler, 26 January 1882, TFP.

24. JGT to Lyon Gardiner Tyler, 8 February 1882, TFP.

25. JGT to Lachlan Tyler, 26 February 1882, TFP.

26. Senator John W. Johnston to JGT, 25 April 1882, TFP.

Gender Relations in Planter Families

————————⚬𝔪𝔪⚬————————

A Postwar Experiment and Its Lost Legacy

AMY FEELY MORSMAN

With the publication in 1970 of *The Southern Lady: From Pedestal to Politics, 1830–1930*, Anne Firor Scott emphasized change versus continuity across the Civil War era, and she did so in exploring a group that had been largely ignored by historians up to that point: white women.[1] Her work has inspired a generation of historians to investigate how women—from a variety of racial and economic backgrounds—helped to shape the postwar years. Scott's concentration on women has also encouraged scholars to ask new, broader questions about the influence of gender relations on Southern society. For Virginia planters and their wives, the challenges of the postwar years prompted them to reexamine their conceptions of gender roles and restructure their marital relationships.[2]

Family letters, Southern periodicals, and census data of the time indicate that in the wake of emancipation, many white plantation elites had no choice but to accept new work responsibilities in both domestic and field-oriented labor and that these changes in the labor regime had broad manifestations in both the private and public realm. Planters, frustrated by the problems of running their farms with free labor, and emotionally bruised by war-related financial losses, watched their wives work harder and economize more than they ever had needed to before the war. These men lamented their loss of status and power as traditional providers. They acknowledged that having to depend on their wives' financial assistance called into question their identity as patriarchs and challenged elite notions of proper manhood and womanhood.[3]

The elite husbands and wives who survived the war and reared their families in troubled times made up the last generation of Virginia's landed elite. The adaptations that masters and mistresses reluctantly made after the war to keep their families and their businesses afloat signal a decline in the patriarchal order and suggest that gender roles were in flux during this period, similar to the "unstable interlude," the "time of experiment, testing, and uncertainty" that C. Vann Woodward discovered for race relations in these same years.[4] Regardless of how emasculated planters felt or how often their wives complained of being overburdened, the alterations that they made to gender roles within their homes are noteworthy, because they reflected a shift in the balance of power, giving more weight to women's influence than had existed in the antebellum period. Such change did not endure.

By the late 1880s and 1890s, a new generation of white Southerners had grown up, and these men and women—many of them the children of Virginia's last plantation elite—abandoned their families' plantations and pursued professional lives in the cities of the New South. The decisions made by people of this next generation about their place in the social order and their attitudes about gender relations reveal that they did not embrace their parents' rural world and were not strongly influenced by their parents' experimenting with marital partnership. Instead of following "the alternative course" that their parents had made in gender relations, these members of the New South took a different path that in some ways resembled the behavior of their *grand*parents in the antebellum years.[5]

White Virginians had suffered greatly during the Civil War: they lost their young men; saw their homes, fields, and roads destroyed; and, with the abolition of slavery, had to relinquish much of their wealth and their labor force. Those who continued to plant had to reconfigure their own work and that of their households before they could attain any degree of financial success. A planter's options included hiring far fewer servants and field hands, putting his own physical labor and that of his family members to practical use, abandoning labor-intensive crops, and selling off the plantation or renting part of it to tenants. A popular agricultural journal published in Virginia advised planters to "begin the good work" to remake their plantations into viable enterprises. To do so often meant employing a combination of these courses.[6]

Fulwar Skipwith, a Virginia planter from Mecklenburg County, noted in his annual farm log his strategies for saving money. In 1869 he figured that he saved over $1,000 by not employing ten more farm hands. Four years later, he measured the time and money that could be saved by working grain crops instead of tobacco.[7] Thomas Watson, the owner of a tobacco and wheat plantation in Louisa County, chose to abandon labor-intensive crops altogether after the war. He hoped, instead, to generate more farm produce using only labor-saving farm machinery and the work of his own family. "Our troubles with the Darkies multiply!" he reported in 1867; "I now look forward to converting Bracketts [Plantation] into a Grazing and Hay Farm—the girls can milk and churn and boys and I herd and feed—and Hay Harvest (with a mower) will be a frolic!"[8] This scenario seemed more appealing to Watson than depending entirely on unreliable servant labor to raise a more valuable, yet vulnerable, tobacco crop.

Watson at first seemed optimistic about his family's future farming endeavors, but he and other former slaveholders soon expressed frustration with the constraints of the postwar economic world. George Munford, for instance, diversified the crops on his Tidewater plantation and added his own hands to the labor of their production. He was not quite prepared, however, for the overwhelming volume of work he had to assume in the absence of slaves. He complained to a relative in 1867: "Farmers have no time to spare in these times. Oats to cut, hay to secure, corn to lay by, . . . potatoes to work—Irish and sweet—Melons to work—turnips to sow . . . I tell you when night comes I drop to bed without much ceremony and I find the nights too short for my naps—I rise at four in the morning and am going it all day long."[9]

Old Virginia gentlemen found their financial troubles and new labor responsibilities emasculating as well as exhausting. George Munford, despite his hard work, experienced great difficulty making ends meet and therefore could not fulfill his responsibilities to provide for and protect his family from want. "Nothing would contribute more to my happiness than to be able to help all [my children]," Munford wrote to his oldest son, but "I have arrived at that crisis both of age and pecuniary necessities as to be almost unable to help myself."[10]

James Hubard, a Nelson County planter, fretted about his wife's appearance and how it might reflect poorly on him as a man. Isaetta was attempting to stretch the family finances by working hard around the household and farmyard and by making do with old clothing, but Hubard wished that the rest of the neighborhood would instead see her "looking trim and fixed up," as her appearance was a means of maintaining their class status. Even when Isaetta complied with James's request that she dress according to elite standards, he was painfully aware of how, because of his precarious postwar financial circumstances—"the surrounding and overpowering circumstances due to the times in which I live"—he had been "doubtless presented . . . to many as a poor provider for my family."[11]

As if altering the size and function of their plantations was not enough to discourage Virginia planters, most of these men had to employ the labor of their wives to further aid in production and management. Editors of the *Southern Planter and Farmer* advised planters to "press into . . . service every other product to which farm and labor is suited. He [the planter] must also throw around himself and his family, all the luxuries and comforts which he can produce at home, and so the more easily dispense with those that have to be purchased with money."[12] Yet, home production of that sort required enormous attention from women. Before the Civil War, white women on plantations had assumed responsibility for all the sewing and darning of clothes in their households. After the war, they expanded their scope of work on the plantation to include cooking, cultivating kitchen gardens, and tending the dairy, the orchard, and the henhouse, anything to contribute to the financial security of the family. Even when families were able to afford some hired help, white women performed much more real labor than simply supervising servants as they had done in the antebellum years.[13]

Women, by their words and actions, demonstrated that they knew their help was essential to the household and that they were willing to contribute a greater effort. Mindful of cutting as many costs as possible, Sarah Hubard of Buckingham County was pleased that the fruits of her hard labor could keep her socialite daughter dressed in the latest styles and finest fabrics. She made vinegar and catsup to sell locally for cash or to trade for credit with Richmond merchants. Sarah's distant relation, Lila Hubard, bragged to her sister-in-law about her "very fine" garden and how "it has added much to our comfort, something to our purses and helps wonderfully in feeding our white folks." Elizabeth Watson was equally successful with her work in the dairy. She made so much extra butter that her husband set up a direct trading relationship between her and Richmond grocers, so that she could command better prices in a larger market.[14]

In addition to helping sustain the financial end of Virginia plantations, women were encouraged to enhance as best they could the appearance of the domestic sphere. In fact, making the plantation household a comfortable home seemed even more essential to the happiness of postwar families than it had been in the antebellum years. The writer of an 1867 agricultural journal article explained: "While our farmers are busy adding to their material prosperity . . . , it is the duty of the ladies to improve and beautify their homes. . . . We, as a people are poor, very poor, and are consequently denied many pleasures and luxuries of former times, still the careful hand of woman can, with little expense, do much to add to the attractions and enjoyments of home." This author suggested that "a row of shade-trees along the walk, a few evergreens and flowering shrubs . . . will do much to alleviate the dreariness of the wasted plantation and give cheerfulness to an otherwise lonely and heavy prospect."[15] In a time of trouble, women assumed broader responsibilities for supporting the home and their husband's plantation business, yet they were supposed to work hard to make things appear as if there was no trouble at all.

One could argue that Virginia women residing on postwar plantations were simply continuing in their tradition of service to their husbands and their families. They did not endeavor to take on the plow and thresher by themselves; rather they focused their efforts in the henhouse and the garden, where they or their mothers might have been found twenty years before (albeit in a more supervisory capacity). Certainly, the gendered division of labor as plantation women knew it in 1850 or 1860 was not fundamentally altered in 1865 or 1880, but in the postbellum period elites articulated a greater appreciation of plantation women's work. Such appreciation gave way to marital relations that were defined more by partnership than by patriarchy. For instance, an 1867 article in the *Southern Planter and Farmer*,

describing "a good wife" as one who "sees that her household are pro-
ducers," observed: "A despondent man finds, in her cheerful cooperation, . . . and he is not wise who does not counsel with her in matters of importance. If he is threatened with reverses, why should he not
confide in her who can more fully understand him than any one else?"[16]

Elite women living on plantations *before* the war had their fair share
of labor and played a substantial role in maintaining the health, comfort, and appearance of their families. But the emotional and financial
contributions women made to plantations in the *postwar* period meant
much more to them and their husbands, because they fulfilled real
needs in ways that their husbands could not. Virginia plantation
women were quick to respond to the postwar emergency—even if they
frequently complained about their burdens—and as a result, they
gained more power within their marriages and within their households. This change, to be sure, did not come close to resembling
equality for women. Instead, elite men and women fashioned some
degree of mutuality as a necessity in trying times, but these trying
times lasted for many years, and during this period, elites accepted the
growth of women's power inside *and* outside the home, not just as
moral arbiters but as economic allies.[17]

The transformation of gender roles took place gradually, and most
often behind closed doors, but it also had a public face. Postwar agricultural organizations, to which Virginia planters belonged, echoed
the sentiments that elite men had been making about their wives' expanding domestic role. Planters joined these organizations and attended monthly meetings primarily to benefit from the agricultural
cooperatives. In these meetings, they also heard a social message that
encouraged cooperation with their womenfolk as well as with fellow
farmers. By including women as members, and by addressing domestic and farmyard concerns as well as financial matters, many of these
organizations offered planters a model for gender relationships that
differed substantially from the patriarchal standard of the prewar
years.[18]

Whether planters belonged to local agricultural societies or the
larger, nationally based organizations, they could not help but notice
women's increased presence in their clubs and hear from the mouths
of their own club leaders that women were crucial to the postwar rural

economy. Virginia Grange leaders, for example, addressed planter husbands' anxiety about changing gender roles with this 1874 observation: "To Virginia gentlemen the most formidable objection which has been urged against our Order, is that it takes woman *out of her proper sphere* and will thereby sap the foundations of our social fabric." Yet white women had a "higher sphere of action" than to "stitch and plod and nurse." The Grange leaders went on to ask: "Has she not a mind to cultivate, a heart to educate, that she may be prepared for her true position in society, . . . the companionship of man?" "Can she be his congenial companion, his sympathizing friend, his intelligent co-operator and efficient helpmate along the devious path of life, unless she is prepared for the position?" Through such advice, Grangers reinforced what Virginia planters were already realizing: that abandoning patriarchy was necessary for the future progress of Southern agriculture and that the relationships planters had established with their wives in the antebellum period needed to undergo a certain, though subtle, transformation.[19]

Virginia planters and their wives were not the only people who experienced these changes firsthand. Their children were no doubt affected by the problems their parents faced and the solutions their parents crafted. For postwar white children on plantations, growing up without many luxuries that their parents had enjoyed before the war, the South was a region needing serious repair. The free labor system threatened their family's financial security and seemed to drain agriculture of all its power and planters of all their status. An article in the *Southern Planter and Farmer* raised the alarm to the mothers and fathers of this generation: "You have no idea of the good you might do yourselves and your children . . . by cultivating a taste for the beautiful, and striving to make your homes attractive. As it is, your children grow up under the impression that farming is a vulgar business, and all the beauty, taste, refinement and pleasure is found in town."[20]

Virginia planter parents knew that the eradication of slavery laid the groundwork for the construction of a New South based less on the productive needs of rural areas and more in urban areas, where commercial and industrial opportunity were beginning to flourish. They could not help but fear that their sons, wary of rising to the enormous challenge posed by postwar agriculture, would be lured away by new urban enticements. For example, despite Thomas Watson's desire that his son continue the family tradition of farming, his son had different plans, and Watson could arouse "no interest or working vim" in Tom Jr. The editors of Southern newspapers and periodicals frequently ran warnings about young people moving to urban areas. One such article urged: "Stay away from the city, young man. Why? Because you are not wanted there. Too many young men already are there—too many struggling for the fortune that never comes and acquiring, instead, tastes and habits which lead to perdition." "Are [you] a farmer's son?" the writer asked. "Be a farmer's son—one of the bone and sinew of the land!"[21] Such messages often fell on deaf ears.

Urban areas also held allure for young women looking to escape the doldrums of the plantation. For example, during her visit to Washington, D.C., Sue Hubard wrote home to her parents in Buckingham County. In reporting all the delights she was enjoying in the city, she drew a sharp contrast between the sacrifice and isolation of the countryside and the wealth of opportunity one could experience in a city: "As it is Lent a great many people will not go to places of amusement," she wrote, "but I tell them we have Lent in Buckingham all year round and I can't think it so great a harm to see a little pleasure when I am in town."[22] The city held promise for young Virginians, but their parents feared it would cause "the race of the country gentleman [to] become extinct."

Expanding railroads, perhaps the greatest symbol of the New South, helped carry the children of the plantation elite far away from rural Virginia and connected them with new social and economic opportunities in developing towns and cities. Most Virginians encouraged the development of more far-reaching rail lines in the last three decades of the century; close to 2,500 miles of rail lines were constructed across the state in these years. Yet rural elites had no control over the exodus that this increasingly sophisticated transportation network inspired. During the 1880s, Virginia's urban population increased by 49.5 percent, its rural population by a mere 3.8 percent. The railroad, itself, provided new, better-paying, and interesting employment. For instance, Bob Hubard, the oldest of James and Isaetta Hubard's sons, sent letters *and money* home from nearby Lynchburg, but also from Tennessee and Alabama, where he was riding the rails as baggage master and rear brakeman for a railroad line. His brother, Ben, like many other young men, used the railroad to make a short but permanent trip to Richmond to seek work in manufacturing enterprises, mercantile establishments, or professional offices that the capital city offered. The letters that young Virginians wrote home to their parents show that their interests lay beyond the plantation, but these brief, sketchy sources do not provide much of their personal perspectives on gender roles.[23]

The next generation delayed marriage. Young men expressed concern about the financial burdens that a wife and children would bring. Wilmer Turner, having heard that his brother enjoyed spending time with young ladies, advised him "by all means to haul off. It is no time to be *taken in*. It won't do to marry just now at least. . . . Shun even the slightest semblance of love." Young women also were less anxious to marry early when the model for marriage that they had observed in their own childhood represented great toil and uneasiness. A female contributor to the *Southern Planter and Farmer* reminded young women of what they might find in store for them with marriage: "If I sympathize with any class of persons more than another, it is the young farmer's wife with four or five little ones to be cared for, the house to keep clean, and such a host of duties coming up all day." The author described a woman's sleepless nights as a result of her baby's teething and all the daily responsibilities that awaited her early in the morning regardless of how little rest she had gotten: "Poor girl, in her impatience she says, 'What folly in me to have married. If I had remained single I would have had such a nice time and been saved all this worry.'"[24]

In addition to wanting to avoid the domestic fate of their mothers, young white Virginia women were attracted to numerous areas of employment, including those that grew out of the New South's urban-oriented, industrial economy.[25] Women found work as office clerks and in retail sales but were particularly attracted to teaching. Teaching positions were numerous, geographically varied, and in apparent keeping with women's softer sensibilities. The experience of teaching in urban areas, however, made it easy for young adults to lose interest in and respect for the plantations of their childhood. When Virginia

Watson, who had begun teaching in one of the state's largest cities, visited her parents' plantation for the summer of 1876, she "put aside all her town airs . . . and her best clothes . . . until the Winter" and walked around the plantation only in calico.[26]

When Virginia Watson and other young white women of the New South finally chose to settle down and create their own marital households, they generally did so as members of an emerging urban middle class. This environment was far removed from their parents' homes and did not present young adults with the obstacles their parents had encountered as postwar planters. As a result, they did not need to replicate the changes their parents had made in gender roles, so the partnerships that husbands and wives created on plantations did not necessarily carry over to their children's townhouses in Richmond, Norfolk, and Petersburg.

Living in Virginia's urban areas exposed the rising generation— these children of the plantations—to a variety of influences that helped to shape their concepts of gender roles at the end of the century. Young middle-class white women were emboldened by talk of the "New Woman," were involved in the burgeoning women's club movement, and were aware of the nascent woman suffrage movement in the South. Yet they came of age at the height of the Confederate memorial movement, and thus they learned a sanitized version of the antebellum period and heard romanticized tales of honorable patriarchal families. As young adults in the 1890s, they witnessed or perhaps even participated in the creation of a stronger system of racial oppression in Virginia, where white men often publicly affirmed the protection of white womanhood in order to inflame racial fear and animosity. In 1895 a Southern woman's magazine encouraged its readers to enter the business world but urged them: "Above all, be gentle and courteous, and . . . remember that you are woman whom God and good men will protect and honor."[27]

After gaining independence, working on their own, and moving to cities, many of the children of Virginia's postwar planters ultimately may have chosen to embrace the gender norms of their *grand*parents' generation. Even their parents had demonstrated after the war that those roles were outdated and that new ones might be necessary for both men and women. In the years following the Civil War, new possibilities emerged for Southern gender relations. Yet patriarchy did not die during the postwar financial emergency. The changes that plantation men and women made in crafting working partnerships in the first postwar years got lost in their children's rush to join the New South.

Notes

The author would like to thank Cindy Aron, Ed Ayers, Peter Wallenstein, and Jenry Morsman for their help in shaping this work and the dissertation from which it is drawn.

1. Anne Firor Scott, *The Southern Lady: From Pedestal to Politics 1830–1930* (Chicago, 1970). Also emphasizing change, but not women, is C. Vann Woodward, *Origins of the New South, 1877–1913* (Baton Rouge, La., 1951).

2. This essay stems from my dissertation, "The Big House After Slavery: Virginia's Plantation Elite and Their Postbellum Domestic Experiment," completed in 2004 at the University of Virginia. Scholarship on post–Civil War Southern women since Scott's *The Southern Lady* includes Jacqueline Jones, *Labor of Love, Labor of Sorrow: Black Women and Work from Slavery to the Present* (New York, 1985); George Rable, *Civil Wars: Women and the Crisis of Southern Nationalism* (Urbana, Ill., 1991); Drew Faust, *Mothers of Invention: Women of the Slaveholding South in the American Civil War* (Chapel Hill, N.C., 1996); Tera Hunter, *To 'Joy My Freedom: Southern Black Women's Lives and Labors after the Civil War* (Cambridge, Mass., 1997); Marli Weiner, *Mistresses and Slaves: Plantation Women in South Carolina, 1830–1880* (Urbana, Ill., 1998); and Jane Turner Censer, *The Reconstruction of White Southern Womanhood, 1865–1895* (Baton Rouge, La., 2003).

3. Related scholarship includes the work of Scott, Censer, and Weiner; LeeAnn Whites, *The Civil War as a Crisis in Gender: Augusta, Georgia, 1860–1890* (Athens, Ga., 1995), 144–50; and Laura Edwards, *Gendered Strife and Confusion: The Political Culture of Reconstruction* (Urbana, Ill., 1997), 107–44.

4. C. Vann Woodward, *The Strange Career of Jim Crow*, rev. ed. (New York, 1974), 32–33, 44.

5. The quoted phrase is from Woodward, *Strange Career*, 44.

6. Allen W. Moger, *Virginia: Bourbonism to Byrd, 1870–1925* (Charlottesville, Va., 1968), 4–5, 76–94; "Fruit Growing," in *The Farmer* 2 (March 1867): 359–60.

7. Fulwar Skipwith's notebook no. 6, box 26, folder 6, 111, and notebook no. 12, box 27, folder 2, 194, Skipwith Family Papers, CWM.

8. Thomas S. Watson to Mrs. J. R. Robertson, 18 August 1867, Watson Family Papers, UVA.

9. George Munford to William Munford, 9 July 1867, Munford-Ellis Family Papers, DU.

10. George Munford to Thomas Munford, 14 December 1868, Munford-Ellis Papers.

11. James L. Hubard to Isaetta Randolph Hubard, 6 March 1879, Randolph-Hubard Family Papers, UVA.

12. "Fruit Growing," 359.

13. Isaetta Randolph Hubard to Sallie Randolph, 12 June 1866, 20 October [after 1866], Isaetta Randolph Hubard to Mary Hubard, 4 January 1888, Randolph-Hubard Papers; Elizabeth Watson to Virginia Robertson (enclosed within Thomas Watson's letter), 27 March 1870, Watson Family Papers; Sallie M. Talbott to Charlie Talbott, 22 October 1867, Munford-Ellis Papers. Censer, *Reconstruction of White Southern Womanhood*, 51–90, describes in detail the tremendous postwar changes in the domestic lives of Southern elite women.

14. Sarah Eppes Hubard to Susan Hubard, 5 April 1873, Edmund Wilcox Hubard Papers, SHC; Lila Hubard to Isaetta Randolph Hubard, 1882, Randolph-Hubard Family Papers; Thomas S. Watson to Virginia Robertson, 8 December 1880, Watson Family Papers.

15. "Home Embellishment—Ladies, Make Your Homes Attractive," in *Southern Planter and Farmer* 1 (November 1867): 626 (hereafter cited as *SP&F*).

16. "The Model Wife," *SP&F* 1 (Oct. 1867): 566.

17. For comparison with scholarship on women's work in the antebellum period, see Scott, *Southern Lady*, and Marli Weiner, *Mistresses and Slaves*.

18. Robert McMath, *American Populism: A Social History, 1877–1898* (New York, 1993), 58; Julie Roy Jeffrey, "Women in the Southern Farmers' Alliance: A Reconsideration of the Role and Status of Women in the Late Nineteenth-Century South," *Feminist Studies* 3 (1975): 72–91; D. Wyatt Aiken, "The Patrons of Husbandry," *SP&F* 6 (July 1872): 406; M. E. Ambler to Phoebe Bailey, 9 December 1874, Bailey Family Papers, VHS.

19. Virginia Patrons of Husbandry, "Address to the Farmers of Virginia" (1874), UVA; see Nancy Grey Osterud, *Bonds of Community: The Lives of Farm Women in Nineteenth-Century* New York (Ithaca, N.Y., 1991), 255–56.

20. "A Talk with Farmers on Home Embellishment," *SP&F* 1 (October 1867): 565.

21. Thomas Watson to Mrs. J. R. Robertson, 25 June 1882, Watson Family Papers; "Don't Come to the City," *SP&F* 3 (March 1869): 152. Numerous other examples of such warnings appeared in this periodical and others throughout the postwar years, among them Willoughby Newton, "Address of the President of the Virginia State Agricultural Society," *SP&F* 1 (February 1867): 24; "Some Comments on Col. Beverley's Advice to Our Young Men," ibid. 11 (February 1877): 81; and "The Enrichment of Rural Life in Virginia," *The Virginia Magazine: The New State Magazine* 1 (December 1908): 21–22.

22. Sue Hubard to Edmund Hubard, 5 March 1870, Edmund Wilcox Hubard Papers.

23. Moger, *Virginia*, 124; Donald Dodd and Wynelle Dodd, *Historical Statistics of the South, 1790–1970* (Tuscaloosa, Ala., 1973), 58–61; Edward Ayers, *The Promise of the New South: Life after Reconstruction* (New York, 1992), viii, 56, 62–63, 66; James L. Hubard to Mary Hubard, 12 March 1888, Robert T. Hubard III to Isaetta Randolph Hubard, 18 October 1883, 14 November 1883, 30 December 1883, Bob Hubard to Ben Hubard, 1 August 1882, Randolph-Hubard Papers; Thomas S. Watson to Mrs. J. R. Robertson, 25 February 1882, Watson Family Papers; Beverley Tucker to Lizzie Munford, 27 March 1869, Munford-Ellis Papers; Sally to Fulwar Skipwith, 20 November 1892, Skipwith Family Papers.

24. Wilmer Turner to Tom Turner, 21 April 1866, Turner Family Papers, DU; Kitty Dawson, "Dear Bettie," *SP&F* 13 (August 1879): 446.

25. "Money-Making for Women," *Southern Literary Messenger* 1 (July 1895): 3.

26. Thomas Watson to Mrs. J. R. Robertson, 15 June 1879, Watson Family Papers. Other references to young women and men teaching are Jennie Munford to George W. Munford, 18 September 1880, Elizabeth Munford to George Munford, 25 September 1880, Munford-Ellis Family Papers; James Hubard to Mary Hubard, 12 March 1888, Randolph-Hubard Family Papers. See also Censer, *Reconstruction of White Southern Womanhood*, 151–73.

27. "Money-Making for Women," 4; see Marjorie Spruill Wheeler, *New Women of the New South: The Leaders of the Woman Suffrage Movement in the Southern States* (New York, 1993); Glenda Gilmore, *Gender and Jim Crow: Women and the Politics of White Supremacy* (Chapel Hill, N.C., 1996); Karen L. Cox, *Dixie's Daughters: The United Daughters of the Confederacy and the Preservation of Confederate Culture* (Gainesville, Fla., 2003), 104–5.

To Honor Her Noble Sons

*The Ladies Memorial Association
of Petersburg, 1866–1912*

CAROLINE E. JANNEY

On June 9, 1904, the Ladies Memorial Association (LMA) of Petersburg, Virginia, gathered to honor their Confederate dead. They had been engaged in such memorial ceremonies for thirty-eight years, but on that day the ritual went beyond the laying of wreaths, evergreens, and bouquets of flowers on the graves of those who had gloriously fallen. As a result of wide publicity, white pilgrims, as they might be called, had traveled from nearly every corner of the old Rebel states to dedicate an eighteenth-century church as a Confederate memorial chapel.

Speeches and prayers opened the obsequies downtown before thousands marched to the chapel. There, the LMA unveiled three stained glass windows that Tiffany & Co. had crafted in memory of fallen soldiers from Virginia, Missouri, and Louisiana. "No nobler band of women ever performed a more beautiful service to posterity than did the Ladies Memorial Association of Petersburg," boasted descendants of the planners in 1957.[1]

The traditional narrative argues that, in unbroken continuity, such celebrations of the Confederacy as this commemoration emerged with the die-hards in the 1860s, flourished in the mid-1880s, and reached a pinnacle of popularity early in the twentieth century. Having emphasized the national organizations, historians have missed the struggle that local communities undertook to keep Confederate flames aglow. How one city's activities developed indicates a much more complicated texture than historians have acknowledged. The story began early, yet the Confederate defeat and subsequent eco-

nomic downturns and political changes made civic efforts a very strenuous and sometimes flagging effort, with memorial efforts revealing
anything but a continuous line of development.[2]

"Petersburg has been a pretty Place," a Union soldier wrote in April
1865, "but it is a hard looking Place now." In 1860 the town had been
a bustling manufacturing and transportation hub for the South, with
a population of 18,266 and the largest free black urban population in
Virginia. The second largest city in Virginia, its five railroads shipped
products from the city's cotton mills, ironworks, and tobacco manufacturers. As a center for provisioning the Army of Northern Virginia,
Petersburg became a crucial object of Union subjugation during the
war, and the town and its inhabitants suffered much. With the end of
slavery, the city's white residents lost $3,500,000 in their human property, and railroad and tobacco companies lost their skilled slave workmen. Although accepting defeat and emancipation, most whites remained tenaciously loyal to the old political values and the principles
of white supremacy.[3]

    After Appomattox, many white women across the South transformed their wartime soldiers' aid societies into Confederate memorial associations. In Petersburg, while the middle- and upper-class
white men toiled "for the upbuilding of a greater South," their wives
and daughters were busy, too. Many of the women had been long active in benevolent organizations such as orphanages, and during the
war they organized the Washington Street Soldiers' Relief Society. On
May 6, 1866, 278 of Petersburg's more prominent women met at Library Hall to organize a Ladies Memorial Association, their purpose
to "honor the bravery and to keep alive the memory of those who fell
in defense of their country." The past was not to be forgotten in any
rush to modernize.[4]

    Proclaiming at their first meeting that "a mysterious providence"
had pointed the way, they established the association's purpose: to
honor the remains of the Confederacy's "noble sons." Their primary
obligation was to "mark more distinctly" the names of the soldiers
buried in each location around the city and annually pay tribute to the
graves. They invited the cooperation of veterans, townsmen, and the
town's Common Council to join them. It was expected that women

should carry out the traditional funereal role of their sex, but they recruited young male volunteers to handle some 25,000 bodies and landscape the burial grounds. As early as June 9, 1866, the LMA organized the group's first grand procession from downtown and a memorial service at the city's largest cemetery, Blandford. According to one observer, "every garden and hillside was robbed to pay tribute to valor and endurance." Another pronounced it "a veritable Sabbath in memory of the dead."[5]

Despite the popularity of the ritual, the LMA desperately needed financial support for reburials. The leaders widened the circle of participants beyond the well-to-do. Knowing that the city treasury was in straits, they ambitiously strove for a state and even regional constituency. For some time after the ten-month wartime siege, the city's services, including gas streetlights and street drainage systems, remained in a deplorable state. Shops, residences, and industrial plants also required repair. But capital was scarce and debts burdensome. A city editor noted the "scarcity of provisions" in the city markets and requested that "our country friends come to our rescue in this our time of need." Given the hard times, the LMA reduced monthly subscriptions from 50 cents to 25 cents. If even the upper- and middle-class residents of Petersburg had difficulty feeding themselves, they could not be expected to donate much money for the LMA's reburial efforts.[6]

Despite the economic hardships, the LMA continued to direct reburial projects. In February 1867 the association resolved that the Old Blandford Cemetery should be the primary spot to bury the city's Confederate dead. They petitioned the Petersburg Common Council, still dominated by conservative former Democrats and Whigs, to appropriate free of charge to the association enough land for the interment of 500 bodies. As soon as the site had been secured, the LMA appealed to the legislatures of all the Southern states requesting aid for the cemetery, which now held nearly 4,000 soldiers. While the LMA members might direct the interment and marking of graves, they could ill afford to finance an ever-increasing project. In May 1867 the common council again supported the cemetery project by donating an acre of Blandford Cemetery to the LMA. With this newly acquired space, the LMA appointed Rev. Thomas H. Campbell and "any sergeants he deemed necessary" to retrieve the bodies of Virginia soldiers from distant battlefields.[7]

Although funds were scare, progress in formally laying out Blandford Cemetery continued with the aid of a few local people. The LMA contracted several men to disinter 277 bodies "hurriedly buried by their comrades" around the battlefield and reinter them in Blandford, while young men and pupils of local schools helped to tidy the grounds. Editors of the city newspapers expressed "courtesy and interest," and railroad officials continued to provide free transportation of soldiers' bodies. In 1868, at the third celebration of June 9, people from outside Petersburg sent flowers, local businesses provided hacks and wagons, and thousands of locals participated in decorating the graves. On that day, support for the LMA and its cemetery seemed to abound, and the Ladies exclaimed, "On no previous occasion has there been manifested by our people more cordial sympathy with the objects of our Society." The LMA rejoiced, "Our hearts are thus encouraged, and we are stimulated to a more lively zeal."[8]

While the tide of support seemed high in June, by the following January, the LMA noted that the cause was losing popular support. At the time, Radical Republicans had risen to power even as the local economy was deteriorating. In 1868 LMA president Mrs. William T. Joynes complained that "the reverses" that had "overtaken the entire community" had ruined "many fortunes." Although pleased with what the LMA had achieved, she deplored "more of the ladies of our city do not lend the aid of their presence and their purses to our sacred undertaking." While not excusing the "luke warmness of Southern men" in honoring the cause, she vowed that she and her friends would never forget those who had "vainly died for Southern independence."[9]

Though the LMA continued to receive financial assistance from subscribers in other states, by early 1869 the monthly meetings had become erratic and membership had decreased. Desperately, the ladies sought means to revive the flagging enterprise, and in preparation for the 1870 Memorial Day celebration, the LMA begged nonmembers for aid. By the spring of 1871, the LMA was meeting only once a year to make preparations for Memorial Day services. Matters grew worse with the onset of the 1873 Panic. Banks were reeling from the withdrawals of deposits, and wages fell by as much as 20 percent. Despite high taxes, the city government had to borrow heavily to finance almost every municipal function from its school system to the dredging of the Appomattox River.[10]

Throughout the political turbulence and fiscal challenges of the postwar years, black and white citizens alike memorialized the war and its dead. As early as 1866, Petersburg blacks had celebrated January 1 as Emancipation Day. The Petersburg Guards, a black militia company organized in 1871, led Emancipation Day parades through the city in 1874 and 1875. Through the 1870s, Northern residents and black citizens of Petersburg gathered at the U.S. military cemeteries at City Point and Poplar Grove to celebrate Northern Decoration day at the end of May. In 1875 the city staged its largest Independence Day celebration since the war with an unusual display of cooperation between the white militia units (the Petersburg Grays and Artillery) and the black Petersburg Guards. By 1876 the city's most prominent newspaper, the *Index-Appeal*, acknowledged May 30 as the national Memorial Day, referring to June 9 merely as a day to decorate Confederate graves.[11]

These promising signs of racial civility notwithstanding, the ways in which blacks and whites, Northerners and Southerners within Petersburg remembered the war are difficult to determine. In spite of the recognition of July 4 as Independence Day, rhetoric of sectional hostilities had not vanished. Municipal Reconstruction of Petersburg had ended in 1874, when the conservatives won a majority of seats on the city council and elected a conservative mayor. Immediately, he began firing Radical Republicans from city jobs, a step that encouraged racial antagonisms on both sides. Soon some Petersburg residents were again flying the Confederate flag. When the *Washington National Republican* blasted the defiant display, the *Index-Appeal* retorted that only "some six-storied Radical jack-ass" would remark on the incident. Further, the editor announced that, "if their exhibition [of the Confederate flag] promotes and keeps alive the bitter feelings of the war, the display of the United States flag is liable in equal measure to the same [objection]."[12] Throughout the 1870s, Rebel sentiments were still very much abroad in Virginia.

Despite these occasional outbursts and the continued popularity of

June 9 celebrations, between the late 1870s and mid-1880s, the celebration of the Confederate past continued to take a back seat to such more pressing issues of the New South as industry, religion, and state and local politics. In the late 1870s, a political struggle regarding repayment of the state debt led to the Readjuster Movement, and Petersburg became the center of activity for city residents like former Confederate general William Mahone.[13]

During the period of Readjuster dominance in state politics, blacks served on Petersburg juries, held positions on the city council, and gained election to the state legislature. The General Assembly voted to locate a black state college and a black mental hospital in Petersburg, and the city council appointed blacks to the Board of Education. These Readjusters improved the city's streets and water system, promoted public health, regulated industry pollution, developed city parks, brought electricity to the city, and developed a horse streetcar line. Along with organizing more militia units than whites, black residents joined fraternal orders and social clubs, established newspapers, created debating and lecture associations, and supported a library.[14]

Perhaps this rejuvenation of black political power, in combination with continual economic difficulties in the city, suppressed participation in celebrations of the Confederate past. According to one historian, the Readjuster era led to a merging of associations in Petersburg between Union and Confederate veterans. Conversely, as the Readjuster Movement declined, so too did racial and Unionist courtesies. After nearly thirteen years of little activity and depressed interest, the Ladies Memorial Association called a meeting on April 26, 1883, to resurrect the society. Eleven women, only three of whom had been members of the original association, gathered to elect an executive committee. In May the LMA slashed its dues to stimulate recruiting, and the scheme worked, as the number of subscribers soon rose to forty-five.[15]

Revival of interest stemmed in part from the ceremonial unveiling of a statue honoring Gen. Robert E. Lee, placed over his tomb in Lexington by the Lee Memorial Association. Memorial organizations across Virginia, such as Richmond's Hollywood Memorial Association, were revitalized during the mid-1880s. Like their counterparts in cities across the South, the Petersburg LMA wished to pay tribute to the dying generation of war heroes while celebrating the traditional privileges of race, gender, and class.[16]

In 1883, with the interments complete and the Memorial Day celebration observed for the year, the revitalized organization needed a new project. In August of that year, the LMA proposed to erect an arch at the entrance of the memorial grounds. Short of funds for the project, once again the LMA approached the public. Despite the Readjuster majority that remained on the common council, the city complied with the LMA's request to aid in widening and grading the road through the cemetery. With improved finances, the members felt "quite encouraged" in the public's response to their efforts.[17]

Yet, all was not well. In the first annual report in over a decade, the president, Mrs. David Callender, described the general feeling of a city under the burden of economic depression. Some people, she recognized, thought more immediate needs than Confederate commemorations ought to be met in "these hard times." William Mahone, though a former supporter of the LMA, declared in 1882, "I have thought it wise to live for the future and not the dead past. . . while cherishing honorable memories of its glories."[18]

Thus, the situation in Petersburg reveals a pattern that contradicts the view that Lost Cause sentiment became increasingly popular throughout the 1880s. Petersburg's economy continued to crumble. Run by out-of-state interests, the railroads often operated at an expense to the city, and unemployment grew. Without a special objective to promote, the LMA could barely hold on to veteran members. By January 1887 the LMA was so desperate for members that it passed a resolution sending a mailing to all the "*old* members of the association urging them to attend the meetings, pay their subscriptions, and to show some interest in our work," yet only two or three "old" subscribers replied.[19] Like much of the city, the former members had more pressing interests than maintaining a Confederate cemetery. Petersburg's economic and political instability helps to explain the lack of enthusiasm for the Lost Cause that was supposedly gaining momentum in the late 1880s and early 1890s.

As in the past, however, when the LMA found a project and funds to support it, membership surged. Following the LMA's erection of the

Confederate Monument on Memorial Hill in 1890, attendance at monthly meetings increased. The LMA noted, "more enthusiasm and interest in the Association was shown than one could have expected, judging from the lack of zeal which has existed for more than three years." Monthly meetings continued throughout the year, and in March 1892 the forty-six members agreed to form an auxiliary society to the A. P. Hill Camp of Confederate Veterans to help aid the widows and orphans of Confederate soldiers. President J. T. Simpson assured the LMA that "this in no wise conflicts with the original design and purpose of our association but to my mind is an additional incentive to the sacred work." Although she expected that the LMA's affiliation with the veterans would increase membership, few of the wives and daughters of the Confederate veterans joined the LMA.[20]

After the peak in participation during the early 1890s, the LMA's membership and participation again declined. Only six members attended the January 1893 annual meeting, and the president noted that "little interest is manifested in our work by the community at large," except on June 9. She stated that "our efforts from time to time to replenish our treasury by means of excursions, entertainment and otherwise have in the main been but poorly supported," and "We have been reduced to the painful necessity of begging, to the City Council and the many private citizens who have so generously aided us." In 1895 the LMA relinquished care of the Memorial Grounds to the Cemetery Committee, and by 1899 membership had dwindled to fifteen— hardly evidence of the extreme enthusiasm and extensive participation in Confederate activities so often attributed to the late nineteenth century. Alternatively, it suggests a transition that was occurring in the ways the past was being remembered.[21]

Historian David Blight has noted the resurgence of Lost Cause enthusiasm in the late 1880s. During this new wave of celebration, new means to reach the public arose: the United Confederate Veterans (UCV), the *Confederate Veteran*, and the United Daughters of the Confederacy (UDC).[22] The UDC had an exceptionally popular appeal among women during the 1890s and was strikingly successful at raising funds. By 1900 it had established 412 chapters, with nearly 17,000 members. While LMAs throughout the South had remained independent organizations, the UDC was a national organization. Like the

LMAs, the UDC believed that tending the graves of the South's fallen soldiers was one of its most important duties. Yet, the UDC assumed much broader social purposes than mere wreath-laying ceremonies. Its members sought "to fulfill the duties of sacred charity to the survivors of the war and those dependent upon them" and "to endeavor to have used in all Southern schools only such histories as are just and true." As UDC historian Mildred Rutherford noted, "the memorial women honor the memory of the dead—the Daughters honor the living."[23]

It may have been the organization of the Petersburg UDC chapter that prompted the Ladies of Petersburg to place a plea in the *Index-Appeal* in 1899 soliciting support. Following this ad, attendance at the May 1899 meeting increased to thirty and in two weeks numbered forty-three. At one meeting, a member suggested transforming the abandoned Blandford Church into a nonsectarian mortuary chapel for all Southern states. Perhaps the fact that the Ladies of Richmond were busy establishing a Confederate museum replete with relics from every Southern state sparked the notion of a shrine in memory of all Confederates.[24] As had been the case each time the association undertook a new project such as the Confederate statue or the Memorial Arch, its membership and local enthusiasm for the Confederate past began to swell.

Built as an Anglican church in 1735 and abandoned by 1803, Blandford Church had been donated to the city of Petersburg by John Grammer in 1819. Left unattended, the church had "gone much to decay: the walls of . . . brick are standing, the roof in part gone, moss and ivy covering the ravages of time." Because the chapel was the focal point for the Confederate cemetery on nearby Memorial Hill, the LMA's first priority was to restore the chapel to its original plan. The most ambitious of the proposals for the church was the installation of stained-glass windows dedicated to the memory of the thousands of soldiers from every Confederate state buried in the cemetery. Within nine months the LMA had decided to employ the services of Louis Comfort Tiffany, the celebrated stained-glass artist, to design "a perfect memorial" for the dead.[25]

In April 1900 the LMA received an invitation from the Southern Memorial Association of Fayetteville, Arkansas, to join a Confederation of Southern Memorial Associations (CSMA). Unwilling to lose their identity as individual memorial associations or merge themselves with the younger Daughters of the Confederacy, the various LMAs aligned themselves with the UCV for the purpose of organizing memorial and historical work across the South. Their objectives, strictly "memorial and historical," included the care of Confederate graves, the erection of monuments, and the compilation of histories of every memorial association. While the Petersburg LMA had requested outside aid since its inception in 1866, the LMA used the history of its association written for the CSMA as a platform to solicit support for the Blandford Church restoration. The Petersburg LMA requested that every Southern state contribute funds for "a memorial window to be placed in this old church to commemorate the mighty deeds wrought in their behalf."[26]

To solicit support across the South for the church restoration, the A. P. Hill Camp of Confederate Veterans volunteered to assist the LMA in preparing and distributing circulars asking for contributions. By October more than 8,000 circulars had been printed, and donations began flooding the LMA. The connection to the CSMA paid off. The LMA exclaimed that "letters from persons in several states" expressed "great interest in the work of restoring 'Old Blandford Church' and also showing that they still cherish loving memories of the Lost Cause that should always be dear to Southern hearts." After a petition from the LMA, in January 1901 the City of Petersburg delegated to the LMA the authority to convert the old church into a mortuary chapel and a Confederate memorial.[27]

If the town council and the veterans camp were willing to support the Blandford project, the LMA felt that perhaps other local organizations might provide support, too. Despite the Petersburg LMA's desire to remain independent of such younger women as the UDC, the group formally invited the Petersburg UDC to cooperate in raising funds to restore the church. The UDC accepted and promptly donated $100 to the project. Nonetheless, the LMA made a concerted effort to remind Petersburg and the nation that they remained distinct from the UDC, evident in the LMA's reaction to the October 1903 *Women's Home Companion* article crediting the UDC with the restoration of Blandford Church.[28]

With a fresh project in which to invest their energies, both the LMA and the citizens of Petersburg expressed a renewed enthusiasm for the Confederate past. At the 1901 memorial celebration, more than 10,000 people participated, and the LMA rejoiced that "36 years after the close of the great struggle for Southern independence popular interest in the annual Confederate Memorial Day celebration is far from diminishing [and] is steadily increasing everywhere throughout Dixie." The LMA insisted that honoring the Confederate dead remained the prime objective, but the day's orator, Gen. Stith Bolling, spoke almost exclusively about the "work of these noble women." He described the women's wartime devotion to the cause and their subsequent "work of gathering from the battlefields the bones of our comrades and giving them a Christian burial." And he declared, "A nobler epitaph could not be theirs." Like many people who spoke for the Lost Cause around the turn of the century, Bolling reminded the crowd not to "forget our helpless living." The LMA and their June 9 speakers found it increasingly unnecessary to dwell on mourning or explain defeat. As David Blight has suggested, champions of the Lost Cause, by the early twentieth century, had converted defeat into a positive narrative about the Southern past.[29]

Throughout 1902 the LMA, the UDC, the UCV, state legislatures, and individuals across the South continued to raise money for the Blandford Church. To prevent disagreements among the donors regarding the content of each memorial window, the LMA requested that Tiffany choose a subject and theme that would unify all fifteen windows. After sending a representative in early 1903 to survey the church, Tiffany decided on the Gothic Revival style of the late nineteenth century. He designed the eleven first-floor compass windows featuring either an evangelist or apostle. Above each figure, he inserted a medallion to designate the window's donor. Below the figures, each donor would be able to choose a memorial verse. The four smaller windows would complement the larger windows. Since individual states would be responsible for acquiring the $400 needed for each window, a Tiffany's associate suggested that the LMA assign one member to work with each state until the necessary funds were raised.[30]

During the next decade, organizations from across the region contributed toward windows for their respective states. On June 3, 1910, an anniversary of the birth of Jefferson Davis, the LMA dedicated eight more windows. On other occasions other windows were installed, and on November 13, 1912, the project was officially concluded with the dedication of the Georgia window.[31]

By transforming the old Blandford Church into a Confederate shrine, the LMA appealed to a national memory of the war dead that invoked an other-worldliness—an eternal life for the martyrs of the lost cause. Like many defenders of the Confederacy, they moved beyond death to celebrate the triumphs of not only their ancestors, but of themselves.

C. Vann Woodward argued in 1951 that one of the most significant inventions of the New South was the Old South—an idea that grew out of the Lost Cause romanticism of the 1880s and 1890s. He claimed that "the deeper the involvements in commitments to the New Order, the louder the protests of loyalty to the Old." A half century later, David Blight argued along a similar vein that the Lost Cause ideology thwarted "threats of populists politics, racial equality, and industrialization."[32] And though Blight acknowledges dissenters, both historians believe that by the late 1890s, the mysticism of the Lost Cause gripped the imagination of white Americans in both the South and the North. While threats to the old social and political world surely compelled white Southerners to invent a past of beautiful plantations, happy slaves, and gallant soldiers, the reality of life in the New South prevented most from spending their everyday lives thinking about the past.

The cyclical popularity of the Ladies Memorial Association suggests that in Petersburg most white citizens were more concerned with the living than with the dead. Enthusiasm for the Confederate past came in waves, rushing forward with great urgency when a project and funds—especially external funds—were at hand, and then dropping off to obscurity. As Petersburg shows, a local community responded to broader influences as it participated in national and regional patterns of Civil War memory. But, as Petersburg also shows, practical matters of local politics and economics shaped how a single community remembered the war. From rough headboards for graves following the war to the magnificent, modern stained-glass windows of the twentieth century, the social, political, and economic conditions of Petersburg continued to moderate the ways in which the Ladies Memorial Association honored the Confederate dead.

Notes

1. *Petersburg Daily Index-Appeal*, 10 June 1904 (cited hereafter as *PDIA*); Janet Bernard Nichols, *Sketch of Old Blandford Church* (Petersburg, Va., 1957).

2. Regarding the Lost Cause, see Gaines M. Foster, *The Ghosts of the Confederacy: Defeat, the Lost Cause, and the Emergence of the New South, 1865 to 1913* (New York, 1987); Rollin G. Osterweis, *The Myth of the Lost Cause, 1865–1900* (Hamden, Conn., 1973); Charles Reagan Wilson, *Baptized in Blood: The Religion of the Lost Cause* (Athens, Ga., 1980); Gary W. Gallagher and Alan T. Nolan, eds., *The Myth of the Lost Cause and Civil War History*, (Bloomington, Ind., 2000); David W. Blight, *Race and Reunion: The Civil War in American Memory* (Cambridge, Mass., 2001); C. Vann Woodward, *The Strange Career of Jim Crow* (1955; 3rd rev. ed. New York, 1974).

3. Suzanne Lebsock, *The Free Women of Petersburg: Status and Culture in a Southern Town, 1784–1860* (New York, 1984), 244–45, 310; William D. Henderson, *Petersburg in the Civil War: War at the Door* (Lynchburg, Va., 1988), 1–20, 136–48; Lawrence L. Hartzell, "The Exploration of Freedom in Black Petersburg, Virginia, 1865–1902," in *The Edge of the South: Life in Nineteenth-Century Virginia*, eds. Edward L. Ayers and John C. Willis (Charlottesville, Va., 1991), 134–56; Nora Fontaine Maury Davidson, *Cullings from the Confederacy* (Washington, D.C., 1903), 10; Nichols, *Old Blandford Church*, 5; Foster, *Ghosts*, 20–21.

4. Mildred Rutherford Scrapbook, XLI, Museum of the Confederacy, Richmond; Elizabeth R. Varon, *We Mean to Be Counted: White Women and Politics in Antebellum Virginia* (Chapel Hill, N.C., 1998); Lebsock, *Free Women*, 195–236, 249; Henderson, *Petersburg in the Civil War*, 1–21.

5. Records of the Memorial Society of the Ladies of the City of Petersburg, 1866–1912, City of Petersburg Museums (hereafter Minutes), 6 May, 11, 18 July, 12, 16 October 1866; *History of the Confederated Memorial Associations of the South* (New Orleans, 1904), 288–90; Davidson, *Cullings*, 160–62.

6. Foster, *Ghosts*, 38; Minutes, 5 December 1866; Hartzell, "Exploration of Freedom," 134–36; *PDIA*, 30 March 1867.

7. Minutes, 6 February, 30 May 1867; Henderson, *Petersburg in the Civil War*, 150–53.

8. Minutes, 7 March, 13 June 1868.

9. Ibid., 16 January 1869.

10. Ibid., 18 May 1870 (according to a later entry, no business was transacted between May 1873 and May 1876); Hartzell, "Exploration of Freedom," 137.

11. *PDIA*, 1 January 1877, 10, 11 June 1878; William D. Henderson, *Gilded Age City: Politics, Life, and Labor in Petersburg, Virginia, 1874–1889* (Lanham, Md., 1980), 258–59, 327–28.

12. *PDIA*, 10 June 1874; Henderson, *Gilded Age City*, 261, 513.

13. *PDIA*, 1 January 1877, 10, 11 June 1878; Minutes, 1 May 1876; Blight, *Race and Reunion*, 292–93; Henderson, *Gilded Age City*, iii; Hartzell, "Exploration of Freedom," 154; Jane Dailey, *Before Jim Crow: The Politics of Race in Postemancipation Virginia* (Chapel Hill, N.C., 2000).

14. Henderson, *Petersburg in the Civil War*, 156–57; Henderson, *Gilded Age City*, iii–v.

15. Henderson, *Gilded Age City*, 258–59; Minutes, 26 April, 3 May 1883; *PDIA*, 27 April 1883.

16. Foster, *Ghosts*, 6, 87–88; John Coski and Amy Feely, "A Monument to Southern Womanhood: The Founding Generation of the Confederate Museum," in *A Woman's War: Southern Women, Civil War, and the Confederate Legacy*, eds. Edward D. C. Campbell Jr. and Kym S. Rice (Charlottesville, Va., 1996), 131–64.

17. Minutes, August 1883–May 1884 (quote 1 May 1884).

18. Henderson, *Gilded Age City*, 476–77; Minutes, 28 June 1884; Blight, *Race and Reunion*, Mahone quotation at 293.

19. Henderson, *Gilded Age City*, 483–84; Minutes, 3 January, 2 May 1887.

20. Minutes, 5 January 1891, January 1893; Coski and Feely, "Monument to Southern Womanhood," 137–38.

21. Minutes, January 1893; Ibid., 1895–April 1899; Foster, *Ghosts*, 6.

22. Blight, *Race and Reunion*, 265, 272–74; Foster, *Ghosts*, 107–44; Thomas Connelly, *The Marble Man: Robert E. Lee and His Image in American Society* (Baton Rouge, La., 1977); *PDIA*, 26 January 1867; Minutes 1, 17 May 1899.

23. Coski and Feely, "Monument to Southern Womanhood," 137–38; Angie Parrott, "'Love Makes Memory Eternal': The United Daughters of the Confederacy in Richmond, Virginia, 1897–1920," in Ayers and Willis, *Edge of the South*, 219–39, UDC constitution (1903) quotation at 221; Rutherford scrapbook XLI.

24. *PDIA*, 26 January 1867; Minutes, 1, 17 May 1899.

25. Quotation from Petersburg historian Charles Campbell in Martha Wren Briggs, *The Compass Windows of Old Blandford Church* (Sedley, Va., 1992), 2–3; Nichols, *Old Blandford Church*, 7.

26. *Confederated Memorial Associations*, 37, 291; Minutes, 21 May 1900.

27. Minutes, 12 October, 16 November 1900.

28. Ibid., 19 November 1903.

29. *PDIA*, 11 June 1901; Blight, *Race and Reunion*, 255–99.

30. Briggs, *Compass Windows*, 4–8; Minutes, 9 April 1903–September 1903.

31. Briggs, *Compass Windows*, 4–8.

32. C. Vann Woodward, *Origins of the New South, 1877–1913* (Baton Rouge, La., 1951), 154–57 (quote 155); Blight, *Race and Reunion*, 291; Minutes, 6 May 1866.

Afterword

⌒νυυ⌒

PETER WALLENSTEIN AND
BERTRAM WYATT-BROWN

This book did not originate with the question: What, of all possible topics and approaches, should be included? Rather, it began with the question: How can the editors make a fine book out of a number of essays that were written by individuals, each of whom had selected and set out to explore some intriguing facet of Virginia's Civil War? Thus, the collection does a good job of indicating the work that is in process, particularly by younger scholars. Less well does it canvass the terrain in a comprehensive manner. It does what it set out to do, not other things that might have been done instead. And thus it suggests what remains undone as well as what is under way.

Charles Dew's innovative recent book, *Apostles of Disunion*, demonstrates that race and slavery were at the core of the secession endeavor. Deep South leaders—in particular, the commissioners to slave states that had not yet seceded—certainly thought an approach emphasizing these themes would prove effective in the Upper South. Among our authors, however, Daniel Kilbride and Charles Irons urge caution in assuming that we fully know to what extent and in what ways slavery informed perceptions and drove decisions through the Civil War era. James McPherson inquires in one of his many insightful books on the Civil War era "what they fought for"—although of course the distinction must be drawn between why a state seceded and why, once it had, so many of its men went off to war in apparent support of secession.[1] Several of our contributors, beginning with Charles Irons, point up the significance of religion for understanding the course of political and military developments during the Civil War era. Jason Phillips and Wayne Hsieh press the question in Virginia of how, on the battle-front or the home front, religion shaped attitudes and behavior in the war. Lisa Frank reexamines a related question of the home front and the battlefront: to what extent Confederate women maintained their original support of the war. The longer works from which these essays were drawn will do much to augment our comprehension of such matters.

The book title itself might have been rendered in the plural—Virginia's Civil Wars—and, either way, it has a number of meanings, each pointing toward a different dimension of the experience of Virginia in the Civil War: how Virginia responded to developments in the Civil War era; how Virginia shaped those developments; how Virginia's experience of the war compared with that of other states; how individuals' experiences of the war in Virginia varied widely; and how the state of Virginia had its own internal war. In recent years a number of authors have emphasized the theme of a civil war within the South—a war within the states, rather than between or among the states. In *The South vs. the South*, William Freehling broadens the theme across time, space, and social group—to include black Unionists as well as white Unionists, throughout the slave states and throughout the war—thus demonstrating how, in cumulative ways, anti-Confederate Southerners undermined the Confederacy's bid for independence.[2] Those themes are yet to be fully explored for Virginia, especially in what remained of Virginia after West Virginia went its separate way. Susanna Michele Lee's innovative use of the Southern Claims Commission records offers one promising approach.

Given how much our essayists have been able to do with various kinds of literary sources, we can only imagine that other such sources remain to be examined or reexamined. Notable for their insights in this collection are Lucinda MacKethan's quest for the slave Marlboro Jones through a range of sources, including a picture that has survived of him; Suzanne Jones's reconsideration of the miscegenation theme through a recent novel about wartime Virginia; and Ian Binnington's exploration of Confederate culture through the *Southern Illustrated News*.

This book does much—and the larger works in process will do much more—to pursue questions of gender roles and women's experiences, especially with regard to elite white Southerners during and after the Civil War. We see Lisa Frank's elite women face a hardening war as it comes to their doorsteps; Amy Feely Morsman's planter men and women—among couples in which the man survived the war—changing their ways as they seek to make their way in the harsh economy of the postwar years; the journey of Theodore DeLaney's "Mrs. Ex-President Tyler" through the same era; and Caroline Janney's women in their efforts in one Virginia city to commemorate the men of the Lost Cause. These four essays highlight one of the key themes of this volume, for, while religion is one theme to generate significant new work on Virginia in the Civil War era, gender is another.

Questions must remain of such matters as wartime Virginia's representativeness and its impact on events outside the state. One essay seeking to demonstrate Virginia's possible impact elsewhere is Ervin L. Jordan Jr.'s quest to determine whether two former slaves in Virginia affected wartime public opinion in Great Britain. Another is David G. Smith's tracking Virginia troops into Pennsylvania who returned with people they claimed to be runaway slaves. As for comparisons, Lisa Frank finds elite Confederate women responding to Union soldiers late in the war in the Shenandoah Valley in much the way that she finds them responding in Georgia along the path of General Sherman's march to the sea.

When all is said and done, much has yet to be done or said. One of the striking observations that might be made of this collection is how seldom black voices are heard. One in three residents of Virginia on the eve of the Civil War was African American, and after the war two in five citizens were. Scholars have not fully explored the experiences and impact of free people of color, slaves, and former slaves within Virginia across the Civil War era—for example, Cornelius Garner, a teenaged slave who became a Union soldier and seven decades later told his story to an interviewer. (See appendix, document 3.) We know too little about developments in politics, literature, religion, and family life among black Virginians. Explorations of the sort that David G. Smith, Ervin L. Jordan, and John McClure have included in this collection surely push the project along. Otherwise, for the most part, black Virginians—by their presence or their absence—appear in other people's fears, desires, arrangements, and agendas. Another book of essays on the topic of Virginia's Civil War might move the perspective and develop the dimension of black Virginians as agents rather than objects, not only during the war but also in its aftermath.

As the opening essays in particular show—those by Emory Thomas, Michael Fellman, Bertram-Wyatt Brown, and Charles Joyner—the personalities and performances of Confederate military leaders, especially Robert E. Lee, continue to beguile historians and their readers. Past generations of scholars have tended to emphasize conventional politics and battlefield developments. Those questions are not going away—the differences among these four students of Lee attest to that. But with essays like the ones in part two of this book, we see in new ways how the political and military events were shaped, and with what consequences, as we look more directly at matters of race, religion, and gender. In the essays on Lee, and in those on the war, we see battlefront and home front in a fresh light.

The many younger scholars whose work is represented in these essays, and their older colleagues in the book—together with platoons of other people, some of them not yet even in graduate school—will continue to inform our understanding of Virginia's Civil War, and by extension the war in other states, Virginia at other times, and the nation's journey through the past and on to the present.

Notes

1. Charles B. Dew, *Apostles of Disunion: Southern Secession Commissioners and the Causes of the Civil War* (Charlottesville, Va., 2001); James M. McPherson, *What They Fought For, 1861–1865* (Baton Rouge, La., 1994); McPherson, *For Cause and Comrades: Why Men Fought in the Civil War* (New York, 1997).

2. William W. Freehling, *The South vs. the South: How Anti-Confederate Southerners Shaped the Course of the Civil War* (New York, 2001).

Appendix

Documents from Virginia's Civil War

1. Conditions for Remaining in the Union, March–April 1861

On March 19, 1861—five weeks into the proceedings of the convention that had been called to consider secession—the Virginia Convention's Committee on Federal Relations reported a series of proposed amendments to the U.S. Constitution—amendments the approval of which, it was understood, would be required to warrant Virginia's remaining in the Union.

The committee had made its way through two sets of recommendations and was offering its synthesis. Among the eight proposed amendments, all but one related directly to slavery; the sole exception would have barred African Americans from voting in federal or territorial elections. One amendment would revive the old 36°30' line of the Missouri Compromise and would bar actions by the federal government to interfere with slavery south of that line. Another would bar state action in the North designed to prevent enforcement of the Fugitive Slave Act. The last of the eight proposals would require unanimous consent of all the states to change (1) any of these proposed amendments, once they had been approved by Congress and ratified by the states; (2) the current three-fifths clause; or (3) the current fugitive slave clause. These proposals can all be found in George H. Reese, ed., *Proceedings of the Virginia State Convention of 1861, February 13–May 1*, 4 vols. (Richmond, 1965), 2:34–37, and subsequent action on each in turn by the Convention can be traced through that source. Here are some of the proposals:

Sec. 6. Congress shall provide by law that the United States shall pay to the owner the full value of his fugitive from labor, in all cases where the marshal, or other officer, whose duty it was to arrest such fugitive, was prevented from so doing by violence or intimidation from mobs, or riotous assemblages, or by violence, or when, after arrest, such fugitive was rescued by like intimidation or violence, and the owner thereby deprived of the same.

Sec. 7. The elective franchise and the right to hold office, whether Federal or Territorial, shall not be exercised by persons who are of the African race.

Sec. 8. No one of these amendments nor the third paragraph of the second section of the first article of the Constitution, nor the third paragraph of the second section of the fourth article thereof, shall be amended or abolished without the consent of all the States.

2. The Virginia Secession Ordinance, April 1861

Virginia considered secession through much of the winter and spring of 1861. After rejecting an ordinance of secession shortly before fighting broke out at Fort Sumter, South Carolina, the convention approved such an ordinance on April 17, right after the news came from Fort Sumter (Reese, *Proceedings* 4:145–46).

AN ORDINANCE

To repeal the Ratification of the Constitution of the United States of America, by the State of Virginia, and to resume all the rights and powers granted under said Constitution.

The people of Virginia, in their ratification of the Constitution of the United States of America, adopted by them in Convention, on the 25th day of June, in the year of our Lord one thousand seven hundred and eighty-eight, having declared that the powers granted under the said Constitution were derived from the people of the United States, and might be resumed whensoever the same should be perverted to their injury and oppression, and the Federal Government having perverted said powers, not only to the injury of the people of Virginia, but to the oppression of the Southern slaveholding states:

Now, therefore, we, the people of Virginia, do declare and ordain that the ordinance adopted by the people of this State, in Convention, on the 25th day of June, in the year of our Lord one thousand seven hundred and eighty-eight, whereby the Constitution of the United States of America, was ratified—and all acts of the General Assembly of this State ratifying or adopting amendments to said Constitution—are hereby repealed and abrogated; that the Union between the State of Virginia and the other States under the Constitution aforesaid is hereby dissolved, and that the State of Virginia is in the full possession and exercise of all the rights of sovereignty which belong and appertain to a free and independent State. And they do further declare that the said Constitution of the United States of America is no longer binding on any of the citizens of this State.

This ordinance shall take effect and be an act of this day when ratified by a majority of the votes of the people of this State, cast at a poll to be taken thereon on the fourth Thursday in May next, in pursuance of a schedule hereafter to be enacted.

Done in Convention, in the City of Richmond, on the seventeenth day of April, in the year of our Lord one thousand eight hundred and sixty one, and in the eighty-fifth year of the Commonwealth of Virginia.

3. "Slave Narratives" of Virginia's Civil War

Particularly since the early 1970s, historians have made substantial use of surviving accounts of interviews conducted in the late 1930s with elderly black Southerners, most of them former slaves. The accounts, generated by a variety of writers, often are presented in dialect as the writer represents having heard the words. Published apart from, and a few years after, those of other states, the Virginia narratives have been used less than most.

Some respondents, acknowledging that they were too young to have direct memories of slavery or of the war themselves, tell what they understand from their elders. Most tell what they recalled themselves, often with extraordinary vividness, more than seventy years after the events in question occurred. What follows is a sample of what the Civil War meant for various black Southerners who were interviewed in Virginia.

Charlotte Brown (*Weevils*, 58–59) remembered freedom day:

De news come on a Thursday, an' all de slaves been shoutin' an' car-
ryin' on tell ev'ybody was all tired out. 'Member [I remember] de
fust Sunday of freedom. We was all sittin' roun' restin' an' tryin' to
think what freedom meant an' ev'ybody was quiet an' peaceful. All
at once ole Sister Carrie who was near 'bout a hundred started in to
talkin':

> Tain't no mo' sellin' today,
> Tain't mo more hirin' today,
> Tain't no pullin' off shirts today,
> Its stomp down freedom today.
> Stomp it down!

An' when she says, "Stomp it down," all de slaves commence to
shoutin' wid her:

> Stomp down Freedom today—
> Stomp it down!
> Stomp down Freedom today.

Wasn't no mo' peace dat Sunday. Ev'ybody started in to sing an'
shout once mo'. Fust thing you know dey done made up music to
Sister Carrie's stomp song an' sang an' shouted dat song all de res' de
day. Chile, dat was one glorious time!

Cornelius Garner was interviewed in Norfolk on May 18, 1937 (*Weevils*, 102–4).

Good mornin'. How are you all.... I'se glad to tell you anything I
can. What you wan's to know. Cose you know I was a slave. Did I
fight in de war? Well if I hadn' you wouldn' be sittin' dere writin' today. Les' start at de beginnin'.

I was born in St. Mary's County, Maryland, February 11,
1846.... Dey didn' whup you much. Mos' o' dat was done down
souf. Dere bigges' punishment was to tell you, "I'll sell you down
souf to Georgia." Dat wus wersen a lickin'....

I came to Norfolk in 1864. I was eighteen on a Friday February
11, and 'listed on a Monday morning in Donaldville. I fit in de battle
o' Deep Bottom on de James River wid de ole 38th regiment. We

had colored sojers an' white officers. We licked de 'federate good an' made 'em treat [retreat] up to a Place called Chaff's farm. Never will I fergit dat battle. It come on a Thursday, Sept. 29, 1864. Friday, October 7, 1864 Lee charged us seven times, tryin' to break our line an' git out. All he did was slaughtered his a'my. Monday. April 5, 1865, Grant made his las' charge on Lee. It were de Petersbu'g 'sault. De whole line charged ev'ywhere, an' Lee flew. Our regiment was de fust into Richmond when Lee surrendered. Grant had Lee all bottled up. Lee couldn' go back, he couldn' go forward, an' he couldn' go sideways. Grant gave him five minutes to surrender. He surrendered too. Den Grant tol' dem rebels to go home an' be good citizens. After de war my regiment was sen' souf way down in Texas for to ketch a rebel general whut was still fightin'. We got down dere an' chased him over into Mexico. Den I come home er back to Virginny an' left de a'my in 1867.

My mother an' father was down heah at a place called Taylor's farm. De lower part of No'folk had plenty o' houses on it den, but up heah wasn' much mo' den a hawg path. De fust school was Nicholson Street School. Dey had white teachers f'om Norf. School was held in an ole buildin'. Dey had dat school an' two or three other schools heah den. Dat was while I was still in de a'my. Dere was an auction block down on de co'ner o' White an' Water Street where dey useta sell slaves e'ry New Yeah's Day. Dat day, New Yeah's Day, should be kept by all de colored people. Dat is de day o' freedom. An' dey ought to 'member Frederick Douglass too. Frederick Douglass tol' Abe Lincun, "Give de black man guns an' let him fight." Abe Linkun say, "Ef I give him gun, when he come to battle, he run." Frederick Douglass say, "Try him an' you'll win de war." Abe said, "Alright, I try him."

Every general 'fused de nigger troops but one. Dat general was General Butler. He say, "I'll take dem." After dey fight dere fust battle, ev'y general wan' 'em. Dey won de war fer de white man. Yessuh.

Garner was injured while on duty in Texas, and he spent years trying to get a pension. The papers are at the National Archives.

Charles Grandy, born in 1842 (*Weevils*, 117), recalled:

Slaves was some kind o' glad when dey 'mancipated, all dey sing was:

> Slavery chain is broke at las'
> Broke at Las, broke at las'
>
> Slavery chain is broke at las'
> Praise God 'till I die.

Anna Harris, who was born in 1846 (*Weevils*, 128), insisted:

No white man ever been in my house. Don't 'low it. Dey sole my sister Kate. I saw it wid dese eyes. Sole her in 1860, and I ain't seed nor heard of her since. Folks say white folks is all right dese days. Maybe dey is, maybe dey isn't. But I can't stand to see 'em. Not on my place.

Caroline Hunter, born about 1847 and interviewed in Portsmouth in January 1937 (*Weevils*, 149, 150), reported:

. . . I can' never forgit how my massa beat my brothers cause dey didn wuk. He beat 'em so bad dey was sick a long time, an' soon as dey got a smatterin' better he sold 'em. Two of 'em I seen agin after we was freed, but de oldes' one I ain' never seen since. . . .

. . . When de war ended and we was free, mama an' I came to Portsmouth, Virginia, to live. We foun' two of my brothers an' my papa here, 'cause [of course] I told you I ain' never seen my oldes' brother agin.

William I. Johnson Jr., born on February 14, 1840, was interviewed on May 28, 1937, in Richmond, where he lived in retirement after many years as a building contractor. Among the topics he covered (*Weevils*, 167–68) was his wartime experience:

. . . I was houseman when the War started. First old master went, then his four sons—Sam, Carter, Beverly, and William, my own young master. They left me in complete charge of the plantation house in Albemarle County, because they knew that I could be trusted to protect Mistress Nancy and her two daughters.

On January 15, 1863, master William was back home on leave, and when he returned he carried me along as servant and horseman.

Soon after we joined Lee's army, I learned from another slave that Lincoln had freed all of us, and I wondered whether young master had taken me in the army to keep the Yankees from getting me. They kept us busy there. Whenever there was fighting, all of us Negroes had the camp to look after and when the shooting was over we had to help bring in the wounded. . . .

In July, 1864 my master's regiment captured a gang of Yankee soldiers and brought them into camp to keep them until they could be transferred to Libby Prison in Richmond. We were in camp up near Fredericksburg. At that time the Rebels were trying to take Washington.

I didn't know what the war was all about nor why they were fighting, but when the "Rebels" were out on the battlefield a few pickets were left to guard the prisoners and the servants got a chance to talk to the Yankee prisoners. They explained to us about slavery and freedom. They told us if we got a chance to steal away from camp and got over on the Yankee's side we would be free. They said, "If we win (the Yankees) all your colored folks will be free, but if the 'Rebels' win you will always be slaves." These words got into our heads—we got together five of us, and decided to take the chance one night, and we made it. . . .

I remember three of the men, Joe Roberts, Sam Smith, myself and two other whose names I didn't know. We reached Washington the next day and Yankee pickets took us to the military headquarters. Roberts, Smith, the other two men were enlisted into the fighting regiments, but I was lucky enough to be sent with another group of men to Boston, Massachusetts, where I was assigned to General Butler's division, and to the Quartermasters Corps, in charge of food and rations.

Our regiments saw active service around Petersburg, Danville and Manassas. We were active between Petersburg and Danville to cut off the Rebels from the Norfolk and Western Railroad. I never took part in any active fighting 'cause I was always busy behind the lines keeping the rations in readiness. We were always posted as to battles and battle plans so that we would know how and where to set up the camp kitchen for the regiment.

George Lewis was born free in Richmond about 1859 (*Weevils*, 196–97). He was interviewed there April 9, 1937.

I was born in the city of Richmond just before the Civil War.

My mother was set free by her young mistress two years before I was born. She came to Richmond along with her sister; here they met two young men and married. My father was a business man (free), hiring boats on the James River.

I know little of the War, but I will tell you of that I do know. We lived on Grace Street near First. On the morning of April 3rd, there was so much noise and so much excitement that my mother took me out of bed—changed my night clothes, dressed me for my day ones—and started with me out of the house. Just as we left the porch three or four Yankee soldiers with guns on their soldiers stopped us, and told my mother that they wanted her to cook breakfast for them. I never shall forget the look that came across my mother's face, but she turned around, took me in her arms and returned to our house. I was frightened and hid behind the kitchen door. After they had finished eating the cakes and fish, they got up from the table and took money out of their pockets and paid my mother for her food and for the trouble. These were Negro troops! They asked her the way to some place; she told them, and they were gone. Later the city was on fire and for a time it rocked. This was all I remembered of the War.

Immediately after the War the Yankees from the New England states sent teachers down to the South to teach the children of the ex-slaves. Such schools were opened in the different colored churches of the city; namely, First Baptist, 3rd Street, Second Baptist, and Ebenezer Baptist.

The first colored school I entered during this era was Second Baptist Church between First and Second Streets on Byrd Street. I remained there for about four years. Then I entered Dills' Bakery; this was also a school conducted by Yankees. The next school I attended was Navy Hill and then to the Old High and Normal. I graduated in 1877 from this school.

During this time I was in school I had several jobs to help myself. I worked along with my lifelong friend, Mr. Eddie R. Carter, selling newspapers. We also had a contract to fold papers and put them up for mailing.

In 1878 I became a teacher in Henrico County. . . . I taught in the country for eight years. The school ran for eight months, and my salary was thirty dollars a month. I came to Richmond once or twice a month. During the time I was teaching, I also did private study. I took up very nearly all the studies taught in leading universities of the day.

In 1886 I entered Howard University Law School. While there I had as my fellow students, Judge Robert H. Terrell, Prof. W. H. H. Heart, and others. I graduated from the law department in the class of May 30, 1888.

I started the practice of law in the city of Richmond in October, 1888 immediately after I passed the bar, and I have continued up to the present time. No, I cannot tell you about any of my cases. I never talk of them.

I was married September 9, 1891 to Miss Lucy Brooks. Her father was a business man in the city, having bought his freedom long before the War. Her brother, Robert Peel Brooks, was the first Negro lawyer admitted to the bar in Richmond; another brother, Rev. Walter H. Brooks, is a hospital minister in Washington, D.C. We have two daughters, Leah and Lucille. One teaches at Virginia Union University, and the other at Virginia State College.

I think you have all the important things in my life, and if you will excuse me, I shall get to work.

When he was born shortly before the Civil War, a state law banned schools for black Virginians, whether they were enslaved or not.

Rev. Ishrael Massie, was born in 1849 and interviewed by Susie Byrd in Petersburg in April 1937 (*Weevils*, 211).

Some nights house servants would come down to de quarters wid long faces an' tell de fiel' hands Marsa and Missus been talkin' 'bout money. Dey know dat mean dey gonna sell some slaves to de nex' nigger-trader dat come 'roun'. Sometime dey would hear dem discussin' what slaves to sell. Den sech prayin', honey. Dem what ain't named would pray to God ole Marsa ain't gonna sell dem, an' dem what been named would pray dey get a good Marsa. Nobody wantin' to be sol'; but Marsa he ain't ask you nothin' 'bout wantin' to be sol'; he gwine sell you, an' you got to go whar dey take you. I don't know how much my sister Sadie was sol' for, but 'twas right much money. De man dat bought my sister took her to Southampton.

Name was some kinda Hood. Po' gal. We didn't see her no mo' till Lee's surrender. Den my father went after her. You chillun what come 'long since don't know jus' what us slaves went through.

Georgianna Preston, born about 1855 (*Weevils*, 233–34), recalled the first night of freedom:

Us young folks carried on somep'n awful. Ole Marse let us stay up all night, an' didn't seem to mind at all. Saw de sun sot an' befo' we know it, it was a-risin' again. Ole foks was shoutn' an' singin' songs. Dar's one dey sung purty nigh all night. Don't know who started it, but soon's dey stopped, 'nother one took it up an' made up some mo' verses. Lawdy, chile, I kin hear dat song a-ringin' in my haid now:
Ain't no mo' blowin' dat fo' day horn,
Will sing, chillun, will sing,
Ain't no mo' crackin' dat whip over John,
Will sing, chillun, will sing.

Louise Bowes Rose, born in 1853, recalled the day word came to her Ashland plantation that slavery had ended (*Weevils*, 242):

Daddy was down to de creek. He jumped right in de water up to his neck. He was so happy he jus' kep' on scooping up han'fulls of water an dumpin' it on his haid an' yellin', "I'se free, I'se free! I'se free!"

Mrs. Virginia Hayes Shepherd, born in 1854, was interviewed in Norfolk (*Weevils*, 257, 262):

... The auction block where the sale took place was right down there between the Portsmouth Ferry and the Monument. And let me tell you one thing that Lee's Monument stands for all the devilment and cruelty that was done to the Negro during the days of slavery.
... We come to Norfok durin' the war. Come for freedom an' [to] be safe. When the war was goin' on, Norfolk was full of soldiers, an' everythin' else. They either came to Norfolk or Hampton. That's why the Hampton school started. Slaves wasn't quite free. Abe Lin-

coln said they was, but Lee hadn't surrendered yet. Mos' o' them thought they was free.

4. Robert E. Lee in Myth and Memory

Biographers of Lee and historians of Virginia and the Civil War continue to draw on a document dating from 1905, and—as three writers in this volume demonstrate—they differ in their understandings of the event reported therein. Whether the four key individuals in the story all attended the church service in question is uncertain, as is whether they actually did or observed what is reported in the document—just as the interpretations are divergent. The document is generally said to have been "reprinted," but the two versions differ in intriguing ways. Both carry the title "Negro Communed at St. Paul's Church." The paired documents offer glimpses of various Virginians' Civil War, as experienced in the 1860s or as recalled four decades later.

The *Richmond Times-Dispatch* of April 16, 1905, carried this version, on page B5:

> Colonel T. L. Broun, of Charleston, W. Va., is in the city stopping on Floyd Avenue. He was present at St. Paul's Church just after the war, when a negro marched to the communion table ahead of the congregation.
>
> Colonel Broun, in speaking of the matter on yesterday, said:
>
> "Two months after the evacuation of Richmond, business called me to Richmond for a few days, and on Sunday morning, in June, 1866, I attended St. Paul's Church. Dr. Minnegerode preached to a congregation fairly good. It was communion day. When the minister was ready to administer the Holy Communion, amongst those who first arose and advanced to the communion table was a tall, well dressed negro man, very black. He walked with an air of military authority. This was a great surprise and shock to the communicants and others present, who frequented that most noted of the Episcopal Churches in Virginia. Its effect upon the communicants was startling, and for several moments they retained their seats in solemn silence, and did not move, being deeply chagrined at this attempt of the Federal authorities, to offensively humiliate them

during their most devoted church services. Dr. Minnegerode looked embarrassed.

"General Robert E. Lee was present, and he, ignoring the action and very presence of the negro, immediately arose, in his usual dignified and self-possessed manner, walked up the aisle of the church to the chancel rail and reverently knelt down to partake of the communion and not far from where the negro was.

"This lofty conception of duty by General Lee, under such provoking and irritating circumstances, had a magic effect upon the other communicants, who immediately went forward to the communion table. I, being one of the number, did likewise.

"By this action of General Lee, the services were concluded, as if the negro had not been present. It was a grand exhibition of superiority shown by a true Christian and great soldier under the most trying offensive circumstances."

A few months later, the piece reappeared in *Confederate Veteran* (August 1905): 360, as follows:

Colonel T. L. Broun, of Charleston, W. Va., writes of having been present at St. Paul's Church, Richmond, Va., just after the war when a negro marched to the communion table ahead of the congregation. His account of the event is as follows:

"Two months after the evacuation of Richmond business called me to Richmond for a few days, and on a Sunday morning in June, 1865, I attended St. Paul's Church. Dr. Minnegerode preached. It was communion day; and when the minister was ready to administer the holy communion, a negro in the church arose and advanced to the communion table. He was tall, well-dressed, and black. This was a great surprise and shock to the communicants and others present. Its effect upon the communicants was startling, and for several moments they retained their seats in solemn silence and did not move, being deeply chagrined at this attempt to inaugurate the 'new regime' to offend and humiliate them during their most devoted Church services. Dr. Minnegerode was evidently embarrassed.

"Gen. Robert E. Lee was present, and, ignoring the action and presence of the negro, arose in his usual dignified and self-possessed manner, walked up the aisle to the chancel rail, and reverently knelt down to partake of the communion, and not far from the negro.

This lofty conception of duty by Gen. Lee under such provoking and irritating circumstances had a magic effect upon the other communicants (including the writer), who went forward to the communion table.

"By this action of Gen. Lee the services were conducted, as if the negro had not been present. It was a grand exhibition of superiority shown by a true Christian and great soldier under the most trying and offensive circumstances."

Contributors

IAN BINNINGTON is Visiting Assistant Professor of History at Eastern Illinois University in Charleston, Illinois, and book review editor for H-South. He earned his Ph.D. in 2004 at the University of Illinois at Urbana-Champaign with a dissertation directed by Orville Vernon Burton on the creation of Confederate nationalism.

THEODORE C. DELANEY, Associate Professor of History at Washington and Lee University, earned his Ph.D. at the College of William and Mary and is completing a biography of Julia Gardiner Tyler.

MICHAEL FELLMAN is Professor of Liberal Arts and Director of the Graduate Liberal Studies Program at Simon Fraser University. His books include *Inside War: The Guerrilla Conflict in Missouri during the American Civil War* (1989), *Citizen Sherman* (1995), *The Making of Robert E. Lee* (2000), and the coauthored *"This Terrible War": The Civil War and Its Aftermath* (2002).

LISA TENDRICH FRANK received her Ph.D. from the University of Florida in 2001 and teaches in the History Department at Florida Atlantic University in Boca Raton. Her book *Home Fires Burning: The Gendered Implications of Sherman's March* is to be published by the University of Georgia Press.

MONTE HAMPTON earned his Ph.D. in 2004 at the University of North Carolina at Chapel Hill, where his dissertation, "'Handmaid' or 'Assailant': Debating Science and Scripture in the Culture of the Lost Cause," was directed by Donald Mathews.

WAYNE WEI-SIANG HSIEH earned his Ph.D. in 2004 at the University of Virginia, where his dissertation, "American Soldiers and American Armies: West Pointers and the Civil War," was codirected by Gary W. Gallagher and Edward L. Ayers. He is an Andrew W. Mellon Postdoctoral Fellow at the Whitney Humanities Center, Yale University.

CHARLES F. IRONS, the author of two prize-winning essays, is an Assistant Professor of History at Elon University. His 2003 dissertation at the University of Virginia, "'The Chief Cornerstone': The Spiritual Foundations of Virginia's Slave Society, 1776–1865," was directed by Edward L. Ayers.

CAROLINE E. JANNEY is a Ph.D. candidate at the University of Virginia. Her dissertation, "The Ladies Memorial Associations of Virginia," directed by Gary W. Gallagher, explores the significance of the associations for Civil War memory and gender relations in the postbellum period.

SUZANNE W. JONES is Professor of English at the University of Richmond. The author of *Race Mixing: Southern Fiction since the Sixties* (2004) and many essays on Southern literature, she has edited two collections of essays, *South to a New Place: Region, Literature, Culture* (2002; with Sharon Monteith) and *Writing the Woman Artist* (1991), and two collections of stories, *Crossing the Color Line: Readings in Black and White* (2000) and *Growing up in the South* (1991, 2003).

ERVIN L. JORDAN JR. is an Associate Professor and Research Archivist at the University of Virginia. He is the author of three books, including *Black Confederates and Afro-Yankees in Civil War Virginia* (1995), a History Book Club selection, and he was a historical adviser for the 2003 motion picture *Gods & Generals.*

CHARLES JOYNER is Burroughs Distinguished Professor of History at Coastal Carolina University. He is the author of *Down by the Riverside: A South Carolina Slave Community* (1984), *Shared Traditions: Southern History and Folk Culture* (1999), and "'Forget Hell!' The Civil War in Southern Memory," in *Legacy of Disunion: The Enduring Significance of the American Civil War,* eds. Susan-Mary Grant and Peter J. Parish (2003). He also wrote and produced the television documentary series *Legacy of Conflict: South Carolina in the Civil War.*

DANIEL KILBRIDE, Associate Professor of History at John Carroll University, earned his Ph.D. at the University of Florida in 1997 under the direction of Bertram Wyatt-Brown. His publications include three articles in the *Journal of Southern History* (1993, 1999, 2003), and he is writing a book on Americans on the grand tour, 1750–1870.

SUSANNA MICHELE LEE is a Ph.D. candidate in history at the University of Virginia, where her dissertation, directed by Edward L. Ayers, is on reconciliation and citizenship in the South during Reconstruction.

LUCINDA H. MACKETHAN is Professor of English at North Carolina State University. She is the author of *The Dream of Arcady: Time and Place in Southern Literature* (1980) and *Daughters of Time: Creating Woman's Voice in Southern Story* (1990). She has edited Eugenia Jones Bacon's *Lyddy: A Tale of the Old South* (1998) and Cornelia Jones Pond's *Recollections of a Southern Daughter* (1999), and coedited *The Com-*

panion to Southern Literature: Themes, Genres, Places, People, Movements, and Motifs (2002).

John M. McClure, after twice winning the James Tice Moore Graduate Essay Award, earned his master's degree in history from Virginia Commonwealth University in 2003. His essay stems from his thesis, directed by Ted Tunnell, "Men in the Middle: Freedmen's Bureau Agents in Lexington, Virginia, 1865–1869."

Amy Feely Morsman, Assistant Professor of History at Middlebury College, completed her dissertation in 2004 at the University of Virginia, "The Big House after Slavery: Virginia's Plantation Elite and Their Postbellum Domestic Experiment," directed by Cindy Aron. She is coauthor of "A Monument to Southern Womanhood: The Founding Generation of the Confederate Museum," in *A Woman's War: Southern Women, Civil War, and the Confederate Legacy* (1996).

Jason Phillips is Assistant Professor of History at Mississippi State University. He received his Ph.D. in history in 2003 at Rice University, where John B. Boles directed his dissertation, "Peculiar Defeat: Warfare and the Confederate Culture of Invincibility."

David G. Smith is a Ph.D. candidate in history at Penn State University, writing his dissertation under the direction of William Blair. He also works for Booz Allen Hamilton as a defense consultant and has authored several technical articles.

Emory M. Thomas is Regents Professor of History Emeritus at the University of Georgia and Mark W. Clark Distinguished Visiting Professor of History at The Citadel. His many books on the Civil War include *The Confederacy as a Revolutionary Experience* (1970), *The Confederate State of Richmond: A Biography of the Capital* (1971), *The Confederate Nation, 1861–1865* (1979), and *Robert E. Lee: A Biography* (1995).

Peter Wallenstein teaches history at Virginia Polytechnic Institute and State University. His books include *From Slave South to New South: Public Policy in Nineteenth-Century Georgia* (1987), *Virginia Tech, Land-Grant University, 1872–1997: History of a School, a State, a Nation* (1997), *Tell the Court I Love My Wife: Race, Marriage, and Law — An American History* (2002), and *Blue Laws and Black Codes: Conflict, Courts, and Change in Twentieth-Century Virginia* (2004).

Bertram Wyatt-Brown, Richard J. Milbauer Professor of History, University of Florida, is the author of *Lewis Tappan and the Evangelical War against Slavery* (1969), *Southern Honor: Ethics and Behavior in the Old South* (1982), *Yankee Saints and Southern Sinners* (1985), *The House of Percy: Honor, Melancholy, and Imagination in a Southern Family* (1994), *The Shaping of Southern Culture: Honor, Grace, and War, 1760s–1880s* (2001), and *Hearts of Darkness: Wellsprings of a Southern Literary Tradition* (2003).

Index